Niall Anderson

A SCHOOL COURSE
IN
VECTORS

BY THE SAME AUTHOR

ELEMENTARY ANALYSIS

(with A. Dakin)

4th Edition, Metricated

FURTHER ELEMENTARY ANALYSIS

4th Edition, Metricated

FURTHER MATHEMATICS

2nd Edition, Metricated

A SCHOOL COURSE IN VECTORS

By
R. I. PORTER
M.B.E., M.A.
Formerly Headmaster, Queen Elizabeth Grammar School, Penrith

BELL & HYMAN
LONDON

Published by
Bell & Hyman Limited
Denmark House
37–39 Queen Elizabeth Street
London SE1 2QB

First published in 1970 by
G. Bell & Sons Ltd
Reprinted 1973, 1977, 1978, 1980, 1983 (twice)

ISBN 0 7135 1585 6

Printed in Great Britain by
Biddles Ltd, Guildford, Surrey

PREFACE

THE object of this book is to provide a simple introduction to the algebra of vectors and to show how vector methods can be applied with advantage in Geometry and Mechanics. It is hoped that the treatment given here of this important subject will prove suitable for students of mathematics and science in the upper forms of schools not only in their preparation for advanced level examinations but also as an introduction to the more advanced aspects of the subject required in college and university courses. With the latter object in mind a brief reference has been made to the calculus of vector functions of more than one scalar variable and in particular the differential operators, gradient, divergence and curl have been defined.

As in my previous books, the aim is to introduce readers as quickly as possible to new ideas and techniques. To achieve this aim and at the same time limit the size and cost of the book it has been necessary in some instances to dispense with formal proofs and rigid lines of approach.

Long experience of teaching mathematics has proved the need for large numbers of carefully graded examples and it will be seen that this requirement is very adequately met.

I am indebted to my pupil, John Little, for the admirable assistance he has given in reading the proofs and checking the answers.

Also I would like to record my sincere appreciation of the encouragement and help given me in my venture as an author by the late A. W. Ready, for many years managing director of G. Bell and Sons Ltd.

R. I. PORTER

CONTENTS

I

DEFINITIONS AND SIMPLE PROCESSES

Definitions Physical quantities are of two kinds: (i) *scalar quantities* or *scalars* which have magnitude but no associated direction (ii) *vector quantities* or *vectors* which have both magnitude and an associated direction. Such physical quantities as mass, volume, work and energy are scalars whilst displacement, velocity, acceleration and force are vectors.

Scalar quantities being just numbers obey the fundamental laws of elementary algebra; vector quantities obey different laws which form the basis of vector algebra.

A characteristic of a vector is that it can be represented completely by a straight line, the direction of the line being the direction of the vector and the length of the line a representation of the magnitude of the vector.

It should be noted that the definition of a vector quantity makes no reference to position so that such a quantity can be represented by any one of a series of parallel lines of equal length. The need will arise later to consider special vector quantities whose positions are restricted; to avoid confusion, vectors as defined above should be thought of as *free vectors* and the first two chapters of this book will be solely concerned with such vectors. One restricted form of vector, the position vector, will be dealt with in chapter III, whilst another, the force vector will be considered in chapter V.

Notation In print and throughout this book, a vector quantity will be shown in heavy type viz. **a**; in a student's written work such a quantity should be denoted by a letter over a bar, $\underline{a}$.

When a vector **a** is represented by the straight line joining a point P to a point Q, the notation $\overline{PQ}$ can be used to denote it. So $\overline{PQ} = \mathbf{a}$ (Fig. 1).

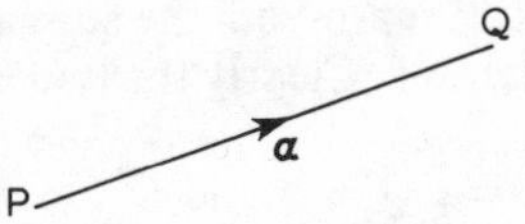

FIG. 1.

Further definitions and notation The *modulus* of a vector is its magnitude. Although the standard notation for the modulus of the vector **a** is $|\mathbf{a}|$, the modulus is usually denoted in print simply as a or in script as the letter a without underline.

The modulus of the vector $\overline{PQ}$ is written PQ.

Unit vectors Vectors with unit magnitude are called unit vectors. They are usually distinguished from other vectors by the use of a circumflex; as for example $\hat{\mathbf{a}}$ represents a unit vector in the direction of the vector **a**. Unit vectors in the directions of mutually perpendicular axes $\overline{OX}$, $\overline{OY}$, $\overline{OZ}$ are however usually taken as **i**, **j**, **k**.

Clearly,

$$\mathbf{a} = a\hat{\mathbf{a}}.$$

Zero or null vector It is convenient to introduce a vector with zero magnitude; this is denoted by **0** and has no directional property.

Negative vector The negative of a vector **a** is written as $-\mathbf{a}$ and defined as a vector with the same modulus as **a** but in the opposite direction.

Equal vectors Vectors are said to be equal if they have the same modulus and the same direction. For example, vectors $\overline{AB}$, $\overline{DC}$ represented by the opposite sides AB, DC of a parallelogram $ABCD$ are equal.

Vector addition and subtraction Let the vectors **a**, **b** be represented respectively by the straight lines $\overline{PQ}$, $\overline{QR}$ (Fig. 2 (*a*)). Then the vector represented by the straight line $\overline{PR}$ is defined as the sum of **a** and **b** and

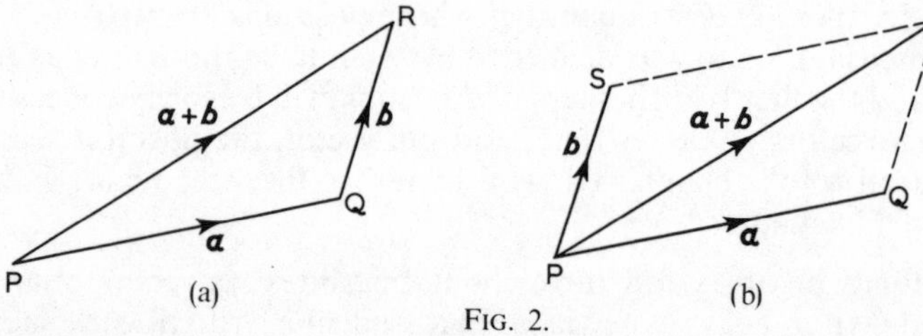

FIG. 2.

is written $\mathbf{a}+\mathbf{b}$. This is called *the triangle law of vector addition.* Alternatively, if the vectors **a**, **b** are represented by straight lines $\overline{PQ}$, $\overline{PS}$ respectively and the parallelogram $PQRS$ be completed, Fig. 2 (*b*), then the diagonal $\overline{PR}$ through P represents the sum $\mathbf{a}+\mathbf{b}$. This is *the parallelogram law of vector addition.* Clearly the two laws are equivalent and either may be used.

From Fig. 2(*b*), as $\overline{SR} = \overline{PQ} = \mathbf{a}$ and $\overline{QR} = \overline{PS} = \mathbf{b}$, it is clear that the commutative law of addition,

$$a+b = b+a,$$

which is true for scalar quantities, is also true for vector quantities.

For

$$\mathbf{b}+\mathbf{a} = \overline{PS}+\overline{SR} = \overline{PR} = \overline{PQ}+\overline{QR} = \mathbf{a}+\mathbf{b}.$$

The difference between the vectors **a**, **b** is expressed as $\mathbf{a}-\mathbf{b}$ and following the rules of scalar algebra this is written as the sum $\mathbf{a}+(-\mathbf{b})$. Representing **a**, **b** by line elements $\overline{PQ}$, $\overline{QR}$ as before, then $\overline{QR'}$, where $QR' = QR$ (Fig. 3), will represent $-\mathbf{b}$. Consequently $\mathbf{a}-\mathbf{b}$ or $\mathbf{a}+(-\mathbf{b})$ is represented by $\overline{PR'}$ or $\overline{SQ}$.

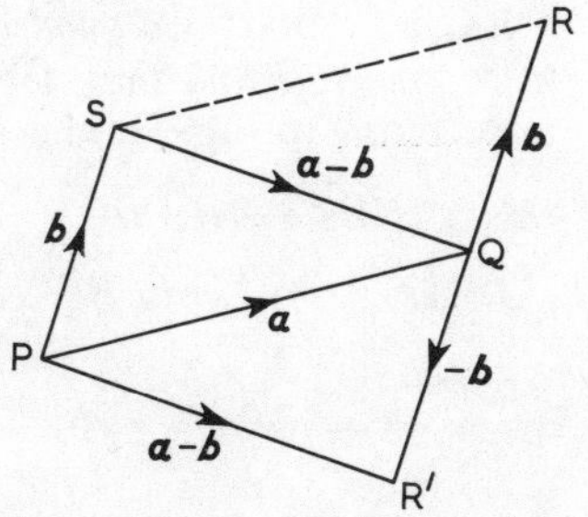

FIG. 3.

Sum of more than two vectors Suppose there are n vectors $\mathbf{a}_1$, $\mathbf{a}_2$, $\mathbf{a}_3$, ... $\mathbf{a}_n$. Let $\mathbf{a}_1$ be represented by $\overline{OA_1}$, $\mathbf{a}_2$ by $\overline{A_1A_2}$, $\mathbf{a}_3$ by $\overline{A_2A_3}$ and so on as far as $\mathbf{a}_n$ represented by $\overline{A_{n-1}A_n}$ (Fig. 4).

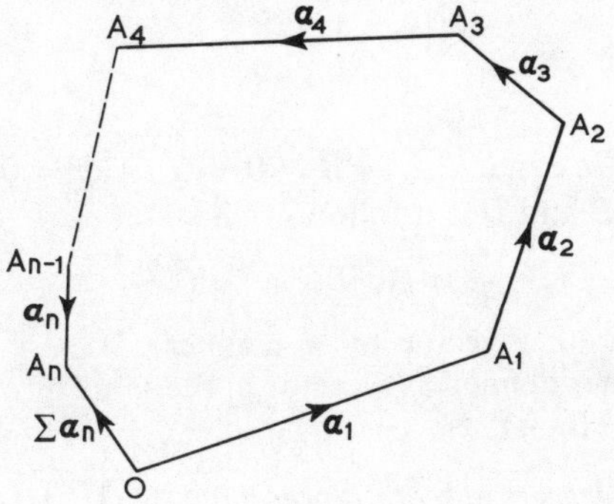

FIG. 4.

Then

$$\overline{OA_2} = \overline{OA_1}+\overline{A_1A_2} = \mathbf{a}_1+\mathbf{a}_2;$$
$$\overline{OA_3} = \overline{OA_2}+\overline{A_2A_3} = \mathbf{a}_1+\mathbf{a}_2+\mathbf{a}_3;$$
$$\overline{OA_4} = \overline{OA_3}+\overline{A_3A_4} = \mathbf{a}_1+\mathbf{a}_2+\mathbf{a}_3+\mathbf{a}_4;$$
$$\cdots\cdots\cdots\cdots\cdots\cdots\cdots\cdots\cdots\cdots\cdots\cdots$$
$$\overline{OA_n} = \overline{OA_{n-1}}+\overline{A_{n-1}A_n} = \mathbf{a}_1+\mathbf{a}_2+\mathbf{a}_3 \ldots +\mathbf{a}_n.$$

This is *the polygon of vectors*, a result which applies equally well in two or three dimensions. From the diagram, Fig. 4, it is evident that

$$\overline{OA_3} = \overline{OA_2}+\overline{A_2A_3} = (\mathbf{a}_1+\mathbf{a}_2)+\mathbf{a}_3 \text{ and } \overline{OA_3} = \overline{OA_1}+\overline{A_1A_3}$$
$$= \mathbf{a}_1+(\mathbf{a}_2+\mathbf{a}_3).$$

Hence $$(\mathbf{a}_1+\mathbf{a}_2)+\mathbf{a}_3 = \mathbf{a}_1+(\mathbf{a}_2+\mathbf{a}_3),$$

a result establishing that the associative law of addition true for scalar quantities is also true of vectors.

Ex. 1 *ABCD is a quadrilateral; P, Q are the mid-points of AB, DC respectively. Prove that* $\overline{AD}+\overline{BC} = 2\overline{PQ}$.

Referring to Fig. 5 and using the polygon of vectors,

$$\overline{PA}+\overline{AD}+\overline{DQ} = \overline{PQ} \quad \text{and} \quad \overline{PB}+\overline{BC}+\overline{CQ} = \overline{PQ}.$$

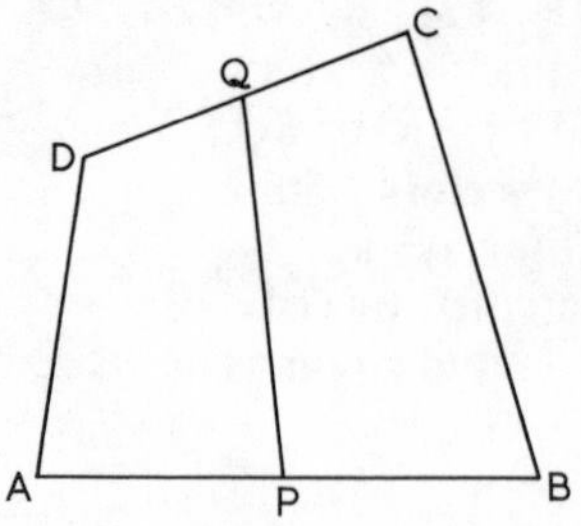

FIG. 5.

Adding and noting that $\overline{PA}+\overline{PB} = 0$, $\overline{DQ}+\overline{CQ} = 0$ as P and Q are mid-points of AB and DC, it follows that

$$\overline{AD}+\overline{BC} = 2\overline{PQ}.$$

Multiplication of a vector by a number If m is a positive real number, then $m\mathbf{a}$ is defined as a vector in the same direction as $\mathbf{a}$ having a modulus equal to ma.

Theorem *If vectors* **a**, **b** *are represented by* $\overline{OP}$, $\overline{OQ}$ *respectively and* m, n *are positive constants, then* $m\mathbf{a}+n\mathbf{b} = (m+n)\mathbf{c}$, *where* **c** *is represented by* $\overline{OR}$; *R being the point of PQ such that* $mPR = nRQ$.

In Fig. 6,

$$\overline{OP}+\overline{PR} = \overline{OR},$$

$$\therefore \quad m\overline{OP}+m\overline{PR} = m\overline{OR}.$$

Similarly,

$$n\overline{OQ}+n\overline{QR} = n\overline{OR}.$$

Adding,

$$m\overline{OP}+n\overline{OQ}+m\overline{PR}+n\overline{QR} = (m+n)\overline{OR}.$$

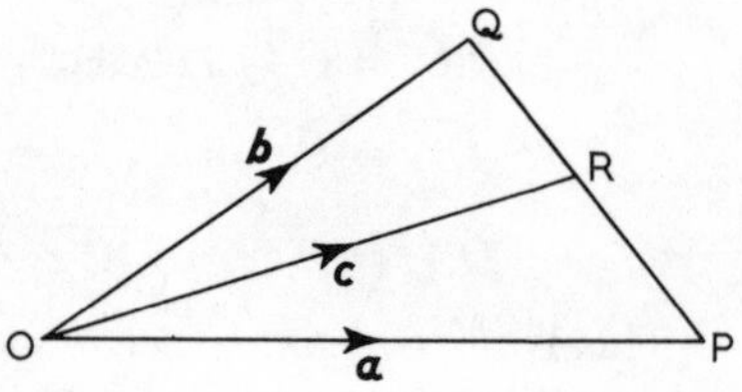

FIG. 6.

But as $mPR = nRQ$, $m\overline{PR}+n\overline{QR} = 0$.

$$\therefore \quad m\overline{OP}+n\overline{OQ} = (m+n)\overline{OR},$$

or

$$m\mathbf{a}+n\mathbf{b} = (m+n)\mathbf{c}.$$

N.B In the special case $m = n = 1$, vectors **a**, **b**, **c** represented respectively by $\overline{OP}$, $\overline{OQ}$ and $\overline{OM}$, where M is the mid-point of PQ, are such that

$$\mathbf{a}+\mathbf{b} = 2\mathbf{c},$$

a result which also follows from the ordinary parallelogram law.

Ex. 2 *ABCD is a plane or skew quadrilateral. Show that the sum of the vectors* $\overline{AB}$, $\overline{CB}$, $\overline{CD}$ *and* $\overline{AD}$ *is* $4\overline{PQ}$ *where P, Q are the mid-points of AC, BD respectively.*

Using the result just established,

$$\overline{AB}+\overline{AD} = 2\overline{AQ} \quad \text{and} \quad \overline{CB}+\overline{CD} = 2\overline{CQ}.$$

But

$$\overline{AQ}+\overline{CQ} = -(\overline{QA}+\overline{QC}),$$
$$= -2\overline{QP}$$
$$= 2\overline{PQ}.$$
$$\therefore \quad \overline{AB}+\overline{AD}+\overline{CB}+\overline{CD}$$
$$= 2(\overline{AQ}+\overline{CQ})$$
$$= 4\overline{PQ}.$$

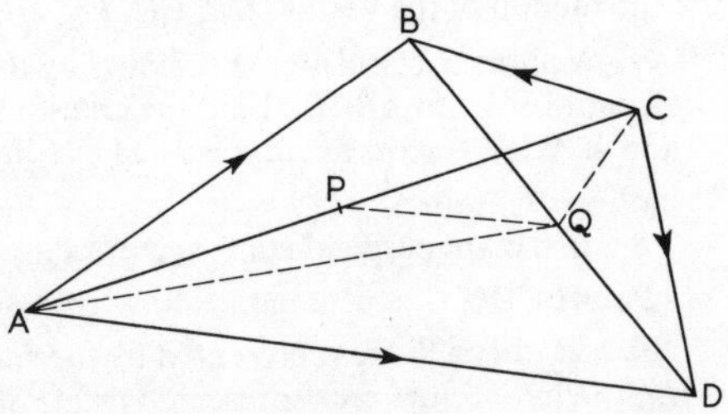

FIG. 7.

Ex. 3 *In a triangle ABC, the points D, E, F divide the sides BC, CA, AB internally in the ratio k:1. Prove that the sum of the vectors represented by* $\overline{AD}$, $\overline{BE}$, $\overline{CF}$ *is zero.*

As $BD = kCD$,

$$(1+k)\overline{AD} = \overline{AB}+k\overline{AC},$$

using the above theorem.

Similarly,

$$(1+k)\overline{BE} = \overline{BC}+k\overline{BA};$$
$$(1+k)\overline{CF} = \overline{CA}+k\overline{CB}.$$

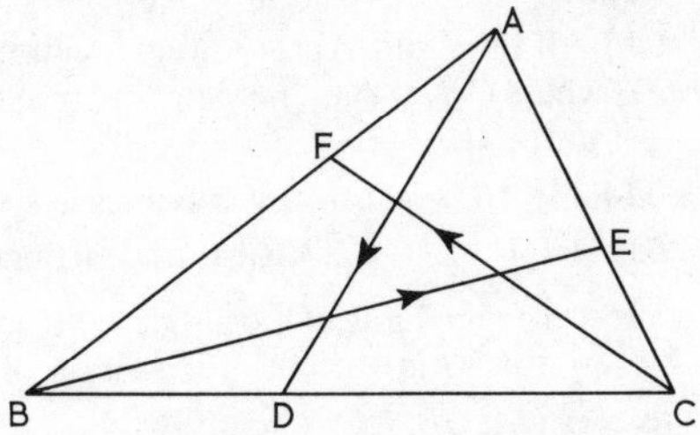

FIG. 8.

Adding,

$$(1+k)(\overline{AD}+\overline{BE}+\overline{CF}) = \overline{AB}+\overline{BC}+\overline{CA}+k(\overline{AC}+\overline{BA}+\overline{CB}).$$

But $$\overline{AB}+\overline{BC}+\overline{CA} = \overline{AC}+\overline{CB}+\overline{BA} = 0.$$

$$\therefore \quad \overline{AD}+\overline{BE}+\overline{CF} = 0.$$

EXAMPLES 1a

1 Taking line elements $\overline{PQ}$, $\overline{RS}$ to represent the vectors **a**, **b** respectively, show how to construct line elements to represent the vectors 2**a**, 2**a**+**b**, **a**−2**b**.

2 If ABC is a triangle what is the sum of the vectors represented by $\overline{BC}$, $\overline{CA}$ and $\overline{AB}$?

3 $ABCD$ is a parallelogram and vectors **a**, **b** are represented by $\overline{AB}$, $\overline{BC}$ respectively. What vectors are represented by (i) $\overline{AC}$; (ii) $\overline{CA}$; (iii) $\overline{BD}$?

4 Referred to rectangular axes the coordinates of the points A, B are (1,1), (4, 5) respectively. Find the value of $|\overline{AB}|$.

5 If vectors **a**, **b** are represented by the sides $\overline{AB}$, $\overline{AC}$ respectively of a triangle ABC, what vectors are represented by (i) $\overline{BC}$; (ii) $\overline{CB}$; (iii) $\overline{AD}$, where D is the mid-point of BC?

6 Points P, Q have coordinates (−2, −1), (3, 11) respectively; find the values of the moduli of the vectors $\overline{OP}$, $\overline{OQ}$, $\overline{PQ}$, $\overline{OP}+\overline{OQ}$, where O is the origin.

7 Vectors **a**, **b**, **c**, **d** are represented by the sides $\overline{AB}$, $\overline{BC}$, $\overline{CD}$, $\overline{AD}$ respectively of a parallelogram $ABCD$. Find the relationships existing between (i) **a** and **c**; (ii) **b** and **d**. What vectors are represented by (iii) $\overline{AC}$; (iv) $\overline{DB}$? What is the sum of the vectors **a**, **b**, **c**?

8 If **a**, **b** are perpendicular vectors show that $|\mathbf{a}+\mathbf{b}| = \sqrt{(a^2+b^2)}$.

9 $ABCDE$ is a pentagon; show that $\overline{AB}+\overline{BC}+\overline{CD} = \overline{AE}+\overline{ED}$.

10 Vectors **a**, **b** are represented by the sides $\overline{AB}$, $\overline{AC}$ respectively of a triangle ABC. What vectors are represented by $\overline{AP}$ if (i) P is the point of trisection of BC nearest B; (ii) P divides BC internally in the ratio 2:3?

11 In triangle ABC a point P on BC is such that $2BP = 3PC$, show that $5\overline{AP} = 2\overline{AB}+3\overline{AC}$.

12 D, E, F are the mid-points of the sides BC, CA, AB respectively of a triangle ABC, show that $\overline{AD} = \frac{1}{2}(\overline{AB}+\overline{AC})$ and deduce that $\overline{AD}+\overline{BE} = \overline{FC}$.

13 If **i** is a unit vector in the direction $\overline{OX}$ and **j** a unit vector in the direction $\overline{OY}$, where OX, OY are perpendicular axes, find the modulus and direction of the vector 3**i**+4**j**.

14 If AB, $A'B'$ are any two lines in space and G, G' are their mid-points, show that $\overline{AA'} = \overline{AG}+\overline{GG'}+\overline{G'A'}$ and deduce that $\overline{AA'}+\overline{BB'} = 2\overline{GG'}$.

15 The medians of a triangle ABC intersect at the centroid G of the triangle. Noting that G is a point of trisection of the medians, show that the sum of the vectors $\overline{GA}$, $\overline{GB}$, $\overline{GC}$ is zero.

16 If O is any point in the plane of triangle ABC and G is the centroid of the triangle, prove that $\overline{OA}+\overline{OB}+\overline{OC} = 3\overline{OG}$. Does the result hold if O is not in the plane of the triangle?

17 The points D, E, F divide the sides BC, CA, AB of triangle ABC internally in the ratios 1:4, 3:2, 3:7 respectively. Show that the sum of the vectors $\overline{AD}$, $\overline{BE}$, $\overline{CF}$ is a vector parallel to $\overline{CX}$ where X is the point dividing AB internally in the ratio 1:3.

18 AB, BC, CD are consecutive sides of a regular hexagon. If $\overline{AB}$ represents the vector **a** and BC represents the vector **b**, find the vector represented by $\overline{CD}$.

19 The points H, K are the mid-points of the sides BC, CD of a parallelogram $ABCD$, prove that $3(\overline{AB}+\overline{AC}+\overline{AD}) = 4(\overline{AH}+\overline{AK})$.

20 If O, A, B, C are points such that $l\overline{OA}+m\overline{OB}+n\overline{OC} = 0$ where $l+m+n = 0$, prove that C is the point dividing AB in the ratio $m:l$.

Components of a vector *A vector* **r** *can be expressed in two dimensions as the sum of two other vectors parallel to given vectors* **a**, **b** *which are coplanar with* **r**.

For taking $\overline{OP}$ to represent **r** (Fig. 9), a parallelogram $OAPB$ can be constructed with OP as a diagonal and sides $\overline{OA}$, $\overline{OB}$ parallel to the vectors **a**, **b** respectively. As $\overline{OA}$ is a vector in the direction of **a** it can be expressed as $\lambda\mathbf{a}$, where λ is a scalar multiplier. Similarly $\overline{OB}$ can be expressed as $\mu\mathbf{b}$, where μ is a scalar multiplier.

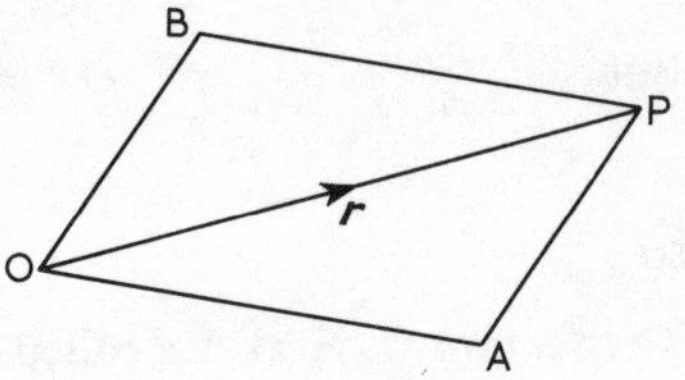

FIG. 9.

Clearly,

$$\overline{OP} = \overline{OA}+\overline{AP} = \overline{OA}+\overline{OB},$$

so

$$\mathbf{r} = \lambda\mathbf{a}+\mu\mathbf{b}.$$

Extending to three dimensions, a vector **r** *can be expressed as the sum of three other vectors parallel to three non-coplanar vectors* **a**, **b**, **c**.

For taking OP to represent **r** (Fig. 10), a parallelepiped $OAQBCSPR$ can be constructed with OP as a diagonal and edges $\overline{OA}, \overline{OB}, \overline{OC}$ parallel to the vectors **a**, **b**, **c** respectively. Then $\overline{OA} = \lambda\mathbf{a}$; $\overline{OB} = \mu\mathbf{b}$; $\overline{OC} = \nu\mathbf{c}$, where λ, μ, ν are scalar multipliers.

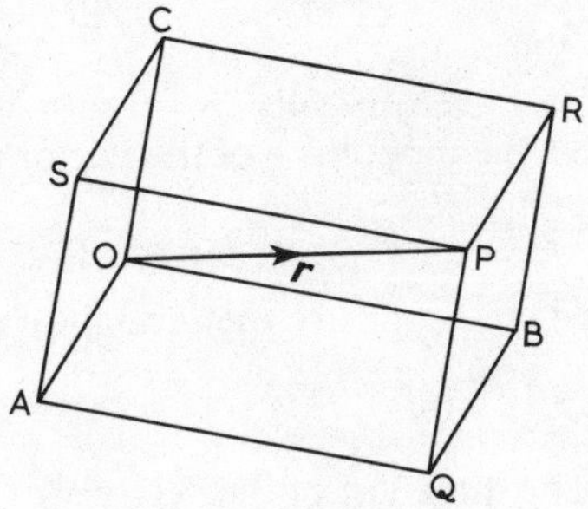

FIG. 10.

Clearly,

$$\overline{OP} = \overline{OA}+\overline{AQ}+\overline{QP}$$
$$= \overline{OA}+\overline{OB}+\overline{OC},$$

so

$$\mathbf{r} = \lambda\mathbf{a}+\mu\mathbf{b}+\nu\mathbf{c}.$$

Components of a vector in mutually perpendicular directions Suppose $\overline{OP}$ represents the vector $\mathbf{r}$ (Fig. 11). Through O draw three mutually perpendicular lines OX, OY, OZ to form a right-handed coordinate frame in the sense that a right-handed screw rotation from $\overline{OY}$ to $\overline{OZ}$ is along $\overline{OX}$ and so on with cyclic interchange of the letters X, Y, Z. Drop perpendiculars PQ, PR, PS to the planes YOZ, ZOX, XOY respectively and complete the rectangular parallelepiped $OASBCRPQ$. Taking $OA = x$, $OB = y$, $OC = z$ and letting unit vectors in the directions $\overline{OX}$, $\overline{OY}$, $\overline{OZ}$ be $\mathbf{i}$, $\mathbf{j}$, $\mathbf{k}$ respectively, then

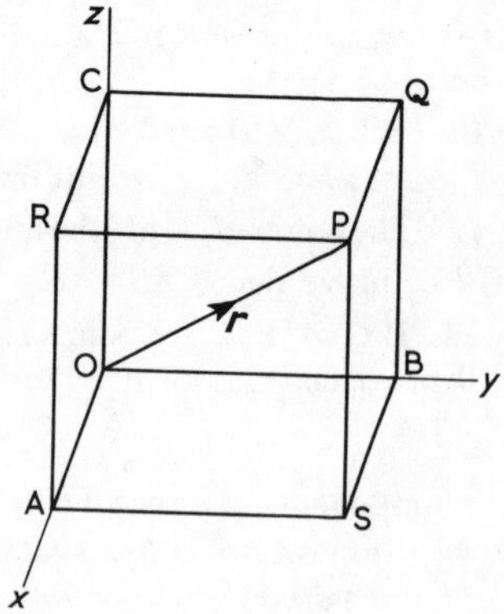

FIG. 11.

$$\overline{OA} = x\mathbf{i}; \quad \overline{OB} = y\mathbf{j}, \quad \overline{OC} = z\mathbf{k}.$$

But
$$\overline{OP} = \overline{OA}+\overline{AS}+\overline{SP}$$
$$= \overline{OA}+\overline{OB}+\overline{OC},$$

so
$$\mathbf{r} = x\mathbf{i}+y\mathbf{j}+z\mathbf{k}.$$

The vectors $x\mathbf{i}$, $y\mathbf{j}$, $z\mathbf{k}$ are called the *components* of $\mathbf{r}$ in the directions of the axes. This resolution of $\mathbf{r}$ into components in the directions of the axes is unique as only one parallelepiped can be drawn as above and hence if two vectors are equal, their respective components in the directions of the axes must also be equal.

In two dimensions, if $\mathbf{r}$ lies in the plane XOY, the above result reduces to

$$\mathbf{r} = x\mathbf{i}+y\mathbf{j}.$$

Modulus and direction cosines of a vector in terms of its components Referring to Fig. 11, it is clear that

$$OP^2 = OA^2+OB^2+OC^2.$$

So the modulus r of the vector $\mathbf{r}$ is given by

$$r^2 = x^2+y^2+z^2,$$

where x, y, z are the moduli of the components of $\mathbf{r}$.

$$\therefore \quad r = \sqrt{(x^2+y^2+z^2)}.$$

The direction of the vector $\mathbf{r}$ or $\overline{OP}$ is determined by the cosines of the angles $\overline{OP}$ makes with the directions of the axes $\overline{OX}$, $\overline{OY}$, $\overline{OZ}$. If these angles are α, β, γ respectively,

$$\cos\alpha = \frac{OA}{OP} = \frac{x}{r}; \quad \cos\beta = \frac{OB}{OP} = \frac{y}{r}; \quad \cos\gamma = \frac{OC}{OP} = \frac{z}{r}.$$

$\cos\alpha$, $\cos\beta$, $\cos\gamma$ are called the *direction cosines* of $\overline{OP}$; they are not independent as

$$\cos^2\alpha + \cos^2\beta + \cos^2\gamma = \frac{x^2+y^2+z^2}{r^2} = 1.$$

In two dimensions, if $\mathbf{r}$ lies in the plane XOY, we have the corresponding results

$$r = \sqrt{(x^2+y^2)}; \quad \cos\alpha = x/r: \quad \cos\beta = y/r, \quad \text{where } \cos^2\alpha + \cos^2\beta = 1.$$

Sums and differences of vectors in terms of components Suppose vectors $\mathbf{r}_1, \mathbf{r}_2, \mathbf{r}_3, \ldots$ are expressed in terms of their components in the directions of rectangular axes $\overline{OX}$, $\overline{OY}$, $\overline{OZ}$.

Then

$$\mathbf{r}_1 = x_1\mathbf{i} + y_1\mathbf{j} + z_1\mathbf{k};$$
$$\mathbf{r}_2 = x_2\mathbf{i} + y_2\mathbf{j} + z_2\mathbf{k};$$
$$\mathbf{r}_3 = x_3\mathbf{i} + y_3\mathbf{j} + z_3\mathbf{k};$$
$$\ldots\ldots\ldots\ldots\ldots\ldots$$

$$\begin{aligned}\therefore \quad \mathbf{r}_1 + \mathbf{r}_2 + \mathbf{r}_3 + \cdots &= (x_1\mathbf{i} + y_1\mathbf{j} + z_1\mathbf{k}) + (x_2\mathbf{i} + y_2\mathbf{j} + z_2\mathbf{k}) \\ &\quad + (x_3\mathbf{i} + y_3\mathbf{j} + z_3\mathbf{k}) + \cdots \\ &= (x_1 + x_2 + x_3 + \cdots)\mathbf{i} + (y_1 + y_2 + y_3 + \cdots)\mathbf{j} \\ &\quad + (z_1 + z_2 + z_3 + \cdots)\mathbf{k}.\end{aligned}$$

A result which shows that vectors can be added by simply adding their like components. Clearly a similar result will apply in the case of subtraction of vectors.

Ex. 4 *Coplanar vectors are given by* $\mathbf{r}_1 = 3\mathbf{i} + 4\mathbf{j}$, $\mathbf{r}_2 = 2\mathbf{i} - 3\mathbf{j}$, *where* $\mathbf{i}$, $\mathbf{j}$ *are unit vectors in the directions of rectangular axes* $\overline{OX}$, $\overline{OY}$. *Find the moduli and direction cosines of* (i) $\mathbf{r}_1 + \mathbf{r}_2$; (ii) $2\mathbf{r}_1 - 3\mathbf{r}_2$.

(i)
$$\mathbf{r}_1 + \mathbf{r}_2 = (3\mathbf{i} + 4\mathbf{j}) + (2\mathbf{i} - 3\mathbf{j}) = 5\mathbf{i} + \mathbf{j},$$
$$\therefore \quad |\mathbf{r}_1 + \mathbf{r}_2| = |5\mathbf{i} + \mathbf{j}| = \sqrt{26},$$

and the direction cosines of $\mathbf{r}_1 + \mathbf{r}_2$ are $\cos\alpha = 5/\sqrt{26}$, $\cos\beta = 1/\sqrt{26}$.

(ii)
$$2\mathbf{r}_1 - 3\mathbf{r}_2 = 2(3\mathbf{i} + 4\mathbf{j}) - 3(2\mathbf{i} - 3\mathbf{j}) = 17\mathbf{j},$$
$$\therefore \quad |2\mathbf{r}_1 - 3\mathbf{r}_2| = |17\mathbf{j}| = 17,$$

and the direction cosines of $2\mathbf{r}_1 - 3\mathbf{r}_2$ are $\cos\alpha = 0$, $\cos\beta = \frac{17}{17} = 1$, the vector being in the direction of $\overline{OY}$.

Ex. 5 *Find the modulus and direction cosines of the vector* $\mathbf{r} = 2\mathbf{i}+\mathbf{j}-2\mathbf{k}$, *where* **i**, **j**, **k** *are unit vectors in the directions of rectangular coordinate axes.*

$$\text{Modulus of } \mathbf{r},\quad r = \sqrt{\{2^2+1^2+(-2)^2\}} = 3;$$

$$\text{direction cosines of } \mathbf{r} \quad \text{are} \quad \tfrac{2}{3}, \tfrac{1}{3}, -\tfrac{2}{3}.$$

Ex. 6 *Unit vectors along the axes* $\overline{OX}$, $\overline{OY}$ *are represented by* **i**, **j** *and* $\overline{OP}$ *represents a vector of magnitude OP in the direction O to P. If* $\overline{OA} = 2\mathbf{i}+3\mathbf{j}$, $\overline{OB} = 3\mathbf{i}-2\mathbf{j}$ *and* $3\overline{OA}+2\overline{OB}+\overline{OC} = 0$, *find the magnitude and direction of* $\overline{OC}$.

Substituting for $\overline{OA}$, $\overline{OB}$ we have

$$3(2\mathbf{i}+3\mathbf{j})+2(3\mathbf{i}-2\mathbf{j})+\overline{OC} = 0.$$

$$\therefore \quad 12\mathbf{i}+5\mathbf{j}+\overline{OC} = 0; \quad \overline{OC} = -12\mathbf{i}-5\mathbf{j}.$$

So the magnitude of $\overline{OC}$ is $\sqrt{\{(-12)^2+(-5)^2\}} = 13$ and the direction cosines of $\overline{OC}$ are $-\frac{12}{13}, -\frac{5}{13}$.

The direction of $\overline{OC}$ which makes obtuse angles with the directions of $\overline{OX}$ and $\overline{OY}$ is as shown in Fig. 12, where $\theta = \tan^{-1}\frac{5}{12}$.

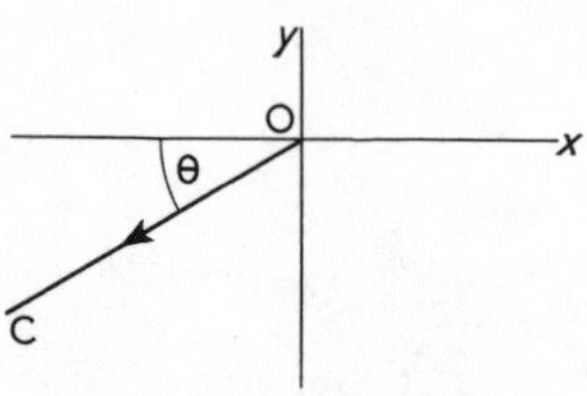

FIG. 12.

Vector proof of trigonometrical addition theorems Referring to the two-dimensional diagram (Fig. 13), suppose $\hat{\mathbf{l}}$, $\hat{\mathbf{m}}$ are unit vectors in perpendicular directions $\overline{OP}$, $\overline{OQ}$ where $\overline{OP}$ makes an angle A with $\overline{OX}$. Then if **i**, **j** are unit vectors in the directions $\overline{OX}$, $\overline{OY}$,

$$\hat{\mathbf{l}} = \cos A\mathbf{i}+\sin A\mathbf{j};$$

$$\hat{\mathbf{m}} = \cos(\tfrac{1}{2}\pi+A)\mathbf{i}+\sin(\tfrac{1}{2}\pi+A)\mathbf{j}$$

$$= -\sin A\mathbf{i}+\cos A\mathbf{j}.$$

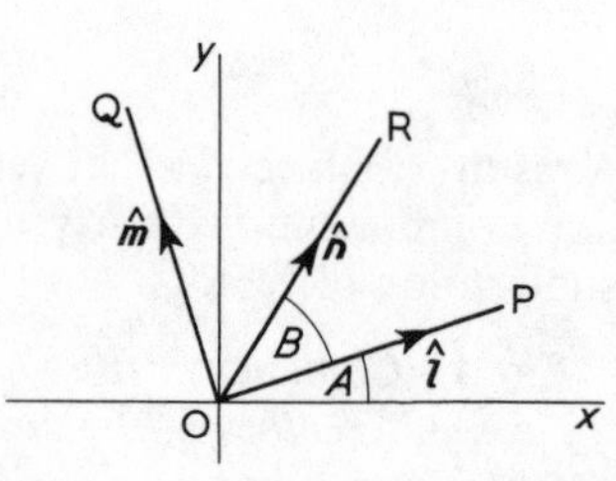

FIG. 13.

Let $\hat{\mathbf{n}}$ be a unit vector in the direction $\overline{OR}$, where angle $ROP = B$. Then resolving $\hat{\mathbf{n}}$ into components in the perpendicular directions $\overline{OP}$, $\overline{OQ}$,

$$\hat{\mathbf{n}} = \cos B\hat{\mathbf{l}}+\sin B\hat{\mathbf{m}}$$

$$= \cos B(\cos A\mathbf{i}+\sin A\mathbf{j})+\sin B(-\sin A\mathbf{i}+\cos A\mathbf{j})$$

$$= (\cos A\cos B-\sin A\sin B)\mathbf{i}+(\sin A\cos B+\cos A\sin B)\mathbf{j} \qquad \text{(i)}$$

But $\hat{\mathbf{n}}$ can be resolved into components in the directions $\overline{OX}, \overline{OY}$, giving

$$\hat{\mathbf{n}} = \cos(A+B)\mathbf{i} + \sin(A+B)\mathbf{j}. \qquad \text{(ii)}$$

From (i) and (ii), equating components in the directions of the axes $\overline{OX}, \overline{OY}$,

$$\cos(A+B) = \cos A \cos B - \sin A \sin B;$$

$$\sin(A+B) = \sin A \cos B + \cos A \sin B.$$

EXAMPLES 1b

[In the following exercises, **i**, **j**, **k** denote unit vectors in the directions of rectangular axes.]

1 A vector has a modulus of 5 and its direction makes angles of 30°, 60° with the axes $\overline{OX}$, $\overline{OY}$. Express the vector in terms of **i** and **j**.

2 Find the modulus of each of the following vectors: (i) $3\mathbf{i}+4\mathbf{j}$; (ii) $\mathbf{i}+\sqrt{3}\mathbf{j}$; (iii) $-2\mathbf{i}-5\mathbf{j}$; (iv) $\mathbf{i}\cos\theta+\mathbf{j}\sin\theta$; (v) $\mathbf{i}\sin\theta-\mathbf{j}\cos\theta$.

3 Find the sum of the vectors $3\mathbf{i}+2\mathbf{j}-4\mathbf{k}$, $\mathbf{i}-5\mathbf{j}+3\mathbf{k}$, $6\mathbf{i}-2\mathbf{j}+7\mathbf{k}$.

4 Find the modulus of the vector $2\mathbf{i}+\mathbf{j}-3\mathbf{k}$.

5 Find the modulus and direction cosines of the vector $\mathbf{i}-2\mathbf{j}+2\mathbf{k}$.

6 A vector **r** makes an angle of 120°, measured counterclockwise, with the direction $\overline{OX}$. Find the modulus of **r** if its component in the direction $\overline{OX}$ has a modulus of 3.

7 Find a if the vectors $a\mathbf{i}+4\mathbf{j}$, $-2\mathbf{i}+6\mathbf{j}$ are parallel.

8 Vectors **a**, **b**, **c** are given by $\mathbf{a} = 3\mathbf{i}$, $\mathbf{b} = \mathbf{i}+2\mathbf{j}$, $\mathbf{c} = -2\mathbf{i}+\mathbf{j}$. Find the moduli of the vector **r** where (i) $\mathbf{r} = \mathbf{a}+\mathbf{b}+\mathbf{c}$; (ii) $\mathbf{r} = 2\mathbf{a}-\mathbf{b}-\mathbf{c}$; (iii) $\mathbf{r} = \mathbf{a}-3\mathbf{b}+2\mathbf{c}$.

9 If the following pairs of vectors are equal find the values of a, b, c: (i) $a\mathbf{i}+b\mathbf{j}$, $3\mathbf{i}-4\mathbf{j}$; (ii) $a\mathbf{i}+b\mathbf{j}+c\mathbf{k}$, $2\mathbf{i}-\mathbf{j}+3\mathbf{k}$; (iii) $(a-1)\mathbf{i}+(b+2)\mathbf{j}$, $-b\mathbf{i}+(a-1)\mathbf{j}$.

10 If $\mathbf{r}_1 = 7\mathbf{i}+3\mathbf{j}-\mathbf{k}$, $\mathbf{r}_2 = 2\mathbf{i}-5\mathbf{j}+4\mathbf{k}$, find the moduli and direction cosines of (i) $\mathbf{r}_1+\mathbf{r}_2$; (ii) $\mathbf{r}_2-\mathbf{r}_1$.

11 In each of the following cases, express the given vector in terms of its rectangular components: (i) modulus 12, direction cosines $\frac{2}{3}, -\frac{2}{3}, \frac{1}{3}$; (ii) modulus $2\sqrt{14}$, direction cosines $1/\sqrt{14}, 3/\sqrt{14}, -2/\sqrt{14}$; (iii) modulus 1, direction cosines l, m, n.

12 Find the unit vector which is in the direction of the vector $2\mathbf{i}-2\mathbf{j}+\mathbf{k}$.

13 Express in component form the vector of modulus 5 which has the direction of the vector $\mathbf{i}+2\mathbf{j}-2\mathbf{k}$.

14 Find the unit vector in the direction of the vector $\mathbf{r}_1-\mathbf{r}_2$, where $\mathbf{r}_1 = 3\mathbf{i}-\mathbf{j}+5\mathbf{k}$, $\mathbf{r}_2 = \mathbf{i}-2\mathbf{j}-\mathbf{k}$.

15 Find the modulus and direction cosines of the vector $\overline{PQ}$ if the vectors $\overline{OP}$, $\overline{OQ}$ are respectively equal to $7\mathbf{i}+3\mathbf{j}-\mathbf{k}$, $2\mathbf{i}-5\mathbf{j}+3\mathbf{k}$.

16 Vectors $\overline{OA}$, $\overline{OB}$ make angles, measured counterclockwise, of 30°, 120° respectively with the axis $\overline{OX}$. Find the magnitudes of $\overline{OA}$, $\overline{OB}$ if $2\overline{OA}+3\overline{OB} = 6\mathbf{i}+4\mathbf{j}$.

17 Vectors $\mathbf{a}, \mathbf{b}, \mathbf{c}, \mathbf{d}$ are given by $\mathbf{a} = \mathbf{i}+\mathbf{j}+\mathbf{k}$, $\mathbf{b} = 2\mathbf{i}+3\mathbf{j}$, $\mathbf{c} = 3\mathbf{i}+5\mathbf{j}-2\mathbf{k}$, $\mathbf{d} = \mathbf{k}-\mathbf{j}$. Prove that the vectors $\mathbf{b}-\mathbf{a}$, $\mathbf{d}-\mathbf{c}$ are parallel and find the ratio of their moduli.

18 Vectors $\mathbf{v}_1, \mathbf{v}_2$ are given by $\mathbf{v}_1 = 3\mathbf{i}-4\mathbf{j}+\mathbf{k}$, $\mathbf{v}_2 = \mathbf{i}+\mathbf{j}-\mathbf{k}$. Find (i) the modulus and direction cosines of the vector $\mathbf{v}_1-\mathbf{v}_2$; (ii) the unit vector in the direction of the vector $\mathbf{v}_1+\mathbf{v}_2$.

19 The vector $(a-4)\mathbf{i}-b\mathbf{j}$ is parallel to the axis $\overline{OY}$ and the vector $(a-8)\mathbf{i}+b\mathbf{j}$ is parallel to the vector $-\mathbf{i}-\mathbf{j}$. Find the values of a and b.

20 Prove that the vectors $a\mathbf{i}+b\mathbf{j}$, $b\mathbf{i}-a\mathbf{j}$ have equal moduli and perpendicular directions.

21 Vectors $\mathbf{a}, \mathbf{b}, \mathbf{c}$ are such that $2\mathbf{a}-\mathbf{b}+\mathbf{c} = 0$. If $\mathbf{a} = 4\mathbf{i}-\mathbf{j}+\mathbf{k}$, $\mathbf{b} = \mathbf{i}-2\mathbf{k}$, find the unit vector in the direction of $\mathbf{c}$.

22 If $\overline{OA} = 2\mathbf{i}+6\mathbf{j}+3\mathbf{k}$, $\overline{OB} = \mathbf{i}+2\mathbf{j}+7\mathbf{k}$, $\overline{OC} = 4\mathbf{i}+14\mathbf{j}-5\mathbf{k}$, show that the vectors $\overline{BA}$, $\overline{AC}$ are in the same direction and deduce that A, B, C are collinear points.

23 If $\mathbf{r}_1 = x_1\mathbf{i}+y_1\mathbf{j}+z_1\mathbf{k}$, $\mathbf{r}_2 = x_2\mathbf{i}+y_2\mathbf{j}+z_2\mathbf{k}$ and $\mathbf{r}_1+\mathbf{r}_2+\mathbf{r}_3 = 0$, find the modulus and direction cosines of $-\mathbf{r}_3$.

24 If $\overline{OP} = 3\mathbf{i}-2\mathbf{j}+\mathbf{k}$, $\overline{OQ} = 4\mathbf{i}+\mathbf{j}-2\mathbf{k}$, express in component form the vector $\overline{OR}$ where (i) R is the mid-point of PQ; (ii) R divides PQ internally in the ratio 2:1.

25 If $\mathbf{a}$, $\mathbf{b}$ are given vectors and $\overline{OP} = \mathbf{a}+\mathbf{b}$, $\overline{OQ} = 2\mathbf{a}+3\mathbf{b}$, $\overline{OR} = 5\mathbf{a}+9\mathbf{b}$, express $\overline{PQ}$, $\overline{QR}$ in terms of $\mathbf{a}$, $\mathbf{b}$ and deduce that these vectors act in the same line and have moduli in the ratio 1:3.

26 Find, in component form, the vector $\mathbf{r}$ if $\mathbf{r}+\mathbf{j}-2\mathbf{k}$ is parallel to the axis $\overline{OX}$ and $\mathbf{r}-2\mathbf{i}$ is parallel to the vector $4\mathbf{k}-2\mathbf{j}$.

27 Use a vector method to obtain the expanded forms of $\cos(A-B)$ and $\sin(A-B)$.

28 Given $\overline{OA} = 4\mathbf{i}+6\mathbf{j}$, $\overline{OP} = \mathbf{i}2\cos\theta+\mathbf{j}2\sin\theta$ where θ is variable and $\overline{OA}+\overline{OP} = 2\overline{OQ}$, show that the locus of Q is a circle and find its centre and radius.

II

PRODUCTS OF VECTORS

Products of two vectors After examining the ways in which two vector quantities enter into combination in geometrical and physical applications, two distinct types of product are defined, the one a scalar quantity referred to as the *scalar product* of the two vectors and the other a vector quantity referred to as the *vector product* of the two vectors.

Scalar product *The scalar product of two vectors* **a**, **b** *whose directions are inclined at an angle* θ *to each other is defined as the scalar quantity* $ab \cos \theta$ *and is denoted symbolically by* $\mathbf{a} \cdot \mathbf{b}$.

It is evident that scalar multiplication of vectors is commutative as

$$\mathbf{b} \cdot \mathbf{a} = ba \cos \theta = ab \cos \theta = \mathbf{a} \cdot \mathbf{b}.$$

Vector product *The vector product of two vectors* **a**, **b** *whose directions are inclined at an angle* θ *to each other is defined as the vector whose modulus is* $ab \sin \theta$ *and whose direction is perpendicular to the directions of both* **a** *and* **b** *in the sense that a right-handed screw rotated from the direction of* **a** *to the direction of* **b** *moves in the direction of the vector product. The vector product of* **a** *and* **b** *is denoted by* $\mathbf{a} \wedge \mathbf{b}$ *or* $\mathbf{a} \times \mathbf{b}$*—the former notation will be used in this book.* The relationship between the direction of $\mathbf{a} \wedge \mathbf{b}$ and the directions of **a** and **b** is shown in Fig. 14. It is important to note that although the product $\mathbf{b} \wedge \mathbf{a}$ has a magnitude equal to that of the product $\mathbf{a} \wedge \mathbf{b}$ its direction is opposite to that of $\mathbf{a} \wedge \mathbf{b}$ as the screw rotation is from the direction of **b** to the direction of **a**, the reverse of that in the case of the product $\mathbf{a} \wedge \mathbf{b}$.

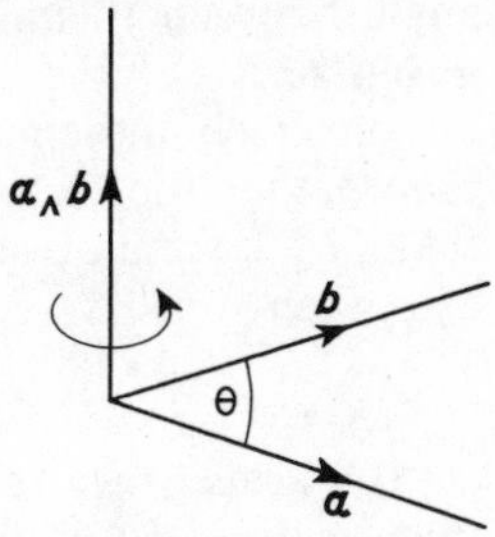

FIG. 14.

So $\mathbf{b} \wedge \mathbf{a} = -\mathbf{a} \wedge \mathbf{b}$ and consequently vector multiplication is non-commutative.

Ex. 1 *If M is the mid-point of side BC of triangle ABC show that* (i) $\overline{MB} \cdot \overline{MA} = -\overline{MC} \cdot \overline{MA}$; (ii) $\overline{MB} \wedge \overline{MA} = -\overline{MC} \wedge \overline{MA}$.

(i) $\overline{MB} \cdot \overline{MA} = MB.\ MA \cos B\widehat{M}A$; $\overline{MC} \cdot \overline{MA} = MC.\ MA \cos A\widehat{M}C$.

But $\quad MB = MC$

and $\quad \cos B\widehat{M}A = -\cos A\widehat{M}C.$

$$\therefore \quad \overline{MB} \, . \, \overline{MA} = -\overline{MC} \, . \, \overline{MA}.$$

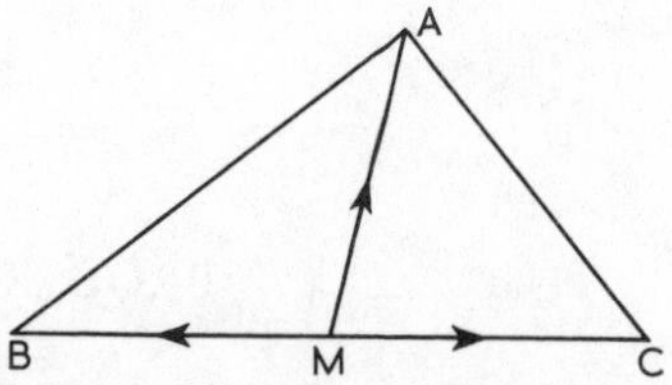

FIG. 15.

(ii) The product $\overline{MB} \wedge \overline{MA}$ has a magnitude of $MB \, . \, MA \sin B\widehat{M}A$ and a direction normal to the plane of the page downwards while the product $\overline{MC} \wedge \overline{MA}$ has a magnitude $MC \, . \, MA \times \sin A\widehat{M}C$ and a direction normal to the plane of the page upwards. Consequently as $\sin A\widehat{M}C$ equals $\sin B\widehat{M}A$ it follows that the vector products $\overline{MB} \wedge \overline{MA}$ and $\overline{MC} \wedge \overline{MA}$ have equal magnitudes and opposite directions. So

$$\overline{MB} \wedge \overline{MA} = -\overline{MC} \wedge \overline{MA}.$$

Ex. 2 *If* $\mathbf{a}$, $\mathbf{b}$ *are non-null vectors such that* $\mathbf{a} \wedge \mathbf{b} = 0$, *show that* $\mathbf{a} = \lambda\mathbf{b}$, *where* λ *is a scalar parameter.*

As $\mathbf{a} \wedge \mathbf{b} = 0$, $ab \sin \theta = 0$ where θ is the angle at which $\mathbf{a}$ and $\mathbf{b}$ are inclined.

But a and b are not zero, so $\sin \theta = 0$ and consequently $\mathbf{a}$ and $\mathbf{b}$ are parallel. Hence $\mathbf{a}$ is a scalar multiple of $\mathbf{b}$ or $\mathbf{a} = \lambda\mathbf{b}$, where λ is a scalar parameter.

Important results involving scalar products

(i) **Perpendicular vectors** If two vectors $\mathbf{a}$, $\mathbf{b}$ are perpendicular, the angle between them θ, is 90°, so $\cos \theta = 0$ and the scalar product $\mathbf{a} \, . \, \mathbf{b}$ is zero.

Conversely if the magnitudes a, b are not zero and the product $\mathbf{a} \, . \, \mathbf{b}$ is zero, then the vectors $\mathbf{a}$, $\mathbf{b}$ are perpendicular. It is important to note that if $\mathbf{i}$, $\mathbf{j}$, $\mathbf{k}$ are unit vectors in the directions of mutually perpendicular axes, then

$$\mathbf{j} \, . \, \mathbf{k} = \mathbf{k} \, . \, \mathbf{i} = \mathbf{i} \, . \, \mathbf{j} = 0.$$

(ii) **Parallel vectors** If $\mathbf{a}$, $\mathbf{b}$ are parallel and in the same direction, then $\mathbf{a} \, . \, \mathbf{b} = ab$; if in opposite directions, then $\mathbf{a} \, . \, \mathbf{b} = -ab$. An important special case arises when $\mathbf{b} = \mathbf{a}$, the scalar product $\mathbf{a} \, . \, \mathbf{a}$ is written $\mathbf{a}^2$ and consequently,

$$\mathbf{a} \, . \, \mathbf{a} = \mathbf{a}^2 = a^2.$$

Note that with the usual definitions of unit vectors $\mathbf{i}$, $\mathbf{j}$, $\mathbf{k}$,

$$\mathbf{i}^2 = \mathbf{j}^2 = \mathbf{k}^2 = 1.$$

(iii) **Angle between two vectors** If vectors **a**, **b** are inclined at an angle θ, then

$$\cos\theta = \frac{\mathbf{a}\,.\,\mathbf{b}}{ab}.$$

Ex 3 *If* **a**, **b** *have equal magnitudes, show that* $\mathbf{a}^2 = \mathbf{b}^2$.

As $\mathbf{a}^2 = a^2$, $\mathbf{b}^2 = b^2$ and $a = b$, the result $\mathbf{a}^2 = \mathbf{b}^2$ follows.

Important results involving vector products

(i) **Parallel vectors** If vectors **a**, **b** are parallel, the sine of the angle θ between them is zero and consequently $\mathbf{a} \wedge \mathbf{b} = 0$. Conversely if $\mathbf{a} \wedge \mathbf{b} = 0$ and a, b are not zero, then **a**, **b** are parallel vectors and so **b** is scalar multiple of **a**.

It is important to note that $\mathbf{a} \wedge \mathbf{a} = 0$ and with the usual definitions of unit vectors **i**, **j**, **k**,

$$\mathbf{i} \wedge \mathbf{i} = \mathbf{j} \wedge \mathbf{j} = \mathbf{k} \wedge \mathbf{k} = 0.$$

(ii) **Mutually perpendicular vectors** As the unit vectors **i**, **j**, **k** form a mutually perpendicular right-handed system, it follows that

$$\mathbf{j} \wedge \mathbf{k} = \mathbf{i}; \quad \mathbf{k} \wedge \mathbf{i} = \mathbf{j}; \quad \mathbf{i} \wedge \mathbf{j} = \mathbf{k};$$

$$\mathbf{k} \wedge \mathbf{j} = -\mathbf{i}; \quad \mathbf{i} \wedge \mathbf{k} = -\mathbf{j}; \quad \mathbf{j} \wedge \mathbf{i} = -\mathbf{k}.$$

(iii) **Angle between two vectors** If vectors **a**, **b** are inclined at an angle θ, then

$$\sin\theta = \frac{|\mathbf{a} \wedge \mathbf{b}|}{ab}.$$

The distributive law for products of vectors

The distributive law for products of scalar quantities

$$a(b+c) = ab+ac,$$

will be shown to hold also for both types of products of vector quantities.

Case (i)—Scalar product In Fig. 16, where vectors **a**, **b**, **c** are represented by $\overline{OA}$, $\overline{OB}$, $\overline{BC}$, clearly the sum $\mathbf{b}+\mathbf{c}$ is represented by $\overline{OC}$. If θ, φ, ψ are the angles of inclination of the pairs of vectors **a**, **b**; **a**, **c**; **a**, $(\mathbf{b}+\mathbf{c})$ respectively, then

$$\mathbf{a}\,.\,\mathbf{b}+\mathbf{a}\,.\,\mathbf{c} = OA\,.\,OB\cos\theta + OA\,.\,BC\cos\varphi$$

$$= OA(OB'+B'C') = OA\,.\,OC'.$$

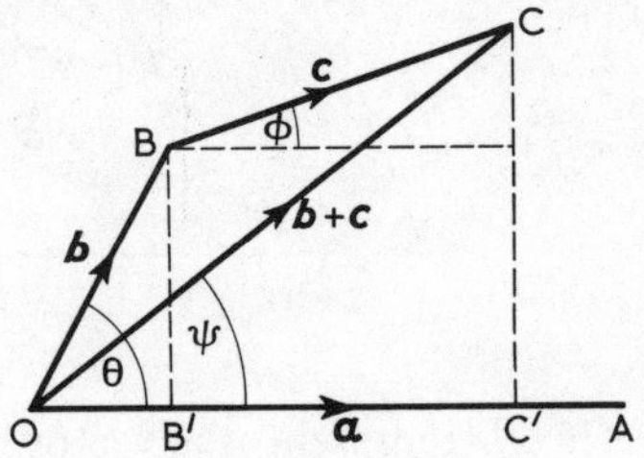

FIG. 16.

Also $$\mathbf{a}\,.\,(\mathbf{b}+\mathbf{c}) = OA\,.\,OC\cos\psi = OA\,.\,OC'.$$

$$\therefore \quad \mathbf{a}\,.\,(\mathbf{b}+\mathbf{c}) = \mathbf{a}\,.\,\mathbf{b}+\mathbf{a}\,.\,\mathbf{c}.$$

This result can be used to establish the more general results

$$\mathbf{a}\,.\,(\mathbf{b}+\mathbf{c}+\mathbf{d}+\cdots) = \mathbf{a}\,.\,\mathbf{b}+\mathbf{a}\,.\,\mathbf{c}+\mathbf{a}\,.\,\mathbf{d}+\cdots;$$

$$(\mathbf{a}+\mathbf{b})\,.\,(\mathbf{c}+\mathbf{d}) = (\mathbf{a}+\mathbf{b})\,.\,\mathbf{c}+(\mathbf{a}+\mathbf{b})\,.\,\mathbf{d}$$
$$= \mathbf{a}\,.\,\mathbf{c}+\mathbf{b}\,.\,\mathbf{c}+\mathbf{a}\,.\,\mathbf{d}+\mathbf{b}\,.\,\mathbf{d}.$$

Thus the distributive law is obeyed in the scalar multiplication of vectors.

Case (ii)—Vector product In Fig. 17 (a), $\overline{OA}$, $\overline{OB}$ represent vectors **a**, **b** inclined at an angle θ, π is the plane through O perpendicular to OA and OB' is the projection of OB on this plane, so $OB' = OB\sin\theta$.

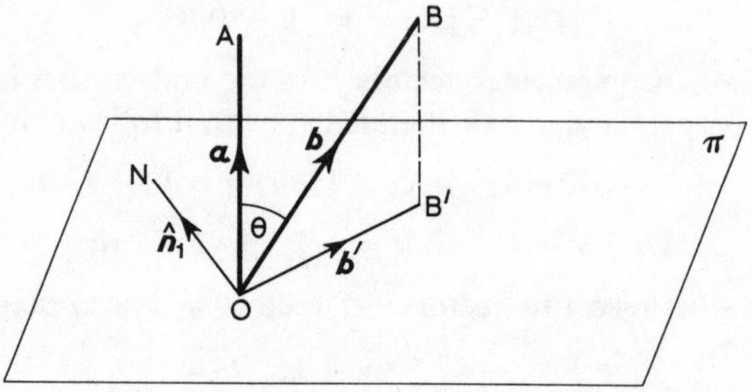

(a)

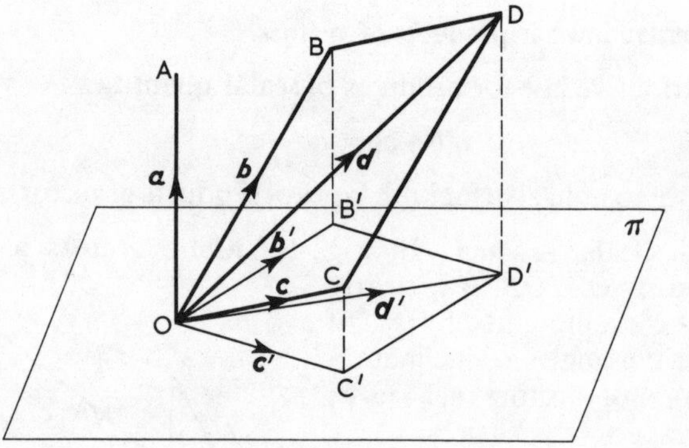

(b)

FIG. 17.

If $\overline{OB'}$ represents the vector $\mathbf{b}'$ and $\overline{ON}$ represents the unit vector $\hat{\mathbf{n}}_1$, perpendicular to both **a** and **b** and such that **a**, **b**, $\hat{\mathbf{n}}_1$, form a right-handed system, then

$$\mathbf{a} \wedge \mathbf{b} = OA\,.\,OB \sin\theta\hat{\mathbf{n}}_1;$$

$$\mathbf{a} \wedge \mathbf{b}' = OA\,.\,OB' \sin\tfrac{1}{2}\pi\,.\,\hat{\mathbf{n}}_1 = OA\,.\,OB \sin\theta\hat{\mathbf{n}}_1.$$

$$\therefore \quad \mathbf{a} \wedge \mathbf{b} = \mathbf{a} \wedge \mathbf{b}' = OA\,.\,OB'\hat{\mathbf{n}}_1. \qquad \text{(i)}$$

In Fig. 17 (*b*) which is an extension of Fig. 17 (*a*), $\overline{OC}$ represents a third vector **c** and $\overline{OD}$, where $OCDB$ is a parallelogram, represents the vector **d** equal to **b**+**c**. OC', OD' are the projections of OC, OD on the plane π.

As OB and CD are equal and equally inclined to π, $OB' = C'D'$.

Similarly, $OC' = B'D'$ and hence $OB'D'C'$ is a parallelogram.

So if $\overline{OC'}$, $\overline{OD'}$ represents vectors **c**′, **d**′, then $\mathbf{d}' = \mathbf{b}' + \mathbf{c}'$. Using result (i) above,

$$\mathbf{a} \wedge \mathbf{b} = \mathbf{a} \wedge \mathbf{b}' = OA\,.\,OB'\hat{\mathbf{n}}_1;$$

$$\mathbf{a} \wedge \mathbf{c} = \mathbf{a} \wedge \mathbf{c}' = OA\,.\,OC'\hat{\mathbf{n}}_2;$$

$$\mathbf{a} \wedge (\mathbf{b}+\mathbf{c}) = \mathbf{a} \wedge \mathbf{d} = \mathbf{a} \wedge \mathbf{d}' = OA\,.\,OD'\hat{\mathbf{n}}_3,$$

where $\hat{\mathbf{n}}_1$, $\hat{\mathbf{n}}_2$, $\hat{\mathbf{n}}_3$ are unit vectors in the plane π perpendicular to OB', OC', OD' respectively, the sense being determined as in the case of $\hat{\mathbf{n}}_1$.

If lines OB'', OC'', OD'' are drawn in the plane π such that $\overline{OB''} = OA\,.\,OB'\hat{\mathbf{n}}_1$, $\overline{OC''} = OA\,.\,OC'\hat{\mathbf{n}}_2$, $\overline{OD''} = OA\,.\,OD'\hat{\mathbf{n}}_3$, then the quadrilateral $OB''D''C''$ will be equiangular to parallelogram $OB'D'C'$ and will have sides proportional in length to the sides of the parallelogram. Therefore $OB''D''C''$ will be a parallelogram, and so

$$\overline{OD''} = \overline{OB''} + \overline{OC''}$$

i.e. $$OA\,.\,OD'\hat{\mathbf{n}}_3 = OA\,.\,OB'\hat{\mathbf{n}}_1 + OA\,.\,OC'\hat{\mathbf{n}}_2,$$

or $$\mathbf{a} \wedge (\mathbf{b}+\mathbf{c}) = \mathbf{a} \wedge \mathbf{b} + \mathbf{a} \wedge \mathbf{c}.$$

This result can be used to establish the more general results

$$\mathbf{a} \wedge (\mathbf{b}+\mathbf{c}+\mathbf{d}+\ldots) = \mathbf{a} \wedge \mathbf{b} + \mathbf{a} \wedge \mathbf{c} + \mathbf{a} \wedge \mathbf{d} + \ldots;$$

$$(\mathbf{a}+\mathbf{b}) \wedge (\mathbf{c}+\mathbf{d}) = (\mathbf{a}+\mathbf{b}) \wedge \mathbf{c} + (\mathbf{a}+\mathbf{b}) \wedge \mathbf{d}$$

$$= \mathbf{a} \wedge \mathbf{c} + \mathbf{b} \wedge \mathbf{c} + \mathbf{a} \wedge \mathbf{d} + \mathbf{b} \wedge \mathbf{d}.$$

Thus the distributive law is obeyed in the vector multiplication of vectors.

Ex. 4 *If* **a**, **b** *are perpendicular vectors, show that* $(\mathbf{a}+\mathbf{b})^2 = (\mathbf{a}-\mathbf{b})^2$.

$$(\mathbf{a}+\mathbf{b})^2 = (\mathbf{a}+\mathbf{b})\,.\,(\mathbf{a}+\mathbf{b}) = \mathbf{a}^2 + \mathbf{a}\,.\,\mathbf{b} + \mathbf{b}\,.\,\mathbf{a} + \mathbf{b}^2$$

$$= \mathbf{a}^2 + \mathbf{b}^2, \quad \text{as} \quad \mathbf{a}\,.\,\mathbf{b} = \mathbf{b}\,.\,\mathbf{a} = 0.$$

Also $(\mathbf{a}-\mathbf{b})^2 = (\mathbf{a}-\mathbf{b}).(\mathbf{a}-\mathbf{b}) = \mathbf{a}^2-\mathbf{a}.\mathbf{b}-\mathbf{b}.\mathbf{a}+\mathbf{b}^2$

$$= \mathbf{a}^2+\mathbf{b}^2.$$

$$\therefore \quad (\mathbf{a}+\mathbf{b})^2 = (\mathbf{a}-\mathbf{b})^2.$$

Ex. 5 *If* $\mathbf{a} \wedge \mathbf{b} = \mathbf{b} \wedge \mathbf{c} \neq 0$, *prove that* $\mathbf{a}+\mathbf{c} = \lambda\mathbf{b}$, *where* λ *is a scalar parameter.*

As $\quad \mathbf{a} \wedge \mathbf{b} = \mathbf{b} \wedge \mathbf{c}, \quad \mathbf{a} \wedge \mathbf{b}-\mathbf{b} \wedge \mathbf{c} = 0.$

$$\therefore \quad \mathbf{a} \wedge \mathbf{b}+\mathbf{c} \wedge \mathbf{b} = 0 \quad \text{or} \quad (\mathbf{a}+\mathbf{c}) \wedge \mathbf{b} = 0.$$

But as neither $\mathbf{a} \wedge \mathbf{b}$ nor $\mathbf{b} \wedge \mathbf{c}$ is zero, then none of $\mathbf{a}$, $\mathbf{b}$, $\mathbf{c}$ is a null vector.

$\therefore$ $\mathbf{a}+\mathbf{c}$ is a vector parallel to $\mathbf{b}$, or $\mathbf{a}+\mathbf{c} = \lambda\mathbf{b}$ where λ is a scalar parameter.

EXAMPLES 2a

1 If a, b are the moduli of vectors $\mathbf{a}$, $\mathbf{b}$ inclined at an angle θ, find the values of $\mathbf{a}.\mathbf{b}$ and $|\mathbf{a} \wedge \mathbf{b}|$ in each of the following cases: (i) $a = 3$, $b = 4$, $\theta = 60°$; (ii) $a = b = \sqrt{2}$, $\theta = 45°$; (iii) $a = 5$, $b = 8$, $\theta = 90°$; (iv) $a = \sqrt{3}$, $b = 1$, $\theta = 120°$; (v) $a = 1$, $b = \sqrt{2}$, $\theta = 135°$.

2 OA, OB are straight lines of lengths 10 cm, 12 cm respectively inclined at an angle of 60°. What are the values of (i) $\overline{OA}.\overline{OB}$; (ii) $\overline{OB}.\overline{OA}$; (iii) $\overline{AO}.\overline{BO}$; (iv) $\overline{AO}.\overline{OB}$; (v) $\overline{BO}.\overline{OA}$?

3 With the data of the previous question and given also that $\hat{\mathbf{n}}$ is a unit vector normal to the plane AOB and such that $\overline{OA}$, $\overline{OB}$, $\hat{\mathbf{n}}$ form a right-handed system, find the values of (i) $\overline{OA} \wedge \overline{OB}$; (ii) $\overline{OB} \wedge \overline{OA}$; (iii) $\overline{AO} \wedge \overline{BO}$; (iv) $\overline{AO} \wedge \overline{OB}$; (v) $\overline{BO} \wedge \overline{OA}$.

4 OAB is a triangle right-angled at A. Prove that (i) $\overline{OA}.\overline{OB} = OA^2$; (ii) $|\overline{OA} \wedge \overline{OB}| = OA.AB$.

5 A, B are points in the plane XOY with coordinates (4, 0), (7, 4) respectively. Express the product $\overline{OA} \wedge \overline{AB}$ in terms of $\mathbf{k}$, the unit vector in the direction of the axis $\overline{OZ}$.

6 If $\mathbf{a} \wedge \mathbf{b} = \mathbf{c}$, what is known about the directions of (i) $\mathbf{a}$ and $\mathbf{c}$; (ii) $\mathbf{b}$ and $\mathbf{c}$? Deduce the values of $\mathbf{a}.\mathbf{c}$ and $\mathbf{b}.\mathbf{c}$.

7 Prove that $(\mathbf{a}-\mathbf{b}) \wedge (\mathbf{a}+\mathbf{b}) = 2\mathbf{a} \wedge \mathbf{b}$.

8 If $\mathbf{p}$, $\mathbf{q}$ are non-null vectors and $\mathbf{p}.\mathbf{q} = 0$ what is the connection between the directions of $\mathbf{p}$ and $\mathbf{q}$? If $\mathbf{p} \wedge \mathbf{q} = 0$, show that $\mathbf{p} = \lambda\mathbf{q}$ where λ is a scalar parameter.

9 If n is a scalar, simplify $\mathbf{a} \wedge (\mathbf{b}+n\mathbf{a})$.

10 If $\mathbf{a}$, $\mathbf{b}$ are perpendicular and λ is a scalar quantity, show that $(\mathbf{a}+\lambda\mathbf{b}).(\mathbf{a}+\mathbf{b}/\lambda) = a^2+b^2$.

11 If vectors $\mathbf{a}+\mathbf{b}$ and $\mathbf{a}-\mathbf{b}$ are perpendicular, show that $\mathbf{a}$, $\mathbf{b}$ are of equal magnitudes.

12 If m is a scalar, verify the results (i) $m(\mathbf{a}\,.\,\mathbf{b}) = (m\mathbf{a})\,.\,\mathbf{b} = \mathbf{a}\,.\,(m\mathbf{b})$; (ii) $m(\mathbf{a} \wedge \mathbf{b}) = (m\mathbf{a}) \wedge \mathbf{b} = \mathbf{a} \wedge (m\mathbf{b})$.

13 If $\overline{OA} = \mathbf{a}, \overline{OB} = \mathbf{b}$, show that the area of triangle OAB is $\frac{1}{2}|\mathbf{a} \wedge \mathbf{b}|$.

14 In the cyclic quadrilateral $OAO'B$, $OA = 2OB$ and $2O'A = O'B$. Prove (i) $\overline{OA}\,.\,\overline{O'A}+\overline{OB}\,.\,\overline{O'B} = 0$. (ii) $\overline{OA} \wedge \overline{O'A} = \overline{OB} \wedge \overline{BO'}$.

15 Given that $\mathbf{x}\,.\,\mathbf{a} = \mathbf{x}\,.\,\mathbf{b}$ where $\mathbf{x} \neq 0$ and $\mathbf{a} \neq \mathbf{b}$, show that $\mathbf{x}$ is perpendicular to $\mathbf{a}-\mathbf{b}$.

16 If vectors $\mathbf{a}, \mathbf{b}, \mathbf{c}$ are represented by the sides $\overline{BC}, \overline{CA}, \overline{AB}$ of a triangle ABC prove that $|\mathbf{b} \wedge \mathbf{c}| = |\mathbf{c} \wedge \mathbf{a}| = |\mathbf{a} \wedge \mathbf{b}| = 2\Delta$, where Δ is the area of triangle ABC. Deduce that $\mathbf{b} \wedge \mathbf{c} = \mathbf{c} \wedge \mathbf{a} = \mathbf{a} \wedge \mathbf{b}$.

17 $\mathbf{a}, \mathbf{b}, \mathbf{c}$ are concurrent vectors such that $\mathbf{c} = \lambda\mathbf{a}+\mu\mathbf{b}$, where λ, μ are scalar quantities. If $\mathbf{n}$ is a vector normal to the plane of $\mathbf{a}, \mathbf{b}$, show that $\mathbf{n}\,.\,\mathbf{c} = 0$ and deduce that the vectors $\mathbf{a}, \mathbf{b}, \mathbf{c}$ are coplanar.

18 If P is a point on the side BC of a triangle ABC, prove that $\overline{BP} \wedge \overline{BA}+\overline{CA} \wedge \overline{CP} = \overline{AB} \wedge \overline{AC}$.

19 Show that the resolved component of a vector $\mathbf{r}$ in the direction of a vector $\mathbf{a}$ has a modulus of $(\mathbf{a}\,.\,\mathbf{r})/a$ and deduce that the resolved component is $(\mathbf{a}\,.\,\mathbf{r})\mathbf{a}/a^2$.

20 Vectors $\mathbf{a}, \mathbf{b}, \mathbf{c}$ are such that $\mathbf{b} \wedge \mathbf{c} = \mathbf{c} \wedge \mathbf{a} \neq 0$, show that $\mathbf{a}+\mathbf{b} = \lambda\mathbf{c}$, where λ is a scalar parameter.

21 If $\mathbf{a} \wedge \mathbf{b} = \mathbf{b} \wedge \mathbf{c} = \mathbf{c} \wedge \mathbf{a} = \mathbf{r} \neq 0$, prove that (i) $\mathbf{a}$, $\mathbf{b}$ and $\mathbf{c}$ are parallel to a plane; (ii) $\mathbf{a} \wedge (\mathbf{a}+\mathbf{b}+\mathbf{c}) = \mathbf{b} \wedge (\mathbf{a}+\mathbf{b}+\mathbf{c}) = \mathbf{c} \wedge (\mathbf{a}+\mathbf{b}+\mathbf{c}) = 0$. What is the value of $\mathbf{a}+\mathbf{b}+\mathbf{c}$?

22 If $\mathbf{a}+\mathbf{b}+\mathbf{c} = 0$, show that $\mathbf{a} \wedge \mathbf{b} = \mathbf{b} \wedge \mathbf{c} = \mathbf{c} \wedge \mathbf{a}$.

Products of two vectors in terms of their components Consider the vectors

$$\mathbf{a} = a_1\mathbf{i}+a_2\mathbf{j}+a_3\mathbf{k}; \quad \mathbf{b} = b_1\mathbf{i}+b_2\mathbf{j}+b_3\mathbf{k},$$

where $\mathbf{i}, \mathbf{j}, \mathbf{k}$ are unit vectors in the directions of three mutually perpendicular axes $\overline{OX}, \overline{OY}, \overline{OZ}$ which form a right-handed system.

Scalar product

$$\mathbf{a}\,.\,\mathbf{b} = (a_1\mathbf{i}+a_2\mathbf{j}+a_3\mathbf{k})\,.\,(b_1\mathbf{i}+b_2\mathbf{j}+b_3\mathbf{k}).$$

Noting that $$\mathbf{i}\,.\,\mathbf{i} \text{ or } \mathbf{i}^2 = 1 = \mathbf{j}^2 = \mathbf{k}^2,$$

and $$\mathbf{j}\,.\,\mathbf{k} = \mathbf{k}\,.\,\mathbf{i} = \mathbf{i}\,.\,\mathbf{j} = 0,$$

the product simplifies to $a_1b_1+a_2b_2+a_3b_3$.

$$\therefore \quad \mathbf{a}\,.\,\mathbf{b} = a_1b_1+a_2b_2+a_3b_3.$$

If the two vectors are inclined at an angle θ,

$$\mathbf{a}\,.\,\mathbf{b} = ab\cos\theta,$$

where $$a = \sqrt{(a_1^2+a_2^2+a_3^2)};\ b = \sqrt{(b_1^2+b_2^2+b_3^2)}.$$

$$\therefore \quad \cos\theta = \frac{a_1b_1+a_2b_2+a_3b_3}{\sqrt{\{(a_1^2+a_2^2+a_3^2)(b_1^2+b_2^2+b_3^2)\}}}.$$

Vector product

$$\mathbf{a} \wedge \mathbf{b} = (a_1\mathbf{i}+a_2\mathbf{j}+a_3\mathbf{k}) \wedge (b_1\mathbf{i}+b_2\mathbf{j}+b_3\mathbf{k}).$$

Noting that $$\mathbf{i} \wedge \mathbf{i} = \mathbf{j} \wedge \mathbf{j} = \mathbf{k} \wedge \mathbf{k} = 0,$$

and $\mathbf{j} \wedge \mathbf{k} = -\mathbf{k} \wedge \mathbf{j} = \mathbf{i};\ \mathbf{k} \wedge \mathbf{i} = -\mathbf{i} \wedge \mathbf{k} = \mathbf{j};\ \mathbf{i} \wedge \mathbf{j} = -\mathbf{j} \wedge \mathbf{i} = \mathbf{k},$

the product simplifies to

$$\mathbf{i}(a_2b_3-a_3b_2)-\mathbf{j}(a_1b_3-a_3b_1)+\mathbf{k}(a_1b_2-a_2b_1).$$

This expression is best remembered by writing it in the form of a determinant where **i**, **j**, **k** are treated in the same way as real algebraic quantities.

So, $$\mathbf{a} \wedge \mathbf{b} = \begin{vmatrix} \mathbf{i} & \mathbf{j} & \mathbf{k} \\ a_1 & a_2 & a_3 \\ b_1 & b_2 & b_3 \end{vmatrix}.$$

As $|\mathbf{a} \wedge \mathbf{b}| = ab\sin\theta$,

$$\sin\theta = \frac{|\mathbf{a} \wedge \mathbf{b}|}{ab}$$

$$= \frac{\sqrt{\{(a_2b_3-a_3b_2)^2+(a_1b_3-a_3b_1)^2+(a_1b_2-a_2b_1)^2\}}}{\sqrt{\{(a_1^2+a_2^2+a_3^2)(b_1^2+b_2^2+b_3^2)\}}}.$$

Ex. 6 *Find the angle at which the vectors* $\mathbf{a} = 3\mathbf{i}+\mathbf{j}-\mathbf{k}$, $\mathbf{b} = 2\mathbf{i}-3\mathbf{j}-2\mathbf{k}$ *are inclined.*

$$\cos\theta = \frac{\mathbf{a}\,.\,\mathbf{b}}{ab} = \frac{(3)(2)+(1)(-3)+(-1)(-2)}{\sqrt{\{(3^2+1^2+1^2)(2^2+3^2+2^2)\}}} = \frac{5}{\sqrt{187}},$$

i.e. $$\text{Angle of inclination} = \cos^{-1}\frac{5}{\sqrt{187}}.$$

Ex. 7 *Given* $\mathbf{p} = \mathbf{i}+\mathbf{j}$, $\mathbf{q} = 2\mathbf{i}-\mathbf{j}+2\mathbf{k}$. *Find the components of the vector* $\mathbf{p} \wedge \mathbf{q}$ *in the directions of the axes. Also find the modulus of the component of the vector* $\mathbf{p} \wedge \mathbf{q}$ *in the direction of the vector* $\mathbf{r} = \mathbf{i}+\mathbf{j}-\mathbf{k}$.

$$\mathbf{p} \wedge \mathbf{q} = \begin{vmatrix} \mathbf{i} & \mathbf{j} & \mathbf{k} \\ 1 & 1 & 0 \\ 2 & -1 & 2 \end{vmatrix} = 2\mathbf{i}-2\mathbf{j}-3\mathbf{k}.$$

So the components of $\mathbf{p} \wedge \mathbf{q}$ in the directions of the axes are $2\mathbf{i}$, $-2\mathbf{j}$, $-3\mathbf{k}$. Writing

$$\mathbf{a} = \mathbf{p} \wedge \mathbf{q} = 2\mathbf{i}-2\mathbf{j}-3\mathbf{k}.$$

The modulus of the component of $\mathbf{a}$ in the direction of the vector $\mathbf{r}$ which is inclined at an angle θ to $\mathbf{a}$ is $a \cos \theta$ or $\frac{1}{r}(\mathbf{a} \cdot \mathbf{r})$.

$$\therefore \quad \text{Modulus of component} = \frac{(2)(1)+(-2)(1)+(-3)(-1)}{\sqrt{(1^2+1^2+1^2)}} = \sqrt{3}.$$

Ex. 8 *Find the unit vectors which are perpendicular to both the vectors* $\mathbf{a} = 2\mathbf{i}+2\mathbf{j}-\mathbf{k}$, $\mathbf{b} = 4\mathbf{i}+\mathbf{j}-\mathbf{k}$.

Vectors $\mathbf{a} \wedge \mathbf{b}$ and $\mathbf{b} \wedge \mathbf{a}$ are perpendicular to both the vectors $\mathbf{a}$, $\mathbf{b}$.

$$\mathbf{a} \wedge \mathbf{b} = \begin{vmatrix} \mathbf{i} & \mathbf{j} & \mathbf{k} \\ 2 & 2 & -1 \\ 4 & 1 & -1 \end{vmatrix} = -\mathbf{i}-2\mathbf{j}-6\mathbf{k}.$$

$$\therefore \quad \mathbf{b} \wedge \mathbf{a} = \mathbf{i}+2\mathbf{j}+6\mathbf{k}.$$

Both these vectors have a modulus of $\sqrt{41}$ and so the required vectors of unit moduli are $\frac{1}{\sqrt{41}}(-\mathbf{i}-2\mathbf{j}-6\mathbf{k})$, $\frac{1}{\sqrt{41}}(\mathbf{i}+2\mathbf{j}+6\mathbf{k})$.

Perpendicular vectors Problems involving perpendicular vectors can be simplified by using components with axes in the directions of the vectors as is illustrated in the following worked example.

Ex. 9 *If* $\mathbf{a}$, $\mathbf{b}$ *are perpendicular vectors, show that the solution of the equation* $\mathbf{x} \wedge \mathbf{a} = \mathbf{b}$ *is* $\mathbf{x} = (\mathbf{a} \wedge \mathbf{b})/a^2 + \lambda\mathbf{a}$, *where* λ *is a scalar parameter.*

Take a right-handed system of axes $\overline{OX}, \overline{OY}, \overline{OZ}$ in the directions of $\mathbf{a}$, $\mathbf{b}$ and the normal to the plane of $\mathbf{a}$ and $\mathbf{b}$. Let unit vectors in the directions of the axes be $\mathbf{i}$, $\mathbf{j}$, $\mathbf{k}$.

So $\mathbf{a} = a\mathbf{i}$; $\mathbf{b} = b\mathbf{j}$; $\mathbf{a} \wedge \mathbf{b} = ab\mathbf{i} \wedge \mathbf{j} = ab\mathbf{k}$.

Let $\qquad \mathbf{x} = x_1\mathbf{i}+x_2\mathbf{j}+x_3\mathbf{k},$

then $$\mathbf{x} \wedge \mathbf{a} = (x_1\mathbf{i}+x_2\mathbf{j}+x_3\mathbf{k}) \wedge a\mathbf{i}$$
$$= -ax_2\mathbf{k}+ax_3\mathbf{j}.$$

But $$\mathbf{x} \wedge \mathbf{a} = \mathbf{b} = b\mathbf{j}.$$

$$\therefore \quad x_2 = 0; \quad x_3 = \frac{b}{a}.$$

Hence $$\mathbf{x} = x_1\mathbf{i}+\frac{b}{a}\mathbf{k} = \frac{x_1}{a}\mathbf{a}+\frac{1}{a^2}\mathbf{a} \wedge \mathbf{b}.$$

As x_1 is an arbitrary scalar, $\dfrac{x_1}{a}$ can be written as a scalar parameter λ.

$$\therefore \quad \mathbf{x} = \frac{1}{a^2}\mathbf{a} \wedge \mathbf{b}+\lambda\mathbf{a}.$$

Triple vector products The quantity $\mathbf{a} \cdot (\mathbf{b} \wedge \mathbf{c})$ is the scalar product of the vectors $\mathbf{a}$ and $\mathbf{b} \wedge \mathbf{c}$; it is called **a scalar triple product.** In terms of vector components,

$$\mathbf{a} \cdot (\mathbf{b} \wedge \mathbf{c}) = (a_1\mathbf{i}+a_2\mathbf{j}+a_3\mathbf{k}) \cdot [\mathbf{i}(b_2c_3-b_3c_2)+\mathbf{j}(b_3c_1-b_1c_3)$$
$$+\mathbf{k}(b_1c_2-b_2c_1)]$$
$$= a_1(b_2c_3-b_3c_2)+a_2(b_3c_1-b_1c_3)+a_3(b_1c_2-b_2c_1).$$

This expression can be written in the determinant form,

$$\begin{vmatrix} a_1 & a_2 & a_3 \\ b_1 & b_2 & b_3 \\ c_1 & c_2 & c_3 \end{vmatrix}.$$

The triple product $(\mathbf{a} \wedge \mathbf{b}) \cdot \mathbf{c}$ is readily seen to be equal to the same determinant and as a consequence either of these products can be written as $[\mathbf{a}, \mathbf{b}, \mathbf{c}]$.

It follows at once from the properties of determinants that the value of a triple product is unchanged by a cyclic interchange of the three elements, i.e.

$$[\mathbf{a}, \mathbf{b}, \mathbf{c}] = [\mathbf{b}, \mathbf{c}, \mathbf{a}] = [\mathbf{c}, \mathbf{a}, \mathbf{b}],$$

but the interchange of two elements will lead to a change of sign, e.g.

$$[\mathbf{a}, \mathbf{b}, \mathbf{c}] = -[\mathbf{c}, \mathbf{b}, \mathbf{a}].$$

Ex. 10 *If* $\mathbf{a}, \mathbf{b}, \mathbf{c}$ *are coplanar vectors, show that* $[\mathbf{a}, \mathbf{b}, \mathbf{c}]$ *is zero.*

The product $\mathbf{b} \wedge \mathbf{c}$ is a vector normal to the plane of $\mathbf{b}$ and $\mathbf{c}$ and therefore normal to $\mathbf{a}$.

Hence $\quad \mathbf{a} \cdot (\mathbf{b} \wedge \mathbf{c}) = 0; \quad \text{i.e. } [\mathbf{a}, \mathbf{b}, \mathbf{c}] = 0.$

Vector triple product The quantity $\mathbf{a} \wedge (\mathbf{b} \wedge \mathbf{c})$ is the vector product of $\mathbf{a}$ and $\mathbf{b} \wedge \mathbf{c}$; it is called a **vector triple product** and can be expressed in terms of $\mathbf{b}$ and $\mathbf{c}$.

For representing the triple product by $\mathbf{v}$, then as $\mathbf{v}$ is perpendicular to $\mathbf{b} \wedge \mathbf{c}$ it can be considered as being in the plane of $\mathbf{b}$ and $\mathbf{c}$ and so it can be expressed as $\mathbf{v} = p\mathbf{b} + q\mathbf{c}$ where p, q are scalars.

Taking rectangular unit vectors $\mathbf{i}, \mathbf{j}, \mathbf{k}$ with $\mathbf{j}, \mathbf{k}$ in the plane of $\mathbf{b}, \mathbf{c}$ and $\mathbf{j}$ parallel to $\mathbf{b}$, then

$$\mathbf{b} = b\mathbf{j}; \quad \mathbf{c} = c_2\mathbf{j} + c_3\mathbf{k}; \quad \mathbf{a} = a_1\mathbf{i} + a_2\mathbf{j} + a_3\mathbf{k}.$$

$$\begin{aligned} \therefore \quad \mathbf{v} &= (a_1\mathbf{i} + a_2\mathbf{j} + a_3\mathbf{k}) \wedge [b\mathbf{j} \wedge (c_2\mathbf{j} + c_3\mathbf{k})] \\ &= (a_1\mathbf{i} + a_2\mathbf{j} + a_3\mathbf{k}) \wedge (bc_3\mathbf{i}) \\ &= -a_2bc_3\mathbf{k} + a_3bc_3\mathbf{j} = -a_2b(\mathbf{c} - c_2\mathbf{j}) + a_3c_3\mathbf{b} \\ &= -a_2b\mathbf{c} + a_2c_2\mathbf{b} + a_3c_3\mathbf{b} \\ &= (a_2c_2 + a_3c_3)\mathbf{b} - a_2b\mathbf{c}. \end{aligned}$$

But $a_2c_2 + a_3c_3 = \mathbf{a} \cdot \mathbf{c}$ and $a_2b = \mathbf{a} \cdot \mathbf{b}$.

$$\therefore \quad \mathbf{a} \wedge (\mathbf{b} \wedge \mathbf{c}) = [\mathbf{a} \cdot \mathbf{c}]\mathbf{b} - [\mathbf{a} \cdot \mathbf{b}]\mathbf{c}.$$

It is important to realise that in a vector triple product the position of the bracket cannot be changed for $\mathbf{a} \wedge (\mathbf{b} \wedge \mathbf{c})$ is a vector expressible in terms of $\mathbf{b}$, $\mathbf{c}$ and is quite different from $(\mathbf{a} \wedge \mathbf{b}) \wedge \mathbf{c}$ or $-\mathbf{c} \wedge (\mathbf{a} \wedge \mathbf{b})$, a vector expressible in terms of $\mathbf{a}$, $\mathbf{b}$.

Ex. 11 *If* $\mathbf{a}, \mathbf{b}$ *are perpendicular vectors, verify that* $\mathbf{x} = \frac{1}{a^2}\mathbf{a} \wedge \mathbf{b} + t\mathbf{a}$, *where t is a scalar parameter, is the solution of the equation* $\mathbf{x} \wedge \mathbf{a} = \mathbf{b}$.

We have
$$\begin{aligned} \mathbf{x} \wedge \mathbf{a} &= \left[\frac{1}{a^2}\mathbf{a} \wedge \mathbf{b} + t\mathbf{a}\right] \wedge \mathbf{a} \\ &= \frac{1}{a^2}(\mathbf{a} \wedge \mathbf{b}) \wedge \mathbf{a} = -\frac{1}{a^2}\mathbf{a} \wedge (\mathbf{a} \wedge \mathbf{b}) \\ &= -\frac{1}{a^2}[\mathbf{a} \cdot \mathbf{b}]\mathbf{a} + \frac{1}{a^2}[\mathbf{a} \cdot \mathbf{a}]\mathbf{b} \\ &= \mathbf{b}, \quad \text{as} \quad \mathbf{a} \cdot \mathbf{b} = 0 \quad \text{and} \quad \frac{1}{a^2}[\mathbf{a} \cdot \mathbf{a}] = 1. \end{aligned}$$

EXAMPLES 2b

1 Find the values of $\mathbf{a}\,.\,\mathbf{b}$ and $\mathbf{a} \wedge \mathbf{b}$ in each of the following cases: (i) $\mathbf{a} = 3\mathbf{i}+\mathbf{j}+\mathbf{k}$, $\mathbf{b} = 2\mathbf{j}-\mathbf{k}$; (ii) $\mathbf{a} = \mathbf{i}+\mathbf{j}+\mathbf{k}$, $\mathbf{b} = \mathbf{i}-2\mathbf{j}-\mathbf{k}$; (iii) $\mathbf{a} = 3\mathbf{i}+\mathbf{j}$, $\mathbf{b} = \mathbf{i}-\mathbf{j}$; (iv) $\mathbf{a} = 4\mathbf{i}+2\mathbf{j}-\mathbf{k}$, $\mathbf{b} = 2\mathbf{i}-3\mathbf{j}+\mathbf{k}$; (v) $\mathbf{a} = 2\mathbf{i}-\mathbf{k}$, $\mathbf{b} = \mathbf{j}+\mathbf{k}$.

2 With the data of example 1, find the values of $(\mathbf{a}+\mathbf{b})\,.\,(\mathbf{a}-\mathbf{b})$.

3 With the data of example 1, find the values of $(\mathbf{a}+2\mathbf{b}) \wedge (2\mathbf{a}+\mathbf{b})$.

4 Show that the vectors $p\mathbf{i}+q\mathbf{j}$, $-q\mathbf{i}+p\mathbf{j}$ are perpendicular and of equal moduli.

5 Find the cosine of the angle of inclination of each of the following pairs of vectors: (i) $\mathbf{i}-\mathbf{j}+\mathbf{k}$, $2\mathbf{i}+\mathbf{j}$; (ii) $2\mathbf{i}+\mathbf{j}+2\mathbf{k}$, $6\mathbf{i}-3\mathbf{j}-2\mathbf{k}$; (iii) $\mathbf{i}-3\mathbf{j}-\mathbf{k}$, $3\mathbf{i}+2\mathbf{j}+\mathbf{k}$; (iv) $-\mathbf{i}-2\mathbf{j}+2\mathbf{k}$, $3\mathbf{i}+4\mathbf{j}$; (v) $2\mathbf{i}+2\mathbf{j}-\mathbf{k}$, $-5\mathbf{i}-12\mathbf{k}$.

6 Find the sines of the angles of inclination of the pairs of vectors: (i) $4\mathbf{i}+\mathbf{j}$, $2\mathbf{i}-\mathbf{j}$; (ii) $\mathbf{i}+\mathbf{j}+\mathbf{k}$, $\mathbf{i}-\mathbf{j}-\mathbf{k}$; (iii) $4\mathbf{i}$, $\mathbf{i}+\mathbf{j}+\mathbf{k}$.

7 Show that the following pairs of vectors are perpendicular: (i) $\mathbf{i}-2\mathbf{j}$, $2\mathbf{i}+\mathbf{j}$; (ii) $2\mathbf{i}-\mathbf{j}+3\mathbf{k}$, $\mathbf{i}-\mathbf{j}-\mathbf{k}$; (iii) $\mathbf{i}+4\mathbf{j}+3\mathbf{k}$, $4\mathbf{i}+2\mathbf{j}-4\mathbf{k}$; (iv) $\mathbf{p}-\mathbf{q}$, $\mathbf{p}+\mathbf{q}$, where $\mathbf{p} = \mathbf{i}\cos\alpha+\mathbf{j}\sin\alpha$, $\mathbf{q} = \mathbf{i}\cos\beta+\mathbf{j}\sin\beta$.

8 If $\hat{\mathbf{n}}$ is a unit vector normal to vectors $\mathbf{a}$, $\mathbf{b}$ and such that $\mathbf{a}$, $\mathbf{b}$, $\hat{\mathbf{n}}$ form a right-handed system, find $\hat{\mathbf{n}}$ in each of the following cases: (i) $\mathbf{a} = 2\mathbf{i}+3\mathbf{j}$, $\mathbf{b} = \mathbf{i}-\mathbf{j}$; (ii) $\mathbf{a} = \mathbf{i}-\mathbf{k}$, $\mathbf{b} = 3\mathbf{i}+2\mathbf{k}$; (iii) $\mathbf{a} = \mathbf{i}+\mathbf{j}-\mathbf{k}$, $\mathbf{b} = \mathbf{i}-\mathbf{j}+\mathbf{k}$; (iv) $\mathbf{a} = 3\mathbf{i}-\mathbf{j}-\mathbf{k}$, $\mathbf{b} = \mathbf{i}+2\mathbf{j}-2\mathbf{k}$.

9 If $\mathbf{a}$, $\mathbf{b}$ are perpendicular vectors of equal moduli, prove that $2\mathbf{a}+\mathbf{b}$, $\mathbf{a}-2\mathbf{b}$ are also perpendicular vectors with equal moduli.

10 Find the modulus of the component of $\mathbf{r}$ in the direction of $\mathbf{a}$ in each of the following cases: (i) $\mathbf{r} = 2\mathbf{i}+\mathbf{k}$, $\mathbf{a} = \mathbf{i}+\mathbf{j}$; (ii) $\mathbf{r} = \mathbf{i}+\mathbf{j}+\mathbf{k}$, $\mathbf{a} = -\mathbf{i}+\mathbf{j}+\mathbf{k}$; (iii) $\mathbf{r} = 4\mathbf{i}-\mathbf{j}+\mathbf{k}$, $\mathbf{a} = \mathbf{i}+3\mathbf{j}-2\mathbf{k}$.

11 If $\mathbf{r} = 2\mathbf{i}+\mathbf{j}-2\mathbf{k}$, $\mathbf{F} = 3\mathbf{i}+6\mathbf{j}+2\mathbf{k}$, find (i) $\mathbf{r} \wedge \mathbf{F}$; (ii) the modulus of the component of $\mathbf{r} \wedge \mathbf{F}$ in the direction of the vector $\mathbf{i}+\mathbf{j}+\mathbf{k}$.

12 Show by using components and expanding that $\mathbf{a}\,.\,(\mathbf{b} \wedge \mathbf{c}) = (\mathbf{a} \wedge \mathbf{b})\,.\,\mathbf{c}$.

13 If $\mathbf{a} = 2\mathbf{i}+\mathbf{j}-\mathbf{k}$, $\mathbf{b} = \mathbf{i}-\mathbf{j}-\mathbf{k}$, $\mathbf{c} = \mathbf{i}+2\mathbf{j}+2\mathbf{k}$, verify that $(\mathbf{c}-\mathbf{a}) \wedge (\mathbf{b}-\mathbf{a}) = (\mathbf{b}-\mathbf{c}) \wedge (\mathbf{a}-\mathbf{c})$.

14 Given $m = 5$, $\mathbf{r} = 3\mathbf{i}-6\mathbf{j}+2\mathbf{k}$, $\mathbf{v} = 2\mathbf{i}-\mathbf{j}+2\mathbf{k}$, find the component of the vector $\mathbf{r} \wedge m\mathbf{v}$ in the direction of the axis of z.

15 Show that $\mathbf{a} = \mathbf{i}\cos\alpha+\mathbf{j}\sin\alpha$, $\mathbf{b} = \mathbf{i}\cos\beta+\mathbf{j}\sin\beta$ are unit vectors in the $x-y$ plane and use the scalar product $\mathbf{a}\,.\,\mathbf{b}$ to obtain a formula for $\cos(\alpha-\beta)$.

16 Prove that $\mathbf{a}\,.\,(\mathbf{a} \wedge \mathbf{b}) = 0$.

17 Find the unit vectors which are perpendicular to each of the following pairs of vectors: (i) $\mathbf{i}+\mathbf{j}+\mathbf{k}$, $2\mathbf{i}-\mathbf{k}$; (ii) $2\mathbf{i}-\mathbf{j}+2\mathbf{k}$, $2\mathbf{i}+6\mathbf{j}-3\mathbf{k}$; (iii) $-\mathbf{i}+2\mathbf{j}+\mathbf{k}$, $4\mathbf{i}-\mathbf{j}+2\mathbf{k}$.

18 The vector $\boldsymbol{\omega}$ is perpendicular to the plane of the vectors $\mathbf{r}$, $\mathbf{v}$. If $\mathbf{v}+\boldsymbol{\omega} \wedge \mathbf{r} = 0$, show by taking the vector product of both sides of the equation with $\boldsymbol{\omega}$ that $\mathbf{r} = \dfrac{1}{\omega^2}\boldsymbol{\omega} \wedge \mathbf{v}$.

19 Find the value of $\mathbf{r} \wedge (\mathbf{v}+\boldsymbol{\omega} \wedge \mathbf{r})$ when $\mathbf{v} = u\mathbf{i}+v\mathbf{j}+w\mathbf{k}$, $\mathbf{r} = x\mathbf{i}+y\mathbf{j}+z\mathbf{k}$, $\boldsymbol{\omega} = \omega\mathbf{k}$.

20 Three mutually perpendicular vectors **a**, **b**, **c** form a right-handed system, prove that (i) $\mathbf{a} = \dfrac{a}{bc}\mathbf{b} \wedge \mathbf{c}$; (ii) the vectors $\mathbf{b}+\mathbf{c}-\mathbf{a}$, $\mathbf{a}+\mathbf{b}-\mathbf{c}$ are inclined at an angle $\cos^{-1}(b^2-c^2-a^2)/(a^2+b^2+c^2)$.

21 Show that the vector $\mathbf{i}(y-z)+\mathbf{j}(z-x)+\mathbf{k}(x-y)$ is perpendicular to each of the vectors $x\mathbf{i}+y\mathbf{j}+z\mathbf{k}$ and $\mathbf{i}+\mathbf{j}+\mathbf{k}$. If the vectors $x\mathbf{i}+y\mathbf{j}+z\mathbf{k}$, $\mathbf{i}+\mathbf{j}+\mathbf{k}$ are themselves perpendicular show that $2(yz+zx+xy) = -(x^2+y^2+z^2)$ and deduce that the modulus of the vector $\mathbf{i}(y-z)+\mathbf{j}(z-x)+\mathbf{k}(x-y)$ is $\sqrt{3}$ times the modulus of the vector $x\mathbf{i}+y\mathbf{j}+z\mathbf{k}$. Hence find two unit vectors which are perpendicular to each other and to $\mathbf{i}+\mathbf{j}+\mathbf{k}$ and also equally inclined to the vector **k**.

22 If vectors $\mathbf{a} = a_1\mathbf{i}+a_2\mathbf{j}+a_3\mathbf{k}$, $\mathbf{b} = b_1\mathbf{i}+b_2\mathbf{j}+b_3\mathbf{k}$ are inclined at an angle θ, obtain expressions for $\cos\theta$ and $\sin\theta$ and deduce the identity

$$(a_2b_3-a_3b_2)^2+(a_1b_3-a_3b_1)^2+(a_1b_2-a_2b_1)^2 \equiv (a_1^2+a_2^2+a_3^2)(b_1^2+b_2^2+b_3^2) - (a_1b_1+a_2b_2+a_3b_3)^2.$$

23 By considering the products $\mathbf{a}\,.\,\mathbf{b}$, $\mathbf{a}\wedge\mathbf{b}$, when $\mathbf{a} = a_1\mathbf{i}+a_2\mathbf{j}+a_3\mathbf{k}$, $\mathbf{b} = b_1\mathbf{i}+b_2\mathbf{j}+b_3\mathbf{k}$, show that for real numbers $a_1, a_2, a_3, b_1, b_2, b_3$,

(i) $(a_1^2+a_2^2+a_3^2)(b_1^2+b_2^2+b_3^2) \geqslant (a_1b_1+a_2b_2+a_3b_3)^2$;

(ii) $(a_1^2+a_2^2+a_3^2)(b_1^2+b_2^2+b_3^2) \geqslant (a_2b_3-a_3b_2)^2+(a_1b_3-a_3b_1)^2 +(a_1b_2-a_2b_1)^2$.

24 Obtain the value of $[\mathbf{a}, \mathbf{b}, \mathbf{c}]$ in each of the following cases: (i) $\mathbf{a} = \mathbf{i}-\mathbf{j}+\mathbf{k}$, $\mathbf{b} = 2\mathbf{j}-\mathbf{k}$, $\mathbf{c} = -\mathbf{i}+\mathbf{j}$; (ii) $\mathbf{a} = 2\mathbf{i}+\mathbf{j}-3\mathbf{k}$, $\mathbf{b} = \mathbf{i}-\mathbf{j}+2\mathbf{k}$, $\mathbf{c} = 3\mathbf{i}-2\mathbf{j}+\mathbf{k}$; (iii) $\mathbf{a} = 2\mathbf{j}+\mathbf{k}$, $\mathbf{b} = 4\mathbf{i}-\mathbf{j}$, $\mathbf{c} = 2\mathbf{j}+\mathbf{k}$.

25 Find the value of the vector triple product $\mathbf{a}\wedge(\mathbf{b}\wedge\mathbf{c})$ in each of the cases of the previous example.

26 Verify the result $\mathbf{a}\wedge(\mathbf{b}\wedge\mathbf{c}) = (\mathbf{a}\,.\,\mathbf{c})\mathbf{b}-(\mathbf{a}\,.\,\mathbf{b})\mathbf{c}$ in the case where $\mathbf{a} = \mathbf{i}+2\mathbf{j}-3\mathbf{k}$, $\mathbf{b} = 3\mathbf{i}-\mathbf{j}-\mathbf{k}$, $\mathbf{c} = 2\mathbf{i}+4\mathbf{j}+\mathbf{k}$.

27 Show that $[\mathbf{c}, \mathbf{b}, \mathbf{a}] = -[\mathbf{a}, \mathbf{b}, \mathbf{c}]$.

28 If **a**, **b**, **c** are non-parallel vectors, what is the geometrical significance of the result $[\mathbf{a}, \mathbf{b}, \mathbf{c}] = 0$?

29 If $\hat{\mathbf{a}}$ is a unit vector, prove that the component perpendicular to $\hat{\mathbf{a}}$ of a vector **b** is $(\hat{\mathbf{a}}\wedge\mathbf{b})\wedge\hat{\mathbf{a}}$.

30 Show that the sum of the vectors $\mathbf{a}\wedge(\mathbf{b}\wedge\mathbf{c})$, $\mathbf{b}\wedge(\mathbf{c}\wedge\mathbf{a})$, $\mathbf{c}\wedge(\mathbf{a}\wedge\mathbf{b})$ is zero.

31 If **a**, **b**, **c** are non-null vectors with **a** not perpendicular to **c** and such that $(\mathbf{a}\wedge\mathbf{b})\wedge\mathbf{c} = \mathbf{a}\wedge(\mathbf{b}\wedge\mathbf{c})$, prove that $(\mathbf{a}\wedge\mathbf{c})\wedge\mathbf{b} = 0$. State the geometrical significance of this result.

32 If **a**, **b**, **c**, **d** are any four vectors, prove that $(\mathbf{a}\wedge\mathbf{b})\,.\,(\mathbf{c}\wedge\mathbf{d}) = (\mathbf{a}\,.\,\mathbf{c})(\mathbf{b}\,.\,\mathbf{d})-(\mathbf{a}\,.\,\mathbf{d})(\mathbf{b}\,.\,\mathbf{c})$.

33 If **a**, **b**, **c**, **d** are non-null vectors such that $(\mathbf{a}\wedge\mathbf{b})\wedge(\mathbf{c}\wedge\mathbf{d}) = 0$, what geometrical possibilities arise?

34 In the equation $\mathbf{a}x+\mathbf{b}y+\mathbf{c}z = \mathbf{d}$, the vectors **a**, **b**, **c**, **d** are given and the scalars x, y, z are unknown. By taking the scalar product of both sides with $\mathbf{b}\wedge\mathbf{c}$, show that $x = [\mathbf{d}, \mathbf{b}, \mathbf{c}]/[\mathbf{a}, \mathbf{b}, \mathbf{c}]$ and state the values of y and z.

III

POSITION VECTORS AND GEOMETRICAL APPLICATIONS

Position vectors When a vector $\overline{OP}$ is used to specify the position of a point P relative to another point O it is called *the position vector* of P for the origin O. This vector uniquely determines the position of P relative to O and consequently if the position vectors of two points P_1, P_2 relative to the same origin are equal, then P_1, P_2 must coincide.

In this and the following chapter the use of the concept of position vectors to deal with geometrical problems will be illustrated. Although examples of two-dimensional geometry will be considered it must be stressed that the main importance of the use of vectors in geometry lies in three-dimensional work.

Basic results The results associated with the addition, subtraction and multiplication of free vectors obtained in the previous chapters apply equally well to position vectors. The following additional results will be useful.

(i) *If the position vectors of points A, B with respect to some origin O are* $\mathbf{a}, \mathbf{b}$ *respectively, then the vector* $\overline{AB} = \mathbf{b}-\mathbf{a}$ *and the vector* $\overline{BA} = \mathbf{a}-\mathbf{b}$.

For in Fig. 18,

$$\overline{OA}+\overline{AB} = \overline{OB}.$$

$$\therefore \quad \overline{AB} = \overline{OB}-\overline{OA} = \mathbf{b}-\mathbf{a}.$$

Also

$$\overline{BA} = -\overline{AB} = \mathbf{a}-\mathbf{b}.$$

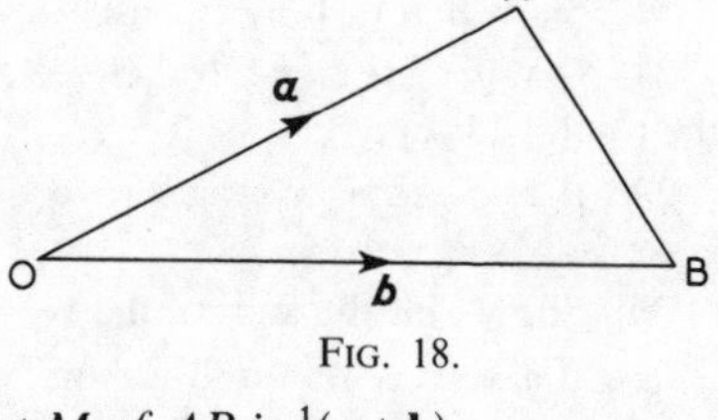

FIG. 18.

(ii) *The position vector of the mid-point M of AB is* $\frac{1}{2}(\mathbf{a}+\mathbf{b})$.

For in Fig. 19,

$$\overline{OM} = \overline{OA}+\overline{AM},$$

and

$$\overline{OM} = \overline{OB}+\overline{BM}.$$

Adding,

$$2\overline{OM} = \overline{OA}+\overline{OB} \quad \text{as} \quad \overline{AM}+\overline{BM} = 0.$$

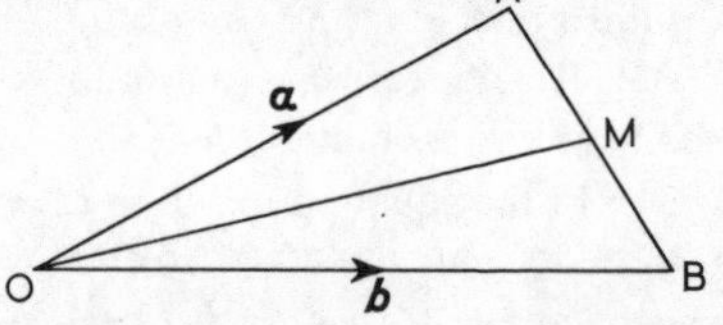

FIG. 19.

$$\therefore \quad \overline{OM} = \tfrac{1}{2}(\overline{OA}+\overline{OB}),$$

or, the position vector of $M = \frac{1}{2}(\mathbf{a}+\mathbf{b})$.

(iii) *The position vector of the point P dividing AB in the ratio m:n is* $(n\mathbf{a}+m\mathbf{b})/(m+n)$.

For in Fig. 20, as $nAP = mPB$,

$$n\overline{OA}+m\overline{OB} = (m+n)\overline{OP},$$

(Theorem, page 4).

$\therefore$

$$(m+n)\overline{OP} = n\mathbf{a}+m\mathbf{b},$$

or $$\overline{OP} = \frac{n\mathbf{a}+m\mathbf{b}}{m+n},$$

i.e. the position vector of $P = \dfrac{n\mathbf{a}+m\mathbf{b}}{m+n}$.

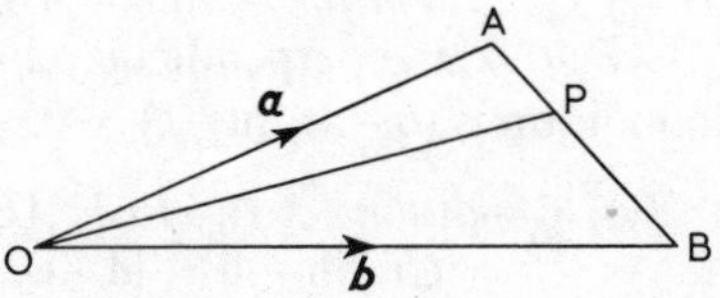

FIG. 20.

Ex. 1 *Use vectors to prove that the diagonals of a parallelogram bisect each other.*

In Fig. 21, $ABCD$ is a parallelogram. Taking A as origin, that is the point whose position vector is zero, let the position vectors of B, D be $\mathbf{b}$, $\mathbf{d}$ respectively. Then as $\overline{AC} = \overline{AB} + \overline{AD}$, the position vector of C is $\mathbf{b}+\mathbf{d}$.

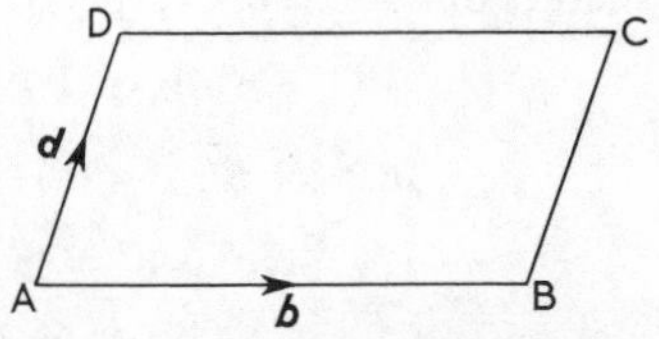

FIG. 21.

Now the position vector of the mid-point of BD is $\frac{1}{2}(\mathbf{b}+\mathbf{d})$ and the position vector of the mid-point of AC is also $\frac{1}{2}(\mathbf{b}+\mathbf{d})$. Therefore the diagonals AC, BD bisect each other.

Ex. 2 *Show that the joins of the mid-points of the opposite edges of a tetrahedron intersect and bisect each other.*

In the tetrahedron $ABCD$, Fig. 22, take A as origin and let the position vectors of B, C, D be $\mathbf{b}$, $\mathbf{c}$, $\mathbf{d}$ respectively. Then P, the mid-point of AB, is the point $\frac{1}{2}\mathbf{b}$ and Q, the mid-point of the opposite edge CD, is the point $\frac{1}{2}(\mathbf{c}+\mathbf{d})$. So the mid-point of PQ has the position vector $\frac{1}{2}[\frac{1}{2}\mathbf{b}+\frac{1}{2}(\mathbf{c}+\mathbf{d})]$, i.e. $\frac{1}{4}[\mathbf{b}+\mathbf{c}+\mathbf{d}]$.

In like manner it is found that the mid-points of the joins of the other two pairs of mid-points of opposite edges is the same point, $\frac{1}{4}[\mathbf{b}+\mathbf{c}+\mathbf{d}]$, and the required result follows.

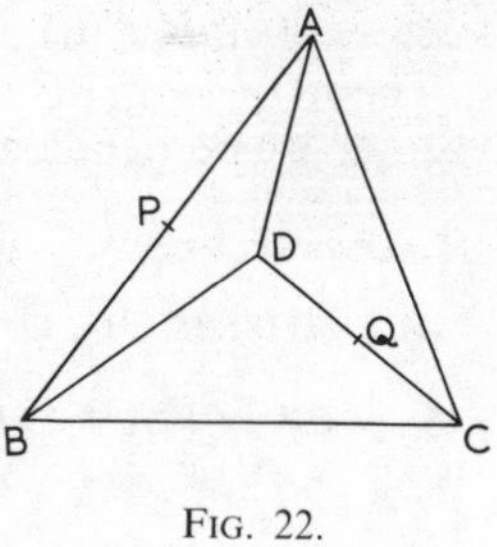

FIG. 22.

Further basic results

(iv) *Condition for two lines AB, CD to be parallel*

Taking the position vectors of A, B, C, D as **a**, **b**, **c**, **d** respectively, then $\overline{AB} = \mathbf{b}-\mathbf{a}$; $\overline{CD} = \mathbf{d}-\mathbf{c}$. So the lines AB, CD are parallel, if $\mathbf{d}-\mathbf{c} = \lambda(\mathbf{b}-\mathbf{a})$, where the scalar λ is the ratio CD/AB.

(v) *Condition for two lines AB, CD to be perpendicular*

AB, CD are perpendicular lines if $\overline{AB} \,.\, \overline{CD} = 0$. So the required condition is $(\mathbf{b}-\mathbf{a}) \,.\, (\mathbf{d}-\mathbf{c}) = 0$.

(vi) *Condition for two lines AB, CD to be equal in length*

As $AB = CD$, $|\mathbf{b}-\mathbf{a}| = |\mathbf{d}-\mathbf{c}|$,

and $$|\mathbf{b}-\mathbf{a}|^2 = |\mathbf{d}-\mathbf{c}|^2.$$

$\therefore \quad (\mathbf{b}-\mathbf{a})^2 = (\mathbf{d}-\mathbf{c})^2 \quad$ as $\quad r^2 = \mathbf{r}^2$, the required condition.

Ex. 3 *In any triangle ABC, prove that* $BC^2 = AB^2+AC^2-2AB\,.\,AC\cos A$—*the cosine rule.*

With A as origin, let the position vectors of B, C be **b**, **c** respectively. Then

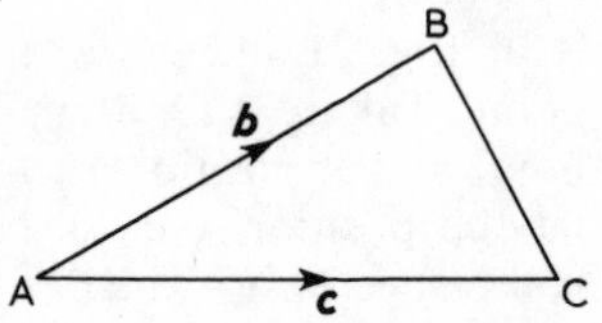

FIG. 23.

$$\overline{BC} = \mathbf{c}-\mathbf{b}.$$

$$\therefore \quad BC^2 = \overline{BC}^2 = (\mathbf{c}-\mathbf{b})^2$$
$$= \mathbf{c}^2+\mathbf{b}^2-2\mathbf{c}\,.\,\mathbf{b}$$
$$= c^2+b^2-2cb\cos A,$$

the vectors **c**, **b** being inclined at an angle A.

As $c = AC$, $b = AB$, the result follows.

Ex. 4 *In the tetrahedron OABC, edges OA, OB are respectively perpendicular to edges BC, CA. Show* (i) *OC is perpendicular to AB*; (ii) $OA^2+BC^2 = OB^2+CA^2 = OC^2+AB^2$.

(i) With O as origin, let the position vectors of A, B, C be **a**, **b**, **c** respectively.

Then $\overline{OA} = \mathbf{a}$, $\overline{BC} = \mathbf{c}-\mathbf{b}$ and as these vectors are perpendicular,

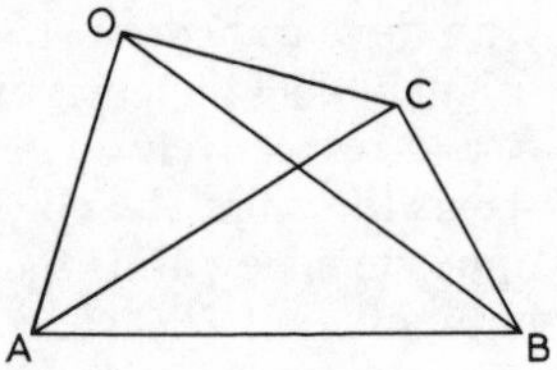

FIG. 24.

$$\mathbf{a}\,.\,(\mathbf{c}-\mathbf{b}) = 0 \quad \text{or} \quad \mathbf{a}\,.\,\mathbf{c} = \mathbf{a}\,.\,\mathbf{b}.$$

Similarly, as $\overline{OB}$, $\overline{CA}$ are perpendicular,

$$\mathbf{b}\,.\,(\mathbf{a}-\mathbf{c}) = 0 \quad \text{or} \quad \mathbf{b}\,.\,\mathbf{a} = \mathbf{b}\,.\,\mathbf{c}.$$

$$\therefore \quad \mathbf{a}\,.\,\mathbf{c} = \mathbf{b}\,.\,\mathbf{c} \quad \text{or} \quad \mathbf{c}\,.\,(\mathbf{b}-\mathbf{a}) = 0.$$

But $\overline{OC} = \mathbf{c}$, $\overline{AB} = \mathbf{b}-\mathbf{a}$ and hence these vectors are perpendicular.

(ii) $$OA^2+BC^2 = \overline{OA}^2+\overline{BC}^2 = \mathbf{a}^2+(\mathbf{c}-\mathbf{b})^2$$
$$= \mathbf{a}^2+\mathbf{b}^2+\mathbf{c}^2-2\mathbf{b}\,.\,\mathbf{c}$$
$$OB^2+CA^2 = \mathbf{b}^2+(\mathbf{a}-\mathbf{c})^2 = \mathbf{a}^2+\mathbf{b}^2+\mathbf{c}^2-2\mathbf{a}\,.\,\mathbf{c}$$
$$OC^2+AB^2 = \mathbf{c}^2+(\mathbf{b}-\mathbf{a})^2 = \mathbf{a}^2+\mathbf{b}^2+\mathbf{c}^2-2\mathbf{b}\,.\,\mathbf{a}.$$

But $$\mathbf{b}\,.\,\mathbf{c} = \mathbf{b}\,.\,\mathbf{a} = \mathbf{a}\,.\,\mathbf{c},$$

so $$OA^2+BC^2 = OB^2+CA^2 = OC^2+AB^2.$$

Ex. 5 *In the tetrahedron ABCD, BC = AD and CA = DB. Show that AB is perpendicular to CD if also AD = BD.*

With A as origin, let the position vectors of B, C, D be **b**, **c**, **d** respectively.

The condition $BC = AD$ can be expressed vectorially as

$$(\mathbf{c}-\mathbf{b})^2 = \mathbf{d}^2 \quad \text{or} \quad (\mathbf{c}-\mathbf{b}-\mathbf{d})\,.\,(\mathbf{c}-\mathbf{b}+\mathbf{d}) = 0. \qquad \text{(i)}$$

Similarly the condition $CA = DB$ leads to the result

$$\mathbf{c}^2 = (\mathbf{b}-\mathbf{d})^2 \quad \text{or} \quad (\mathbf{c}+\mathbf{b}-\mathbf{d})\,.\,(\mathbf{c}-\mathbf{b}+\mathbf{d}) = 0. \qquad \text{(ii)}$$

Subtracting (i) from (ii),

$$2\mathbf{b}\,.\,(\mathbf{c}-\mathbf{b}+\mathbf{d}) = 0$$

or $$\mathbf{b}\,.\,\mathbf{c}+\mathbf{b}\,.\,\mathbf{d} = \mathbf{b}^2. \qquad \text{(iii)}$$

If also $AD = BD$, then $\mathbf{d}^2 = (\mathbf{d}-\mathbf{b})^2$ or $2\mathbf{b}\,.\,\mathbf{d} = \mathbf{b}^2$.

Using this result in (iii), leads to $\mathbf{b}\,.\,\mathbf{c}+\mathbf{b}\,.\,\mathbf{d} = 2\mathbf{b}\,.\,\mathbf{d}$, i.e.

$$\mathbf{b}\,.\,\mathbf{c}-\mathbf{b}\,.\,\mathbf{d} = 0 \quad \text{or} \quad \mathbf{b}\,.\,(\mathbf{c}-\mathbf{d}) = 0.$$

The latter result establishes the perpendicularity of AB and CD.

Ex. 6 *Two skew lines AP, BQ inclined at 60° are intersected by their common perpendicular at A, B; AQ is perpendicular to BP. Prove that AP . BQ = 2AB².*

Take A as origin and let the position vectors of B, P, Q be **b**, **p**, **q** respectively.

As $\overline{AP}\,.\,\overline{BQ} = AP\,.\,BQ \cos 60°$,

$$AP\,.\,BQ = 2\overline{AP}\,.\,\overline{BQ} = 2\mathbf{p}\,.\,(\mathbf{q}-\mathbf{b}).$$

But as AB is perpendicular to AP,

$$\mathbf{p}\,.\,\mathbf{b} = 0;$$

as AB is perpendicular to BQ,

$$(\mathbf{q}-\mathbf{b})\,.\,\mathbf{b} = 0 \quad \text{or} \quad \mathbf{q}\,.\,\mathbf{b} = \mathbf{b}^2;$$

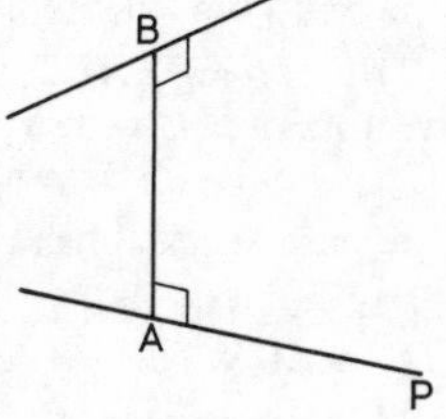

FIG. 25.

as AQ is perpendicular to BP,

$$(\mathbf{p}-\mathbf{b}).\mathbf{q} = 0 \quad \text{or} \quad \mathbf{p}.\mathbf{q} = \mathbf{b}.\mathbf{q}.$$

So
$$2\mathbf{p}.\mathbf{q} = 2\mathbf{b}.\mathbf{q} = 2\mathbf{b}^2 \quad \text{and} \quad 2\mathbf{p}.\mathbf{b} = 0.$$

$$\therefore \quad AP.BQ = 2\mathbf{p}.\mathbf{q} - 2\mathbf{p}.\mathbf{b}$$
$$= 2\mathbf{b}^2 \quad \text{or} \quad 2AB^2.$$

EXAMPLES 3a

1 With origin O, the position vector of a point A is $\mathbf{a}$. Write down the position vectors of (i) the mid-point of OA; (ii) the point dividing OA in the ratio 2:3; (iii) the point B on OA produced such that $AB = 2OA$; (iv) the reflection of A in the origin.

2 The position vectors of points A, B with respect to O are $\mathbf{a}$, $\mathbf{b}$. The points P, Q divide AB internally and externally in the ratio 5:3. Find $\overline{OP}$, $\overline{OQ}$ and $\overline{PQ}$ in terms of $\mathbf{a}$, $\mathbf{b}$.

3 Points A, B, C, D are collinear with $AB = BC = \frac{1}{2}CD$. If the position vectors of A, B are $\mathbf{a}$, $\mathbf{b}$, find the position vectors of C, D and the mid-point of CD.

4 If A, B, C, D have position vectors $\mathbf{a}, \mathbf{b}, \mathbf{c}, \mathbf{d}$ and E, F, G, H are the mid-points of AB, BC, CD, DA respectively, express the following vectors in terms of $\mathbf{a}, \mathbf{b}, \mathbf{c}, \mathbf{d}$: (i) the position vector of E; (ii) $\overline{AC}$; (iii) $\overline{EB}$; (iv) $\overline{GH}$; (v) the position vector of the point dividing FG internally in the ratio 2:3.

5 $ABCD$ is a parallelogram; express the position vector of D in terms of $\mathbf{a}, \mathbf{b}, \mathbf{c}$, the position vectors of A, B, C. Also write down the position vectors of the point of intersection of the diagonals and of the point P in BD such that $BP = 2PD$.

6 The position vectors of A, B, C, D are $\mathbf{a}$, $\mathbf{b}$, $4\mathbf{a}-\mathbf{b}$, $\mathbf{a}+2\mathbf{b}$ respectively. Show that $\overline{CD}$ is parallel to $\overline{AB}$ and find the ratio AB/CD.

7 Points A, B, C, D are such that $\overline{AB}$ and $\overline{CD}$ are parallel and $CD = 2AB$. Express $\mathbf{d}$, the position vector of D, in terms of $\mathbf{a}, \mathbf{b}, \mathbf{c}$, the position vectors of A, B, C and find the position vector of the common point of AD and BC.

8 If $\mathbf{a}, \mathbf{b}, \mathbf{c}$ are the position vectors of the vertices of triangle ABC, find the position vector of the point G which divides the median AD in the ratio 2:1. Deduce that the three medians of the triangle concur at G.

9 In triangle PQR, M and N are the mid-points of sides PQ, PR respectively. Using P as origin, express $\overline{MN}$ in terms of the position vectors of Q, R and deduce the mid-point theorem.

10 Triangle ABC is right-angled at A. Express $\overline{BC}^2$ in terms of the position vectors of B, C with respect to A and deduce the Pythagoras theorem.

11 Points A, B, C have position vectors $\mathbf{a}$, $\mathbf{b}$, $3\mathbf{a}-2\mathbf{b}$. By showing that $\overline{AB}$, $\overline{BC}$ are parallel, establish that the three points are collinear.

12 X is the mid-point of edge BC of tetrahedron $OABC$, prove that $\overline{OA}+\overline{AC}+\overline{OB} = 2\overline{OX}$.

13 In triangle ABC, $AB = AC$ and D is the mid-point of BC. By expressing $\overline{BC}$, $\overline{AD}$ in terms of the position vectors of B, C with respect to A, establish that $\overline{BC}$ is perpendicular to $\overline{AD}$.

14 $ABCD$ is a tetrahedron and P, Q, R are the mid-points of BC, CD, DB respectively. Prove that $\overline{AB}+\overline{AC}+\overline{AD} = \overline{AP}+\overline{AQ}+\overline{AR}$.

15 $ABCD$ is a square. Obtain the position vectors of E, F, the mid-points of AD, DC respectively, in terms of the position vectors of B, D with respect to A and show that $\overline{BE}\,.\,\overline{AF} = 0$, explaining the geometrical significance of the result.

16 $ABCD$ is a trapezium with $\overline{AB}$ parallel to $\overline{DC}$ and P, Q are the mid-points of AD, BC respectively. If the position vectors of A, B, are $\mathbf{a}$, $\mathbf{b}$ and $DC = kAB$ show that $\overline{PQ} = \frac{1}{2}(k+1)(\mathbf{b}-\mathbf{a})$.

17 In triangle ABC, O is the mid-point of AB and $OA = OB = OC$. Express the vectors $\overline{CB}$, $\overline{CA}$ in terms of the position vectors of A, C with respect to O and deduce that angle ACB is a right angle.

18 Prove that the points with position vectors $\mathbf{a}+2\mathbf{b}$, $2\mathbf{a}-\mathbf{b}$, $4\mathbf{a}-7\mathbf{b}$ are collinear.

19 If AM is a median of triangle ABC, show that $2AM^2+2BM^2 = AB^2+AC^2$.

20 In a quadrilateral $ABCD$, plane or skew, prove that the mid-points of the sides are the vertices of a parallelogram.

21 If O is the origin and $\mathbf{a}$, $\mathbf{b}$ the position vectors of A, B, show that the point with position vector $\lambda\mathbf{a}+\mu\mathbf{b}$, where λ, μ are scalars, lies in the plane OAB.

22 If AB, $A'B'$ are any two lines in space and M, M' are their mid-points, show that $\overline{AA'}+\overline{BB'} = 2\overline{MM'}$.

23 $ABCD$ is a rhombus. By expressing $\overline{AC}$, $\overline{BD}$ in terms of the position vectors of B, D with respect to A, show that the diagonals of the rhombus are perpendicular to each other. Also show that the diagonals bisect each other.

24 In a parallelogram, prove that the sum of the squares on the diagonals is twice the sum of the squares on two adjacent sides.

25 If the sum of the scalar multiples p, q, r is zero and $p\mathbf{a}+q\mathbf{b}+r\mathbf{c}$ is also zero, show that the points with position vectors $\mathbf{a}$, $\mathbf{b}$, $\mathbf{c}$ are collinear and also establish the converse result.

26 In the rectangle $ABCD$, $AB = 2AD$ and P is the point on DC such that $DP = 3PC$. Taking $\overline{AB} = \mathbf{b}$, $\overline{AD} = \mathbf{d}$, express $\overline{AC}$, $\overline{BP}$ in terms of $\mathbf{b}$, $\mathbf{d}$ and hence show that $\overline{AC}$, $\overline{BP}$ are perpendicular.

27 Use vectors to prove the converse of Pythagoras theorem that if in triangle ABC, $BC^2 = AB^2+CA^2$, then angle $A = 90°$.

28 If the diagonals of a quadrilateral $ABCD$ bisect each other show that $ABCD$ is a parallelogram.

29 Prove that the sum of the squares on the edges of a tetrahedron is equal to four times the sum of the squares on the joins of the mid-points of opposite edges.

30 In triangle ABC, R divides AB internally in the ratio 2:3, P divides BC externally in the ratio 3:2 and Q is the mid-point of AC. Show that P, Q, R are collinear.

31 If $\mathbf{a}$, $\mathbf{b}$, $\mathbf{c}$ are the position vectors of vertices A, B, C of a regular hexagon $ABCDEF$, find the position vectors of D, E, F in terms of $\mathbf{a}$, $\mathbf{b}$, $\mathbf{c}$.

32 If ABC is a triangle and O a point not necessarily in its plane, show that $\overline{OA}+\overline{OB}+\overline{OC} = 3\overline{OG}$, where G is the centroid of the triangle. Also if G is a point in the plane of the triangle such that $\overline{AG}+\overline{BG}+\overline{CG} = 0$, show that G is the centroid of the triangle.

33 Squares $ACXY$, $BCWZ$ are described externally on the sides AC, BC of triangle ABC making a plane figure. If $\overline{CX} = \mathbf{b}$, $\overline{CA} = \mathbf{a}$, $\overline{CW} = \mathbf{q}$, $\overline{CB} = \mathbf{p}$, prove that $\mathbf{a}\cdot\mathbf{p}+\mathbf{q}\cdot\mathbf{b} = 0$ and also that $\overline{AW}$, $\overline{BX}$ are perpendicular.

34 If A, B have position vectors $\mathbf{a}$, $\mathbf{b}$, show that if P, Q are any two points in the plane OAB where O is the origin, then $\overline{PQ}$ can be expressed in the form $p\mathbf{a}+q\mathbf{b}$ where p, q are scalars. Deduce that if a line OC is perpendicular to OA and OB then it is perpendicular to any line PQ in the plane OAB.

35 The position vectors of the vertices of triangle ABC are $\mathbf{a}$, $\mathbf{b}$, $\mathbf{c}$. Points P, Q, R are taken on BC, CA, AB respectively such that $BP/PC = CQ/QA = AR/RB = \frac{1}{2}$. Prove that the position vector of the mid-point U of AP is $\frac{1}{6}(3\mathbf{a}+2\mathbf{b}+\mathbf{c})$. Also prove that if V, W are the mid-points of BQ, CR, then triangles UVW, ABC have the same centroid.

36 In triangle ABC, AD is an altitude. If the position vectors of B, C, D with respect to A are $\mathbf{b}$, $\mathbf{c}$, $\mathbf{d}$, show that $\mathbf{d} = \mathbf{b}+\lambda(\mathbf{c}-\mathbf{b})$ where $\lambda = \mathbf{b}\cdot(\mathbf{b}-\mathbf{c})/(\mathbf{b}-\mathbf{c})^2$.

37 In tetrahedron $ABCD$, $BC = AD$. Prove that the join of the mid-points of BD, AC is perpendicular to the join of the mid-points of AB, DC.

38 In tetrahedron $ABCD$, $AB = CD$ and $BC = AD$, show that the join of the mid-points of AC, BD is perpendicular to both AC and BD.

39 Prove that the lines joining the vertices of a tetrahedron to the centroids of the opposite faces intersect and divide each other in the ratio 3:1.

40 AB is the common perpendicular of two skew lines AP, BQ. If H is the mid-point of AB and M the mid-point of PQ, prove that HM is perpendicular to AB.

41 Variable points P, Q on each of two given skew lines AP, BQ are a constant distance apart, prove that $\overline{AB}\cdot\overline{PQ} = AB^2$ and hence that PQ makes a constant angle with the common perpendicular AB to the two lines.

42 AB is the common perpendicular of two skew lines AC, BD where $AC = BD$. Prove that the line joining the mid-points of AB, CD cuts both these lines at right angles.

43 Defining the vector area $\mathbf{\Delta}$ of triangle OAB as $\Delta\hat{\mathbf{n}}$, where Δ is the scalar area and $\hat{\mathbf{n}}$ is a unit vector normal to the plane of the triangle and such that $\overline{OA}$, $\overline{OB}$, $\hat{\mathbf{n}}$ form a right-handed system, show that $\mathbf{\Delta} = \frac{1}{2}\mathbf{a}\wedge\mathbf{b}$, where $\overline{OA} = \mathbf{a}$, $\overline{OB} = \mathbf{b}$. Show further that the volume of the tetrahedron $OABC$, where $\overline{OC} = \mathbf{c}$, is $\frac{1}{6}[\mathbf{a}, \mathbf{b}, \mathbf{c}]$.

44 If $\mathbf{a}$, $\mathbf{b}$, $\mathbf{c}$ are the position vectors of the vertices of triangle ABC, show that $\mathbf{b}\wedge\mathbf{c}+\mathbf{c}\wedge\mathbf{a}+\mathbf{a}\wedge\mathbf{b} = 2\mathbf{\Delta}$, where $\mathbf{\Delta}$ is the vector area of the triangle.

Components of a position vector Suppose a point P has coordinates (x, y, z) with respect to rectangular axes OX, OY, OZ and that Q is the foot of the perpendicular from P to the plane XOY (Fig. 26). Then if NQ, MQ are parallel to OX, OY respectively, $OM = x$; $MQ = ON = y$; $QP = z$. So if $\mathbf{r}$ is the position vector of P with respect to O,

$$\mathbf{r} = \overline{OP} = \overline{OM}+\overline{MQ}+\overline{QP}$$

$$= x\mathbf{i}+y\mathbf{j}+z\mathbf{k},$$

where **i**, **j**, **k** are unit vectors in the directions of the axes $\overline{OX}, \overline{OY}, \overline{OZ}$.

The modulus of **r**, $r = \sqrt{(x^2+y^2+z^2)}$. If α, β, γ are the angle $\overline{OP}$ makes with the axes $\overline{OX}, \overline{OY}, \overline{OZ}$, then the direction cosines of **r** are $l = \cos\alpha = x/r$; $m = \cos\beta = y/r$; $n = \cos\gamma = z/r$, where $l^2+m^2+n^2 = 1$.

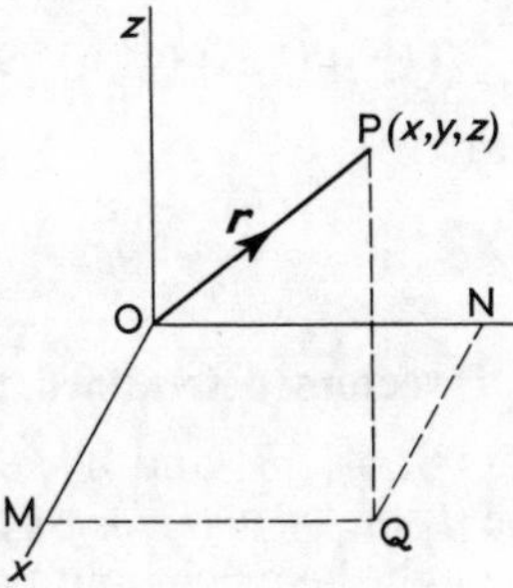

FIG. 26.

Ex. 7 *If the points P, Q have coordinates* (2, −1, 3), (−1, −2, 1) *respectively and O is the origin, find* $\overline{OP}\,.\,\overline{OQ}$ *and* $\overline{OP} \wedge \overline{OQ}$ *in terms of the unit vectors* **i, j, k**.

$$\overline{OP} = 2\mathbf{i}-\mathbf{j}+3\mathbf{k}; \quad \overline{OQ} = -\mathbf{i}-2\mathbf{j}+\mathbf{k}.$$

$$\therefore \quad \overline{OP}\,.\,\overline{OQ} = 2(-1)+(-1)(-2)+(3)(1) = 3.$$

$$\overline{OP} \wedge \overline{OQ} = \begin{vmatrix} \mathbf{i} & \mathbf{j} & \mathbf{k} \\ 2 & -1 & 3 \\ -1 & -2 & 1 \end{vmatrix} = 5\mathbf{i}-5\mathbf{j}-5\mathbf{k}.$$

Modulus and direction cosines of $\overline{AB}$ in terms of the coordinates of A, B

Let the coordinates of A, B be (x_1, y_1, z_1), (x_2, y_2, z_2) respectively.

Then $\quad \overline{OA} = x_1\mathbf{i}+y_1\mathbf{j}+z_1\mathbf{k}; \quad \overline{OB} = x_2\mathbf{i}+y_2\mathbf{j}+z_2\mathbf{k}.$

So $\quad \overline{AB} = \overline{OB}-\overline{OA} = \mathbf{i}(x_2-x_1)+\mathbf{j}(y_2-y_1)+\mathbf{k}(z_2-z_1).$

$\therefore$ Modulus of $\overline{AB} = AB = \sqrt{\{(x_2-x_1)^2+(y_2-y_1)^2+(z_2-z_1)^2\}}$,

and the direction cosines of $\overline{AB}$ are

$$l = \frac{x_2-x_1}{AB}, \quad m = \frac{y_2-y_1}{AB}, \quad n = \frac{z_2-z_1}{AB}.$$

Ex. 8 *The points A, B have coordinates* (3, 1, −1) *and* (2, 0, 2). *Express* $\overline{BA}$ *in terms of unit vectors parallel to the axes and find the direction cosines of this vector.*

$$\overline{BA} = \mathbf{i}(3-2)+\mathbf{j}(1-0)+\mathbf{k}(-1-2)$$
$$= \mathbf{i}+\mathbf{j}-3\mathbf{k}.$$

The modulus $\quad AB = \sqrt{\{(1)^2+(1)^2+(-3)^2\}} = \sqrt{11}.$

Direction cosines of $\overline{AB}$ are

$$l = \frac{1}{\sqrt{11}}; \quad m = \frac{1}{\sqrt{11}} \quad n = -\frac{3}{\sqrt{11}}.$$

Angle of inclination of vectors determined by two pairs of points

Let the two pairs of points be A_1, B_1 and A_2, B_2 and let the direction cosines of $\overline{A_1B_1}, \overline{A_2B_2}$ be $(l_1, m_1, n_1), (l_2, m_2, n_2)$ respectively.

The unit vector $\hat{\mathbf{r}}_1$, through the origin and parallel to $\overline{A_1B_1}$ is $l_1\mathbf{i}+m_1\mathbf{j}+n_1\mathbf{k}$, and the unit vector $\hat{\mathbf{r}}_2$, through the origin and parallel to $\overline{A_2B_2}$ is $l_2\mathbf{i}+m_2\mathbf{j}+n_2\mathbf{k}$.

If θ is the angle of inclination of $\overline{A_1B_1}, \overline{A_2B_2}$, it is also the angle of inclination of $\hat{\mathbf{r}}_1, \hat{\mathbf{r}}_2$.

$$\therefore \cos\theta = \hat{\mathbf{r}}_1 . \hat{\mathbf{r}}_2 = l_1l_2+m_1m_2+n_1n_2.$$
$$\theta = \cos^{-1}(l_1l_2+m_1m_2+n_1n_2).$$

Ex. 9 *The position vectors of A, B, C, D are* $\mathbf{a} = \mathbf{i}+\mathbf{j}+\mathbf{k}$, $\mathbf{b} = 2\mathbf{i}+3\mathbf{j}$, $\mathbf{c} = 3\mathbf{i}+5\mathbf{j}-2\mathbf{k}$, $\mathbf{d} = -\mathbf{j}+\mathbf{k}$. *Show that* $\overline{AB}$, $\overline{CD}$ *are parallel and determine the ratio AB/CD. Also find the cosine of the angle between* $\overline{AC}$ *and* $\overline{BD}$.

$$\overline{AB} = \mathbf{b}-\mathbf{a} = \mathbf{i}+2\mathbf{j}-\mathbf{k}; \quad \overline{CD} = \mathbf{d}-\mathbf{c} = -3\mathbf{i}-6\mathbf{j}+3\mathbf{k}.$$

So $\quad AB = \sqrt{6} \text{ and } CD = 3\sqrt{6}.$

Direction cosines of $\overline{AB}$ are $\frac{1}{\sqrt{6}}, \frac{2}{\sqrt{6}}, \frac{-1}{\sqrt{6}}$ and of $\overline{CD}$ are $\frac{-1}{\sqrt{6}}, \frac{-2}{\sqrt{6}}, \frac{1}{\sqrt{6}}$.

$\therefore$ $\overline{AB}$, $\overline{CD}$ are parallel but in opposite directions and $AB/CD = \frac{1}{3}$.

Also $\overline{AC} = \mathbf{c}-\mathbf{a} = 2\mathbf{i}+4\mathbf{j}-3\mathbf{k}$; $\overline{BD} = \mathbf{d}-\mathbf{b} = -2\mathbf{i}-4\mathbf{j}+\mathbf{k}$. So the direction cosines of $\overline{AC}$ and $\overline{BD}$ are $\frac{2}{\sqrt{29}}, \frac{4}{\sqrt{29}}, \frac{-3}{\sqrt{29}}$ and $\frac{-2}{\sqrt{21}}, \frac{-4}{\sqrt{21}}, \frac{1}{\sqrt{21}}$.

$$\therefore \quad \text{Cosine of angle between } \overline{AC}, \overline{BD} = \frac{1}{\sqrt{(29)(21)}}[-4-16-3]$$
$$= -\frac{23}{\sqrt{609}}.$$

Use of position vector components in geometrical problems Geometrical problems involving cubes or rectangular parallelepipeds are often readily solvable by taking axes along mutually perpendicular edges and using vector components. The method is illustrated in the following worked examples.

Ex. 10 *A cube with an edge of 2a has opposite faces ABCD, PQRS joined by edges AP, BQ, CR, DS; the mid-points of BC, RS are M, L respectively. Find* (i) *the length ML*; (ii) *the angle between* $\overline{AP}$ *and* $\overline{ML}$.

(i) Taking A as origin and letting unit vectors in the directions of axes $\overline{AB}$, $\overline{AD}$, $\overline{AP}$ be **i, j, k** respectively, then

$$\overline{AM} = \overline{AB}+\overline{BM} = 2a\mathbf{i}+a\mathbf{j};$$

$$\overline{AL} = \overline{SL}+\overline{AD}+\overline{DS} = a\mathbf{i}+2a\mathbf{j}+2a\mathbf{k}.$$

$$\therefore \quad \overline{ML} = \overline{AL}-\overline{AM} = -a\mathbf{i}+a\mathbf{j}+2a\mathbf{k},$$

so $\quad ML = \sqrt{(a^2+a^2+4a^2)} = a\sqrt{6}.$

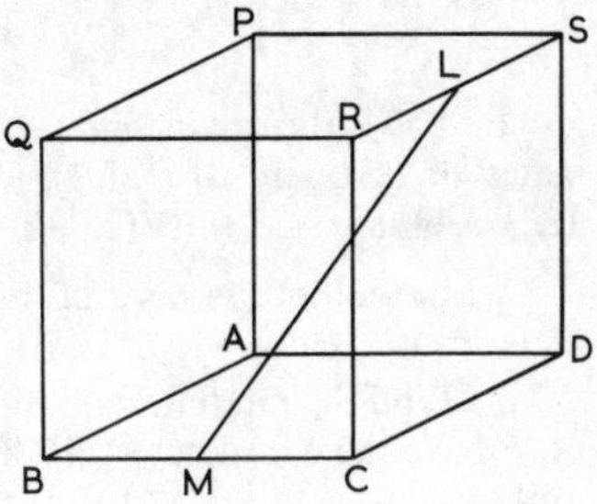

FIG. 27.

(ii) As $\overline{ML}$ has direction cosines $-1/\sqrt{6}$, $1/\sqrt{6}$, $2/\sqrt{6}$ and $\overline{AP}$ is the axis of z, then the cosine of the angle between $\overline{AP}$ and $\overline{ML}$ is $2/\sqrt{6}$.

Ex. 11 *A rectangular parallelepiped has opposite faces ABCD, PQRS joined by edges AP, BQ, CR, DS; AB = 2a, AD = 3a, AP = a. Find the position of a point L in QR such that the vectors* $\overline{AL}$, $\overline{BS}$ *are perpendicular.*

Taking A as origin and AB, AD, AP as axes, then if the position vectors of B, Q, R, S are **b, q, r, s**,

$$\mathbf{b} = 2a\mathbf{i}; \quad \mathbf{q} = 2a\mathbf{i}+a\mathbf{k};$$

$$\mathbf{r} = 2a\mathbf{i}+3a\mathbf{j}+a\mathbf{k};$$

$$\mathbf{s} = 3a\mathbf{j}+a\mathbf{k}.$$

So

$$\overline{BS} = \mathbf{s}-\mathbf{b} = -2a\mathbf{i}+3a\mathbf{j}+a\mathbf{k}.$$

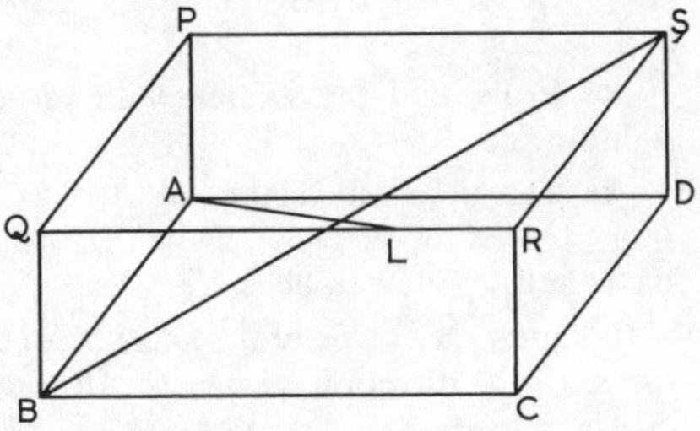

FIG. 28.

Now if L divides QR in the ratio $1:\lambda$, the position vector of L is $(\lambda\mathbf{q}+\mathbf{r})/(\lambda+1)$, i.e. $[2a(1+\lambda)\mathbf{i}+3a\mathbf{j}+a(1+\lambda)\mathbf{k}]/(\lambda+1)$.

So $$\overline{AL} = [2a(1+\lambda)\mathbf{i}+3a\mathbf{j}+a(1+\lambda)\mathbf{k}]/(\lambda+1).$$

As $\overline{AL}$, $\overline{BS}$ are perpendicular, $\overline{AL}\,.\,\overline{BS} = 0$.

$$\therefore \quad (-2a)2a(1+\lambda)+(3a)(3a)+(a)a(1+\lambda) = 0;$$

i.e. $$-4-4\lambda+9+1+\lambda = 0; \quad \lambda = 2.$$

So L divides QR in the ratio 1:2; i.e. $QL = a$, $LR = 2a$.

EXAMPLES 3b

1 If O is the origin, find the values of $\overline{OP}\,.\,\overline{OQ}$ in the cases where the coordinates of P, Q are (i) $(1, 1, 1)$, $(2, -1, 3)$; (ii) $(0, 3, 2)$, $(-1, 0, 4)$; (iii) $(-1, 2, 2)$, $(2, -3, 6)$; (iv) $(3, 3, -1)$, $(2, -2, -1)$; (v) $(a, -a, a)$, $(-a, a, 2a)$.

2 In each of the cases of the previous example express the vector $\overline{OP} \wedge \overline{OQ}$ in terms of the unit vectors **i**, **j**, **k**.

3 Find the modulus and direction cosines of $\overline{AB}$ in each of the cases where A, B have the coordinates: (i) $A(0, 1, 1)$, $B(-1, 2, 0)$; (ii) $A(2, 1, -1)$, $B(1, -1, 1)$; (iii) $A(3, -1, 3)$, $B(-3, 1, 0)$; (iv) $A(2, -2, 1)$, $B(2, -2, -1)$; (v) $A(a, a, 0)$, $B(2a, 0, -a)$.

4 The position vectors of P, Q with respect to the origin O are **p**, **q**. Find the modulus and direction cosines of $\overline{PQ}$ in each of the following cases: (i) $\mathbf{p} = \mathbf{i}-\mathbf{j}+\mathbf{k}$, $\mathbf{q} = \mathbf{j}-2\mathbf{k}$; (ii) $\mathbf{p} = 4\mathbf{i}+\mathbf{j}-2\mathbf{k}$, $\mathbf{q} = \mathbf{i}-2\mathbf{j}+4\mathbf{k}$; (iii) $\mathbf{p} = \mathbf{j}+\mathbf{k}$, $\mathbf{q} = \mathbf{i}+\mathbf{j}+\mathbf{k}$.

5 Find the cosine of the angle between $\overline{OA}$ and $\overline{OB}$ where O is the origin, in each of the following cases: (i) the direction cosines of $\overline{OA}$, $\overline{OB}$ are $1/\sqrt{3}$, $1/\sqrt{3}$, $-1/\sqrt{3}$ and $\frac{2}{3}$, $-\frac{1}{3}$, $-\frac{2}{3}$; (ii) A, B are the points $(-1, 1, 2)$, $(0, 1, -1)$; (iii) A, B are the points $(3, 0, -1)$, $(1, 2, 0)$; (iv) A, B have position vectors $2\mathbf{i}+\mathbf{j}$, $\mathbf{i}-\mathbf{j}+2\mathbf{k}$.

6 If the position vectors of P, Q are $\mathbf{i}+4\mathbf{j}+3\mathbf{k}$, $4\mathbf{i}+2\mathbf{j}-4\mathbf{k}$ relative to the origin O, show that OP, OQ are perpendicular.

7 Find the unit vector in the direction $\overline{AB}$ in each of the cases where A, B have the coordinates: (i) $(0, 1, 0)$, $(3, -1, 6)$; (ii) $(1, -1, 1)$, $(3, -1, 1)$; (iii) $(1, -1, 2)$, $(-1, -2, 0)$.

8 Prove that the triangle with vertices $(3, 1, -1)$, $(1, -2, 0)$, $(-1, 3, 11)$ is right-angled.

9 The position vectors of A, B, C, D are $\mathbf{j}+\mathbf{k}$, $2\mathbf{i}-\mathbf{j}+4\mathbf{k}$, $-\mathbf{i}+2\mathbf{j}-\mathbf{k}$, $-5\mathbf{i}+6\mathbf{j}-7\mathbf{k}$ respectively. Show that $ABCD$ is a trapezium and find the ratio of the lengths of the parallel sides.

10 Find the cosine of the angle between $\overline{AB}$ and $\overline{PQ}$ in each of the following cases: (i) the direction cosines of $\overline{AB}$, $\overline{PQ}$ are 0, 1, 0 and $1/\sqrt{3}$, $-1/\sqrt{3}$, $1/\sqrt{3}$; (ii) $\overline{AB} = 3\mathbf{i}-\mathbf{j}+\mathbf{k}$, $\overline{PQ} = \mathbf{i}+\mathbf{j}-2\mathbf{k}$; (iii) A, B, P, Q are the points $(1, -1, 1)$, $(0, 1, 2)$, $(3, 1, 0)$, $(1, 4, -1)$ respectively; (iv) A is the origin and B, P, Q the points $(0, 0, a)$, $(a, a, 0)$, $(-a, a, a)$ respectively.

11 A, B have position vectors $\mathbf{i}+2\mathbf{j}-\mathbf{k}$, $2\mathbf{j}+3\mathbf{k}$ respectively. Find the position vector of the point dividing AB in the ratio 1:2.

12 A vector **F** of modulus 5 units acts in the direction $\overline{OP}$ where O is the origin and P the point $(1, 2, -2)$. Find the component of the vector in the direction of the x-axis.

13 Find the coordinates of the point dividing the line joining the points $(1, 2, -1)$, $(2, 0, 1)$ in the ratio $2:3$.

14 If P, Q are the points $(0, 3, 2)$, $(2, -1, 0)$ and M is the mid-point of PQ, find the unit vector in the direction $\overline{OM}$, where O is the origin.

15 Points P, Q, R have coordinates $(1, 1, 1)$, $(1, 3, 2)$, $(2, 3, 1)$ respectively. Find (i) $\overline{PQ} \cdot \overline{PR}$; (ii) $\overline{PQ} \wedge \overline{PR}$ in terms of unit vectors along the axes. Deduce the values of the cosine of angle QPR and the area of triangle PQR.

16 The position vectors of the vertices A, B, C of a triangle are $\mathbf{i}+\mathbf{j}-\mathbf{k}$, $2\mathbf{i}+\mathbf{k}$, $-\mathbf{i}+2\mathbf{j}-\mathbf{k}$ respectively. Find (i) the lengths of the sides and (ii) the cosines of the angles of the triangle.

17 Find the unit vector $\hat{\mathbf{n}}$ normal to the plane OAB in the sense that $\overline{OA}$, $\overline{OB}$, $\hat{\mathbf{n}}$ form a right-handed system when A, B are the points $(1, 2, -1)$, $(3, 0, 2)$ respectively, and O is the origin.

18 Defining the vector area of a triangle ABC as the vector with modulus equal to the scalar area of the triangle having a direction normal to the plane of the triangle in the sense of a right-handed screw rotation from $\overline{AB}$ to $\overline{AC}$, express the vector area in terms of the product $\overline{AB} \wedge \overline{AC}$ and find the vector area in the case where A, B, C have coordinates $(0, 2, 2)$, $(3, 1, -1)$, $(-1, 0, 2)$ respectively.

19 $ABCD$, $PQRS$ are opposite faces of a cube with edges AP, BQ, CR, DS. Find (i) the angle between the join of B to the mid-point of PS and the join of D to R; (ii) the angle between the diagonal AR and the edge DC.

20 $P(x, y, z)$ is a point on a sphere of which $A(1, 2, -1)$ and $B(3, 0, 2)$ are the ends of a diameter. Using the fact that AP, PB are perpendicular, show that the equation of the sphere is $(x-1)(x-3)+(y-2)y+(z+1)(z-2) = 0$.

21 Find the unit vector normal to the plane ABC in the sense of a right-handed screw rotation from $\overline{AB}$ to $\overline{AC}$ when A, B, C are the points $(0, 1, 1)$, $(1, 2, 0)$, $(2, -1, 2)$ respectively, expressing the result in terms of unit vectors along the axes.

22 If $\mathbf{s} = \overline{AB}$, find the value of $\mathbf{s} \cdot \mathbf{P}$ in each of the following cases: (i) A, B are the points $(1, 1, -1)$, $(3, 0, 1)$ respectively and $\mathbf{P} = 2\mathbf{i}+\mathbf{j}-\mathbf{k}$; (ii) $\overline{AB} = 3\mathbf{i}-4\mathbf{j}+\mathbf{k}$, $\mathbf{P}$ has a modulus of 21 units and direction cosines $\frac{6}{7}, -\frac{2}{7}, \frac{3}{7}$; (iii) $\overline{AB}$ has a modulus of 10 units and direction cosines $\frac{2}{3}, \frac{1}{3}, -\frac{2}{3}$ and $\mathbf{P}$ has a modulus of 5 units in the direction of the vector $2\mathbf{i}+2\mathbf{j}-\mathbf{k}$.

23 Rectangular axes $\overline{OX}$, $\overline{OY}$ take up directions $\overline{OX'}$, $\overline{OY'}$ when rotated through an angle θ in a counterclockwise sense. If $\mathbf{i}, \mathbf{j}$ are unit vectors in the directions $\overline{OX}, \overline{OY}$, show that unit vectors in the directions $\overline{OX'}, \overline{OY'}$ are $\mathbf{i}\cos\theta+\mathbf{j}\sin\theta$, $-\mathbf{i}\sin\theta+\mathbf{j}\cos\theta$ respectively. P is a point such that its coordinates with respect to OX, OY are (x, y) and with respect to OX', OY' are (x', y'). By expressing $\overline{OP}$ (i) in terms of its components along $\overline{OX}, \overline{OY}$; (ii) in terms of its components along $\overline{OX'}, \overline{OY'}$, show that $x = x'\cos\theta - y'\sin\theta$, $y = x'\sin\theta + y'\cos\theta$.

24 $ABCD$, $PQRS$ are opposite faces of a rectangular parallelepiped with edges AP, BQ, CR, DS; the lengths of edges AB, BC, AP are in the ratios $3:2:1$. Find the cosine of the angle between the diagonal AR and the edge BC.

25 Show that the points A, B, C, D are coplanar if one of the unit vectors normal to the triangle BAC is the same as a unit vector normal to the triangle BDC. Deduce that each of the following sets of points are coplanar: (i) (0, 0, 0), (1, 1, 1), (2, 0, 3), (0, −2, 1); (ii) (1, 0, 0), (2, 1, 0), (−1, −1, 2), (−1, 1, 6); (iii) (4, 5, 1), (−4, 4, 4), (0, −1, −1), (3, 9, 4).

26 If $\mathbf{v} = \boldsymbol{\omega} \wedge \mathbf{r}$ where $\mathbf{r} = \overline{OP}$, find $\mathbf{v}$ when $\boldsymbol{\omega}$ is a vector of modulus 10 units in the direction of the vector $\mathbf{i}+\mathbf{j}+\mathbf{k}$, P is the point (2, 1, 3) and O the origin. What is the modulus of the component of $\mathbf{v}$ in the direction of the vector $2\mathbf{i}-\mathbf{j}+\mathbf{k}$?

27 A cube has opposite faces $ABCD$, $EFGH$ joined by edges AE, BF, CG, DH. The mid-points of AB, BC, CG are respectively P, Q, R. Prove (i) that PQ, QR are both perpendicular to DF; (ii) that angle PQR is 120°.

28 A, B, C have position vectors $\mathbf{i}+\mathbf{j}+\mathbf{k}$, $3\mathbf{i}-\mathbf{j}+2\mathbf{k}$, $\mathbf{j}-4\mathbf{k}$ respectively. If $\mathbf{F}$ is a vector modulus 21 units acting in the direction $\overline{BC}$ and $\mathbf{s} = \overline{AB}$, find the modulus of the component of the product $\mathbf{s} \wedge \mathbf{F}$ in the direction of the x-axis.

29 The position vectors of points A, B are $\mathbf{i}+\mathbf{j}+\mathbf{k}$ and $2\mathbf{i}-\mathbf{j}+3\mathbf{k}$; write down the position vector of a point P dividing AB in the ratio $1:\lambda$. If O is the origin, by expressing vectorially the fact that OP is perpendicular to AB, find the position vector of the foot of the perpendicular from O to AB.

30 Find the position vector of the point in which the perpendicular from the origin meets the line joining the points (2, −1, 0), (1, 1, 2).

31 Find the coordinates of the foot of the perpendicular from the point (5, 2, −1) to the line joining the points (3, 1, 3), (−1, −1, −3).

32 $\overline{OA}$, $\overline{OB}$ are unit vectors perpendicular to each other and inclined at angles α, β respectively to the plane XOY; M is the mid-point of AB. If $\overline{OM}$ is inclined at an angle γ to the plane XOY show that $\sqrt{2}\sin\gamma = \sin\alpha+\sin\beta$.

33 In a cube of edge a, prove that the perpendicular distance of a vertex from a diagonal which does not pass through it is $a\sqrt{\tfrac{2}{3}}$.

IV

VECTOR EQUATIONS OF STRAIGHT LINES AND PLANES

Vector equation of a straight line passing through a given point and parallel to a given vector Suppose the given point A has position vector $\mathbf{a}$ with respect to the origin O and that the given vector is $\mathbf{b}$. Then if P is any point on the straight line drawn through A parallel to $\mathbf{b}$, $\overline{AP}$ is equal to $\lambda\mathbf{b}$, where λ is a scalar multiple or parameter which is positive for points on one side of A and negative for points on the other. Thus if $\mathbf{r}$ is the position vector of P, then

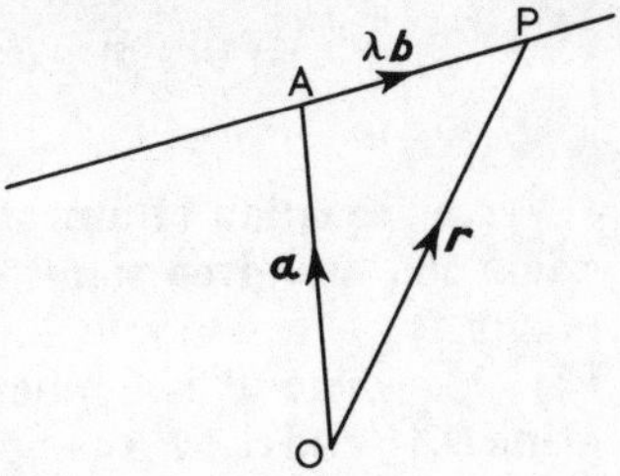

FIG. 29.

$$\mathbf{r} = \overline{OP} = \overline{OA} + \overline{AP};$$

i.e.

$$\mathbf{r} = \mathbf{a} + \lambda\mathbf{b}$$

—the vector equation of the straight line passing through the point $\mathbf{a}$ and parallel to the vector $\mathbf{b}$.

Vector equation of a straight line passing through two given points Let the points A, B have position vectors $\mathbf{a}$, $\mathbf{b}$ with respect to the origin O; so $\overline{AB} = \mathbf{b} - \mathbf{a}$. Hence as the line AB passes through the point with position vector $\mathbf{a}$ and is parallel to the vector $\mathbf{b} - \mathbf{a}$, its vector equation is

$$\mathbf{r} = \mathbf{a} + \lambda(\mathbf{b} - \mathbf{a}),$$

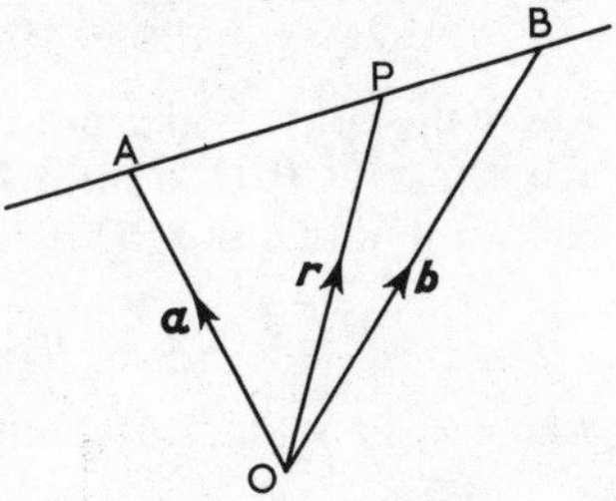

FIG. 30.

where the scalar parameter λ is positive for points on the same side of A as B and negative for points on the other side. It should also be noted that λ is equal to the ratio AP/AB.

Ex. 1 *The position vectors of the vertices B, D of parallelogram $ABCD$ with respect to the vertex A as origin are* $\mathbf{b}$, $\mathbf{d}$. *Find the vector equations of* (i) AC; (ii) BD; (iii) *the straight line through C parallel to* $\overline{BD}$.

(i) As the position vectors of A, C are zero and $\mathbf{b}+\mathbf{d}$ respectively, the vector equation of AC is

$$\mathbf{r} = \lambda(\mathbf{b}+\mathbf{d}).$$

(ii) The vector equation of BD can be expressed as

$$\mathbf{r} = \mathbf{b}+\lambda(\mathbf{d}-\mathbf{b}) = (1-\lambda)\mathbf{b}+\lambda\mathbf{d}.$$

It could of course also be written in the form $\mathbf{r} = \mathbf{d}+\mu(\mathbf{b}-\mathbf{d})$, where both λ and μ are scalar parameters.

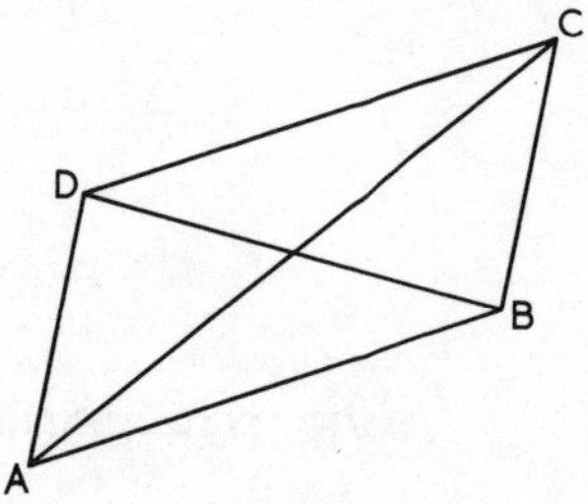

FIG. 31.

(iii) The vector equation of the line through C parallel to $\overline{BD}$ is

$$\mathbf{r} = (\mathbf{b}+\mathbf{d})+\lambda(\mathbf{d}-\mathbf{b}) = (1-\lambda)\mathbf{b}+(1+\lambda)\mathbf{d}.$$

Vector equation of any straight line in the plane determined by the origin and two given points Assume that the origin O and the given points A, B are non-collinear. In Fig. 32, where P is a point in the plane OAB and $OA'PB'$ is a parallelogram,

$$\overline{OP} = \overline{OA'}+\overline{OB'} = u_1\overline{OA}+u_2\overline{OB},$$

where u_1, u_2 are scalar multiples.

Similarly, if Q is some other point in the plane OAB,

$$\overline{OQ} = v_1\overline{OA}+v_2\overline{OB},$$

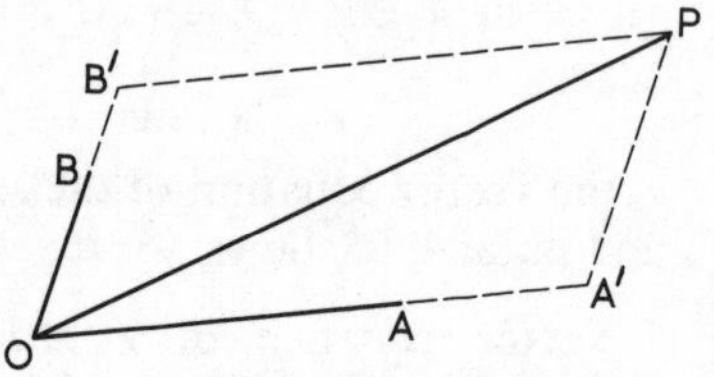

FIG. 32.

where v_1, v_2 are scalar multiples. So, if the position vectors of A, B are $\mathbf{a}$, $\mathbf{b}$, those of P, Q are $u_1\mathbf{a}+u_2\mathbf{b}$, $v_1\mathbf{a}+v_2\mathbf{b}$ respectively and the vector equation of the line PQ is

$$\mathbf{r} = u_1\mathbf{a}+u_2\mathbf{b}+\lambda[(v_1\mathbf{a}+v_2\mathbf{b})-(u_1\mathbf{a}+u_2\mathbf{b})],$$

where λ is a scalar parameter.

Point of intersection of two coplanar lines The position vector of the common point of two coplanar lines is readily determinable if the vector equations of the lines are both expressed in terms of the position vectors, say $\mathbf{a}$, $\mathbf{b}$, of the same two points lying in the plane of the lines. The method, requiring the equating of the coefficients of $\mathbf{a}$ and $\mathbf{b}$ in the separate vector equations of the lines, is illustrated in the following example.

Ex. 2 *PQRS is a parallelogram and M is the mid-point of PQ. With P as origin the position vectors of Q, S are* **q**, **s**. *Find the position vector of the common point N of PR and MS and deduce that N trisects PR.*

As the position vector of R is $\mathbf{q}+\mathbf{s}$, the equation of the line PR is $\mathbf{r} = \lambda(\mathbf{q}+\mathbf{s})$, where λ is a scalar parameter. As the position vector of M is $\frac{1}{2}\mathbf{q}$, the equation of the line MS is $\mathbf{r} = \frac{1}{2}\mathbf{q}+\mu(\mathbf{s}-\frac{1}{2}\mathbf{q})$, where μ is a scalar parameter.

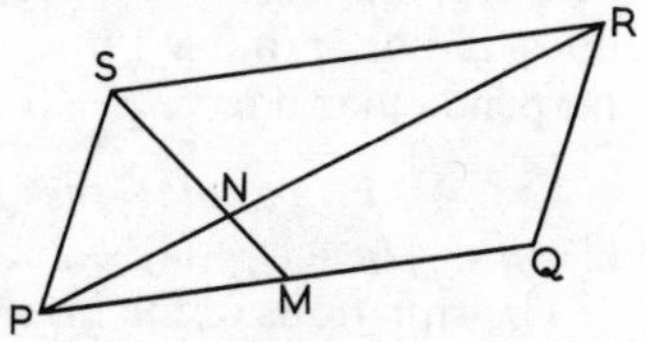

FIG. 33.

At the common point N, the values of $\mathbf{r}$ in the two equations are identical, so,

$$\lambda(\mathbf{q}+\mathbf{s}) = \tfrac{1}{2}\mathbf{q}+\mu(\mathbf{s}-\tfrac{1}{2}\mathbf{q})$$

identically. Equating the coefficients of $\mathbf{q}$ and $\mathbf{s}$ we have

$$\lambda = \tfrac{1}{2}(1-\mu) \quad \text{and} \quad \lambda = \mu.$$

Hence $\lambda = \mu = \frac{1}{3}$ and so the position vector of N is $\frac{1}{3}(\mathbf{q}+\mathbf{s})$. As $\overline{PN} = \frac{1}{3}(\mathbf{q}+\mathbf{s}) = \frac{1}{3}\overline{PR}$, N is a point of trisection of PR.

Condition for three points to be collinear Let the points A, B, C have position vectors $\mathbf{a}$, $\mathbf{b}$, $\mathbf{c}$, then the equation of the line BC is $\mathbf{r} = \mathbf{b}+\lambda(\mathbf{c}-\mathbf{b})$, where λ is a scalar parameter. So the necessary condition for the three points to be collinear, arising from the fact that the position vector of A must satisfy the equation of BC, is

$$\mathbf{a} = \mathbf{b}+\lambda(\mathbf{c}-\mathbf{b}), \qquad \text{or,}$$

$$\mathbf{a}+(\lambda-1)\mathbf{b}-\lambda\mathbf{c} = 0,$$

a result which can be expressed as

$$\alpha\mathbf{a}+\beta\mathbf{b}+\gamma\mathbf{c} = 0,$$

where

$$\alpha+\beta+\gamma = 0.$$

The sufficiency of this latter condition is established by writing $\alpha = 1$, $\beta = -\gamma-1$, leading to the result

$$\mathbf{a} = \mathbf{b}-\gamma(\mathbf{c}-\mathbf{b}),$$

from which it is evident that A lies on the line BC.

Ex. 3 *Prove that the points* $A(3, -1, 2)$, $B(-1, 1, -2)$, $C(5, -2, 4)$ *are collinear.*

As the position vectors of B and C are $-\mathbf{i}+\mathbf{j}-2\mathbf{k}$ and $5\mathbf{i}-2\mathbf{j}+4\mathbf{k}$, the equation of the line BC is

$$\mathbf{r} = -\mathbf{i}+\mathbf{j}-2\mathbf{k}+\lambda(6\mathbf{i}-3\mathbf{j}+6\mathbf{k})$$
$$= (6\lambda-1)\mathbf{i}+(1-3\lambda)\mathbf{j}+(6\lambda-2)\mathbf{k}.$$

The point on BC corresponding to $\lambda = \frac{2}{3}$ has position vector $3\mathbf{i}-\mathbf{j}+2\mathbf{k}$. This is the position vector of A and hence A, B, C are collinear.

Angle between two straight lines With the vector equations of the two lines in the forms $\mathbf{r} = \mathbf{a}_1 + \lambda \mathbf{b}_1$, $\mathbf{r} = \mathbf{a}_2 + \mu \mathbf{b}_2$, where λ, μ are scalar parameters, it follows that the angle between the lines is also the angle between the vectors $\mathbf{b}_1, \mathbf{b}_2$. Consequently the angle between the two lines is $\cos^{-1}(\mathbf{b}_1 . \mathbf{b}_2)/b_1 b_2$. It should be noted that the lines are perpendicular if $\mathbf{b}_1 . \mathbf{b}_2 = 0$ and parallel if $\mathbf{b}_1$ is a scalar multiple of $\mathbf{b}_2$.

Ex. 4 *Prove that the lines* $\mathbf{r} = (2\lambda+1)\mathbf{i}+(1-\lambda)\mathbf{j}+(1-\lambda)\mathbf{k}$, $\mathbf{r} = (3+\mu)\mathbf{i}-(2\mu+1)\mathbf{j}+(4\mu+2)\mathbf{k}$ *are perpendicular.*

The equations of the lines can be written as

$$\mathbf{r} = \mathbf{i}+\mathbf{j}+\mathbf{k}+\lambda(2\mathbf{i}-\mathbf{j}-\mathbf{k}); \quad \mathbf{r} = 3\mathbf{i}-\mathbf{j}+2\mathbf{k}+\mu(\mathbf{i}-2\mathbf{j}+4\mathbf{k}).$$

But $(2\mathbf{i}-\mathbf{j}-\mathbf{k}).(\mathbf{i}-2\mathbf{j}+4\mathbf{k}) = 2+2-4 = 0$. Hence the lines are perpendicular.

Vector equation of the bisector of the angle between two intersecting straight lines Consider first the case where the lines OB_1, OB_2 intersect at the origin O. If $\overline{OB_1}$, $\overline{OB_2}$ are parallel respectively to the vectors $\mathbf{b}_1$, $\mathbf{b}_2$, the equations of the lines OB_1, OB_2 can be expressed as $\mathbf{r} = \lambda_1 \mathbf{b}_1$, $\mathbf{r} = \lambda_2 \mathbf{b}_2$, where λ_1, λ_2 are scalar parameters.

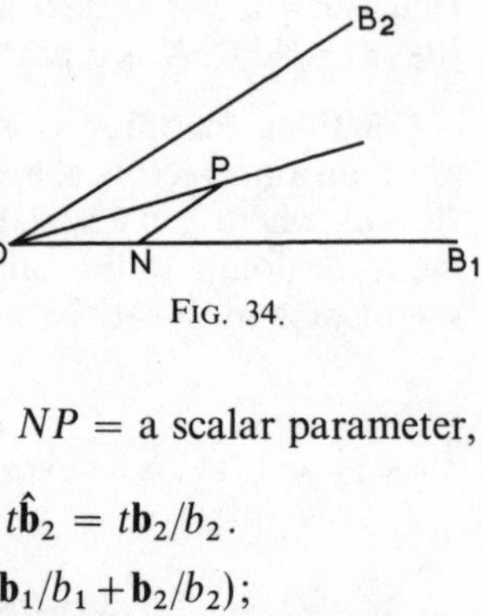

FIG. 34.

Let P, position vector $\mathbf{r}$, be a point on the internal bisector of the angle B_1OB_2 and let $\overline{NP}$ be parallel to $\overline{OB_2}$ (Fig. 34).

Then as OP bisects angle B_1OB_2, $ON = NP =$ a scalar parameter, say t.

So $$\overline{ON} = t\hat{\mathbf{b}}_1 = t\mathbf{b}_1/b_1; \quad \overline{NP} = t\hat{\mathbf{b}}_2 = t\mathbf{b}_2/b_2.$$

$$\therefore \quad \mathbf{r} = \overline{OP} = \overline{ON}+\overline{NP} = t(\mathbf{b}_1/b_1+\mathbf{b}_2/b_2);$$

i.e. the equation of the internal bisector of the angle between the given lines is

$$\mathbf{r} = t\left(\frac{\mathbf{b}_1}{b_1}+\frac{\mathbf{b}_2}{b_2}\right).$$

Replacing $\mathbf{b}_1$ by $-\mathbf{b}_1$, it follows that the bisector of the exterior angle between the lines has a vector equation of the form

$$\mathbf{r} = w\left(\frac{\mathbf{b}_2}{b_2}-\frac{\mathbf{b}_1}{b_1}\right), \quad \text{where } w \text{ is a scalar parameter.}$$

More generally if the given lines intersect at a point with position vector $\mathbf{a}$, then the equations of the angle bisectors will be

$$\mathbf{r} = \mathbf{a}+t\left(\frac{\mathbf{b}_1}{b_1}+\frac{\mathbf{b}_2}{b_2}\right) \quad \text{and} \quad \mathbf{r} = \mathbf{a}+w\left(\frac{\mathbf{b}_2}{b_2}-\frac{\mathbf{b}_1}{b_1}\right).$$

Ex. 5 *Prove that the internal bisector of an angle of a triangle divides the opposite side in the ratio of the sides containing the angle.*

In triangle ABC, take A as origin and let the position vectors of B, C be $\mathbf{b}, \mathbf{c}$. Then the equation of AD, the internal bisector of angle A is

$$\mathbf{r} = t\left(\frac{\mathbf{b}}{b}+\frac{\mathbf{c}}{c}\right).$$

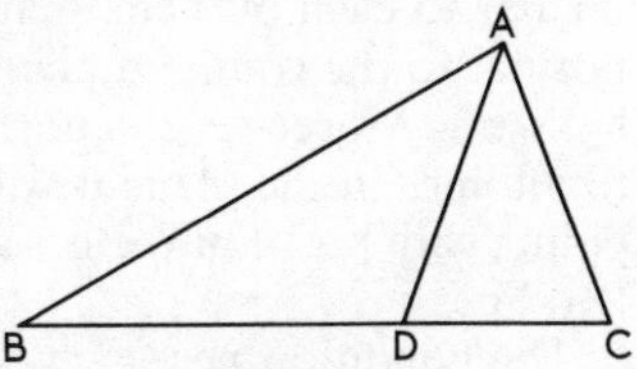

FIG. 35.

The equation of BC is $\mathbf{r} = \mathbf{b}+\lambda(\mathbf{c}-\mathbf{b})$, where the scalar parameter λ is equal to the ratio BD/BC.

For the common point D of these two lines,

$$\frac{t}{b} = 1-\lambda \quad \text{and} \quad \frac{t}{c} = \lambda.$$

Hence $\lambda = \dfrac{b}{b+c}$; i.e. $\dfrac{BD}{BC} = \dfrac{AB}{AB+AC}$ and so $\dfrac{BD}{DC} = \dfrac{AB}{AC}$.

Perpendicular distance of a point from a straight line Suppose the point P has position vector $\mathbf{p}$ and let the given line pass through the point A, position vector $\mathbf{a}$, and have a direction parallel to the vector $\mathbf{b}$. So the equation of the given line is $\mathbf{r} = \mathbf{a}+\lambda\mathbf{b}$. Now AN, the projection of AP on the given line, $= \dfrac{\overline{AP}\,.\,\mathbf{b}}{b}$.

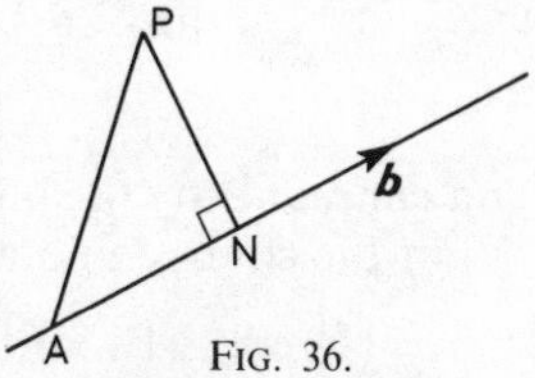

FIG. 36.

$\therefore$ the square of the perpendicular $PN = AP^2 - AN^2$

$$= (\mathbf{p}-\mathbf{a})^2 - \frac{1}{b^2}[(\mathbf{p}-\mathbf{a})\,.\,\mathbf{b}]^2.$$

Ex. 6 *Find the length of the perpendicular from the point* $3\mathbf{i}+2\mathbf{j}-6\mathbf{k}$ *to the line* $\mathbf{r} = \lambda(2\mathbf{i}-\mathbf{j}+2\mathbf{k})$.

In the notation of the general result above, $\mathbf{p} = 3\mathbf{i}+2\mathbf{j}-6\mathbf{k}$, $\mathbf{a} = 0$, $\mathbf{b} = 2\mathbf{i}-\mathbf{j}+2\mathbf{k}$.

$\therefore$ the square of the perpendicular $= (3\mathbf{i}+2\mathbf{j}-6\mathbf{k})^2$

$$-\tfrac{1}{9}[(3\mathbf{i}+2\mathbf{j}-6\mathbf{k})\,.\,(2\mathbf{i}-\mathbf{j}+2\mathbf{k})]^2$$

$$= 49-\tfrac{1}{9}(-8)^2 = \tfrac{377}{9}.$$

i.e. the length of the perpendicular $= \frac{1}{3}\sqrt{377}$ units.

To find the condition that two lines intersect Let the equation of the lines be

$$\mathbf{r} = \mathbf{a}_1+\lambda_1\mathbf{b}_1\,; \quad \mathbf{r} = \mathbf{a}_2+\lambda_2\mathbf{b}_2,$$

where $\mathbf{b}_1$ and $\mathbf{b}_2$ are non-parallel vectors. For the lines to intersect they must be coplanar and a normal to their common plane will be perpendicular to each of them, that is to the vectors $\mathbf{b}_1$, $\mathbf{b}_2$. Consequently a normal to the common plane is in the direction of the vector product $\mathbf{b}_1 \wedge \mathbf{b}_2$. Moreover as a normal to the common plane is perpendicular to all lines in the plane it will be perpendicular to the line joining the points with position vectors $\mathbf{a}_1$, $\mathbf{a}_2$, these points lying separately on the two lines.

The condition necessary for the vectors $\mathbf{b}_1 \wedge \mathbf{b}_2$ and $\mathbf{a}_2 - \mathbf{a}_1$ to be perpendicular is that

$$(\mathbf{a}_2 - \mathbf{a}_1) \cdot (\mathbf{b}_1 \wedge \mathbf{b}_2) = 0,$$

i.e. the scalar triple product $[(\mathbf{a}_2 - \mathbf{a}_1), \mathbf{b}_1, \mathbf{b}_2] = 0$, and this is the required condition for the lines to intersect.

Ex. 7 *Show that the lines* $\mathbf{r} = \mathbf{i}+\mathbf{j}+2\mathbf{k}+\lambda(\mathbf{i}+\mathbf{j}-3\mathbf{k})$, $\mathbf{r} = -2\mathbf{i}-2\mathbf{j}+\mu(\mathbf{i}+\mathbf{j}+\mathbf{k})$ *intersect and find the position vector of their common point.*

Here $\mathbf{a}_1 = \mathbf{i}+\mathbf{j}+2\mathbf{k}$; $\mathbf{a}_2 = -2\mathbf{i}-2\mathbf{j}$; $\mathbf{b}_1 = \mathbf{i}+\mathbf{j}-3\mathbf{k}$; $\mathbf{b}_2 = \mathbf{i}+\mathbf{j}+\mathbf{k}$.

So
$$[(\mathbf{a}_2 - \mathbf{a}_1), \mathbf{b}_1, \mathbf{b}_2] = \begin{vmatrix} -3 & -3 & -2 \\ 1 & 1 & -3 \\ 1 & 1 & 1 \end{vmatrix} = 0$$

and consequently the lines are coplanar and intersect.

For the common point of the two lines

$$(1+\lambda)\mathbf{i}+(1+\lambda)\mathbf{j}+(2-3\lambda)\mathbf{k} = (-2+\mu)\mathbf{i}+(-2+\mu)\mathbf{j}+\mu\mathbf{k}.$$

$$\therefore \quad 1+\lambda = -2+\mu \quad \text{and} \quad 2-3\lambda = \mu;$$

so $\lambda = -\frac{1}{4}$, $\mu = \frac{11}{4}$ and the common point is $\frac{1}{4}(3\mathbf{i}+3\mathbf{j}+11\mathbf{k})$.

EXAMPLES 4a

1 The points A, B, C have position vectors $\mathbf{a}$, $\mathbf{b}$, $\mathbf{c}$, find the vector equations of the following straight lines: (i) AB; (ii) BC; (iii) AM, where M is the mid-point of BC; (iv) the line through A parallel to $\overline{BC}$.

2 Find the vector equation of the line AB in each of the following cases: (i) A, B have position vectors $\mathbf{i}+\mathbf{j}-\mathbf{k}$ and $2\mathbf{i}-\mathbf{j}-\mathbf{k}$; (ii) A, B have coordinates $(-1, 2, 0)$ and $(2, 3, -1)$; (iii) A has position vector $2\mathbf{i}+2\mathbf{j}+\mathbf{k}$ and $\overline{AB}$ is parallel to the vector $3\mathbf{i}-\mathbf{j}-\mathbf{k}$; (iv) B is the point $(2, 1, -1)$ and $\overline{AB}$ is parallel to the line joining the points $(1, 0, -1)$, $(3, 1, 2)$.

3 Find the vector equations of PQ in the cases where P, Q have respectively the following position vectors: (i) 0, $2\mathbf{a}$; (ii) $\mathbf{a}$, $2\mathbf{b}$; (iii) $\mathbf{a}+\mathbf{b}$, $\mathbf{a}-\mathbf{b}$; (iv) $\mathbf{a}+2\mathbf{b}$, $\mathbf{b}+2\mathbf{a}$.

4 Points P, Q, R, S in a plane have position vectors $2\mathbf{i}+3\mathbf{j}$, $3\mathbf{i}+2\mathbf{j}$, $4\mathbf{i}+6\mathbf{j}$,

$9\mathbf{i}+6\mathbf{j}$ respectively. Determine the position vector of the point of intersection of the lines PQ, RS.

5 The position vectors of the vertices B, C of a triangle with respect to the vertex A as origin are $\mathbf{b}$, $\mathbf{c}$; M, N are the mid-points of sides BC, CA respectively. Find the position vector with respect to A of the common point of BN and the line through C parallel to $\overline{MA}$.

6 $ABCD$ is a parallelogram. With A as origin, the position vectors of B, C are $\mathbf{b}$, $\mathbf{c}$. Find the vector equations of the following straight lines : (i) AD; (ii) CD; (iii) the line joining the mid-points of BC and AD; (iv) the line joining D and the mid-point of AC; (v) the line through C parallel to $\overline{DB}$.

7 Find the position vector of the common point of each of the following pairs of coplanar lines: (i) $\mathbf{r} = \lambda(\mathbf{a}+\mathbf{b}), \mathbf{r} = \mathbf{a}+\mu\mathbf{b}$; (ii) $\mathbf{r} = \lambda(\mathbf{a}-\mathbf{b}), \mathbf{r} = \mathbf{a}+\mu(\mathbf{b}-2\mathbf{a})$; (iii) $\mathbf{r} = \mathbf{i}+\mathbf{j}+\lambda(2\mathbf{i}-\mathbf{j})$, $\mathbf{r} = 2\mathbf{i}+\mu(-\mathbf{i}+\mathbf{j})$; (iv) $\mathbf{r} = \mathbf{a}+\lambda(\mathbf{b}-\frac{1}{2}\mathbf{a})$, $\mathbf{r} = \mathbf{b}+\mu(\mathbf{a}-\frac{1}{2}\mathbf{b})$; (v) $\mathbf{r} = 2\mathbf{i}-\mathbf{j}+\mathbf{k}+\lambda(3\mathbf{i}+\mathbf{j})$, $\mathbf{r} = -\mathbf{i}+\mathbf{j}+\mathbf{k}+\mu(2\mathbf{j}-3\mathbf{i})$.

8 Find the vector equation of the line passing through the point $(1, 1, 2)$ and having direction cosines $\frac{2}{3}, -\frac{2}{3}, \frac{1}{3}$. More generally, what is the vector equation of the line passing through the point (a, b, c) and having direction cosines l, m, n?

9 Prove that the point $4\mathbf{b}-3\mathbf{a}$ lies on the line joining the points $\mathbf{a}$, $\mathbf{b}$.

10 Prove that the points $\mathbf{a}+\mathbf{b}$, $\mathbf{a}-\mathbf{b}$, $\mathbf{a}+7\mathbf{b}$ are collinear.

11 The vertex A of triangle ABC is taken as origin and the vertices B, C have position vectors $\mathbf{b}$, $\mathbf{c}$. Find (i) the vector equation of the median AD; (ii) the vector equation of PQ, where P, Q are respectively the mid-points of AB, AC. Deduce that AD bisects PQ.

12 Using the data of the previous example, find also the vector equations of the medians BE and CF. Deduce that the three medians of the triangle have a common point which trisects each of them.

13 The position vectors of the vertices A, B, C, D of a tetrahedron are $\mathbf{0}$, $\mathbf{b}$, $\mathbf{c}$, $\mathbf{d}$ respectively. Find the vector equations of (i) the line joining A and the mid-point of CD; (ii) the line joining B and the mid-point of AD; (iii) the line joining the mid-points of AC and BD.

14 A, B, C have position vectors $\mathbf{i}+\mathbf{j}$, $3\mathbf{i}-2\mathbf{j}$, $2\mathbf{i}+4\mathbf{j}$ respectively, find the vector equations of the lines BC and AM, where M is the mid-point of BC. Also determine the position vector of the common point of AM and CN, where N is the point dividing AB in the ratio $1:2$.

15 Show that the vector equation of the line joining the points $(2, 3, 4)$, $(1, 4, -3)$ is $\mathbf{r} = (2-\lambda)\mathbf{i}+(3+\lambda)\mathbf{j}+(4-7\lambda)\mathbf{k}$ and find the value of the scalar parameter λ at the point where this line meets the plane $z = 0$.

16 In triangle ABC, D is the point of AB such that $2AD = DB$ and E is the point of AC such that $2AE = EC$; the lines BE, CD intersect at P. Using A as origin and taking $\mathbf{b}$, $\mathbf{c}$ as the position vectors of B, C, find the vector equations of the lines BE and CD and hence determine the ratio in which P divides BE and CD.

17 Find the vector equations of (i) the line joining the points $2\mathbf{i}-\mathbf{j}+\mathbf{k}$, $\mathbf{i}+\mathbf{j}-2\mathbf{k}$; (ii) the line joining the points $(-1, 3, 1)$, $(0, 2, 2)$; (iii) the line through the point $(0, 1, 1)$ parallel to the line joining the points $(-1, -1, 2)$, $(3, 1, 3)$.

18 Prove that the points $(1, -1, 0)$, $(2, 0, 3)$, $(0, -2, -3)$ are collinear.

19 Show that each of the following pairs of lines are perpendicular: (i) $\mathbf{r} = 2\mathbf{i}+\mathbf{j}-\mathbf{k}+\lambda(\mathbf{i}+\mathbf{j}-\mathbf{k})$, $\mathbf{r} = \mathbf{i}-\mathbf{j}-\mathbf{k}+\mu(2\mathbf{i}+2\mathbf{k})$; (ii) $\mathbf{r} = (1-2\lambda)\mathbf{i}+(2+\lambda)\mathbf{j}+(3-\lambda)\mathbf{k}$, $\mathbf{r} = (3+\mu)\mathbf{i}-(2+3\mu)\mathbf{j}+(2-5\mu)\mathbf{k}$; (iii) the line joining the points $(1, 1, 1)$, $(3, 2, 0)$ and the line joining the points $(0, 3, -1)$, $(1, 0, -2)$.

20 If M, N are the mid-points of the sides AB, CD of a parallelogram $ABCD$, prove, by using vector equations of lines, that DM, BN trisect the diagonal AC.

21 Find the cosine of the acute angle between the lines $\mathbf{r} = \lambda(2\mathbf{i}+\mathbf{j}-2\mathbf{k})$, $\mathbf{r} = (1-\mu)\mathbf{i}+(1+2\mu)\mathbf{j}+(2\mu-1)\mathbf{k}$.

22 The point A is fixed and $\overline{OA} = 4\mathbf{i}+6\mathbf{j}$; the point P is variable and $\overline{OP} = 2\cos\theta\mathbf{i}+2\sin\theta\mathbf{j}$, where θ varies. If $\overline{OA}+\overline{OP} = 2\overline{OQ}$, show that the locus of Q is a circle.

23 $ABCD$ is a trapezium with $\overline{AB}$ parallel to $\overline{DC}$. Prove that the line joining the mid-points of AB, DC passes through the common point of the diagonals AC, BD.

24 Show that a line which is perpendicular to both the lines $\mathbf{r} = \mathbf{a}_1+\lambda\mathbf{b}_1$, $\mathbf{r} = \mathbf{a}_2+\mu\mathbf{b}_2$ is in one of the directions of $\pm\mathbf{b}_1\wedge\mathbf{b}_2$. Hence find the vector equations of the lines passing through the origin and perpendicular to both the lines $\mathbf{r} = (2+\lambda)\mathbf{i}+(1+\lambda)\mathbf{j}+(\lambda-3)\mathbf{k}$, $\mathbf{r} = (1+2\mu)\mathbf{i}-(1+3\mu)\mathbf{j}-\mu\mathbf{k}$.

25 $ABCD$ is a tetrahedron; with A as origin the position vectors of B, C, D are $\mathbf{b}$, $\mathbf{c}$, $\mathbf{d}$. Find (i) the position vector of the centroid G_1 of triangle BCD; (ii) the position vector of the centroid G_2 of triangle ACD; (iii) the equations of the lines AG_1, BG_2. Show that the lines AG_1, BG_2 intersect each other and state the position vector of their common point.

26 Find the vector equations of the internal bisectors of the angles between the pairs of lines (i) $\mathbf{r} = \lambda(2\mathbf{i}+2\mathbf{j}-\mathbf{k})$, $\mathbf{r} = \mu(3\mathbf{i}-6\mathbf{j}+2\mathbf{k})$; (ii) $\mathbf{r} = \mathbf{i}+\mathbf{j}+\mathbf{k}+\lambda(\mathbf{i}-\mathbf{j}-\mathbf{k})$, $\mathbf{r} = \mathbf{i}+\mathbf{j}+\mathbf{k}+\mu(-\mathbf{i}+\mathbf{j}-\mathbf{k})$; (iii) $\mathbf{r} = (1+3\lambda)\mathbf{i}+4\lambda\mathbf{j}$, $\mathbf{r} = 4\mu\mathbf{i}+(1+3\mu)\mathbf{j}$.

27 Taking A as origin and the position vectors of B, C as $\mathbf{b}$, $\mathbf{c}$, write down the vector equations of the internal bisectors of the angles of triangle ABC and verify that these lines are concurrent.

28 Find the length of the perpendicular from the origin to the line $\mathbf{r} = \mathbf{i}+\mathbf{j}+\mathbf{k}+\lambda(2\mathbf{i}+2\mathbf{j}-\mathbf{k})$.

29 ABC is a triangle and P is a point in its plane lying on the perpendicular bisector of the side AB. If the position vectors of A, B, C, P are $\mathbf{a}$, $\mathbf{b}$, $\mathbf{c}$, $\mathbf{r}$ respectively, prove that $\mathbf{r}\,.\,(\mathbf{a}-\mathbf{b}) = \frac{1}{2}(a^2-b^2)$ and write down the corresponding result if P lies on the perpendicular bisector of CA. From these two results deduce that $\mathbf{r}\,.\,(\mathbf{b}-\mathbf{c}) = \frac{1}{2}(b^2-c^2)$ and hence that the perpendicular bisectors of the sides of the triangle are concurrent.

30 Find the perpendicular distance of a vertex of a cube of side a from a diagonal which does not pass through it.

31 Prove that the distance between the parallel lines $\mathbf{r} = \mathbf{a}_1+\lambda\mathbf{b}$, $\mathbf{r} = \mathbf{a}_2+\mu\mathbf{b}$ is $\frac{1}{b}|(\mathbf{a}_2-\mathbf{a}_1)\wedge\mathbf{b}|$.

32 Show that the lines $\mathbf{r} = (3+2\lambda)\mathbf{i}-(1+3\lambda)\mathbf{j}+(4+6\lambda)\mathbf{k}$, $\mathbf{r} = (1+\mu)\mathbf{i}+4\mu\mathbf{j}+(3\mu-2)\mathbf{k}$ are coplanar and find the position vector of their common point.

33 The position vectors of the vertices A, B, C of a triangle are $\mathbf{a}$, $\mathbf{b}$, $\mathbf{c}$. If $\mathbf{r}$ is the position vector of a point on the altitude AD, show that $\mathbf{r}\,.\,(\mathbf{b}-\mathbf{c}) = \mathbf{a}\,.\,(\mathbf{b}-\mathbf{c})$.

Using the corresponding results for the altitudes BE and CF, deduce that the three altitudes are concurrent.

34 Prove that the foot of the perpendicular from the vertex of a cube onto a diagonal which does not pass through it divides the diagonal in the ratio 1:2.

35 Two non-intersecting straight lines have equations $\mathbf{r} = \mathbf{a}_1 + \lambda\mathbf{b}_1$, $\mathbf{r} = \mathbf{a}_2 + \mu\mathbf{b}_2$. Show that their common normal is parallel to the vector $\mathbf{b}_1 \wedge \mathbf{b}_2$. Show further that the length of the common perpendicular to the two lines is the projection of the line joining the points $\mathbf{a}_1$, $\mathbf{a}_2$ onto the common normal and is equal to $(\mathbf{a}_1 - \mathbf{a}_2) . (\mathbf{b}_1 \wedge \mathbf{b}_2)/|\mathbf{b}_1 \wedge \mathbf{b}_2|$.

36 Using the result obtained in the previous example, find the shortest distance between the skew lines $\mathbf{r} = \lambda\mathbf{k}$, $\mathbf{r} = (1+\mu)\mathbf{i} + \mu\mathbf{j} + \mu\mathbf{k}$.

37 Prove that the shortest distances between a diagonal of a rectangular parallelepiped of sides a, b, c and the edges not meeting it are $bc/\sqrt{(b^2+c^2)}$, $ca/\sqrt{(c^2+a^2)}$, $ab/\sqrt{(a^2+b^2)}$.

38 A regular tetrahedron has sides of length $2a$. Show (i) the opposite edges are perpendicular; (ii) the join of the mid-points of a pair of opposite edges is the shortest distance between these edges; (iii) the shortest distance between two opposite edges is $a\sqrt{2}$.

39 A tetrahedron $ABCD$ is such that $AD = BC = a$, $AB = CD = b$, $AC = BD = c$. If P, Q are the mid-points of AD, BC, prove that PQ is the common normal to these edges and find its length.

The plane The vector equation of a plane will be determined in each of the following cases:

(i) in terms of the position vectors of three non-collinear points in the plane;

(ii) in terms of the position vector of the common point and the directions of two lines lying in the plane;

(iii) in terms of the position vector of a point in the plane and the direction of a line normal to the plane.

Plane passing through three points Let the position vectors of the three points A, B, C which determine the plane be $\mathbf{a}, \mathbf{b}, \mathbf{c}$ and let the position vector of any point P of the plane be $\mathbf{r}$ (Fig. 37). Then the vector $\overline{AP}$ can be resolved into components in the directions $\overline{AB}$, $\overline{AC}$, so $\overline{AP} = s\overline{AB} + t\overline{AC}$, where s, t are scalar multiples. But $\overline{AP} = \mathbf{r} - \mathbf{a}$; $\overline{AB} = \mathbf{b} - \mathbf{a}$; $\overline{AC} = \mathbf{c} - \mathbf{a}$.

So $$\mathbf{r} = \mathbf{a} + s(\mathbf{b} - \mathbf{a}) + t(\mathbf{c} - \mathbf{a})$$

—this is the vector equation of the plane in which a pair of values of the scalar parameters s, t uniquely determines one point of the plane.

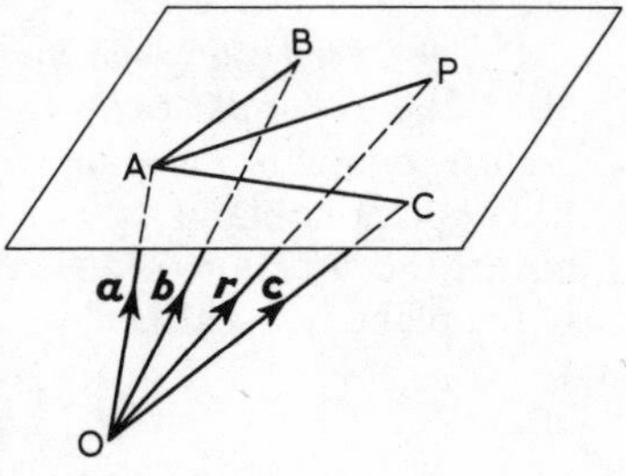

FIG. 37.

Ex. 8 *Find the vector equation of the plane determined by the points* (0, 1, 1), (2, 1, −3), (1, 3, 2) *and also find the coordinates of the point in which this plane intersects the line* $\mathbf{r} = \mathbf{i}(1+2\lambda)+\mathbf{j}(2-3\lambda)+\mathbf{k}(-3-5\lambda)$.

The position vectors of the points are $\mathbf{j}+\mathbf{k}$, $2\mathbf{i}+\mathbf{j}-3\mathbf{k}$, $\mathbf{i}+3\mathbf{j}+2\mathbf{k}$.

∴ The equation of the plane is

$$\mathbf{r} = \mathbf{j}+\mathbf{k}+s(2\mathbf{i}-4\mathbf{k})+t(\mathbf{i}+2\mathbf{j}+\mathbf{k});$$

i.e.
$$\mathbf{r} = \mathbf{i}(2s+t)+\mathbf{j}(1+2t)+\mathbf{k}(1-4s+t),$$

where s, t are scalar parameters.

For the common point of the plane and the given line, the values of the parameters s, t, λ must satisfy the equations

$$2s+t = 1+2\lambda; \quad 1+2t = 2-3\lambda; \quad 1-4s+t = -3-5\lambda.$$

The solution of these simultaneous equations is $s = 2$, $t = -1$, $\lambda = 1$.

Substituting either for s, t in the equation of the plane or for λ in the equation of the line gives the position vector $3\mathbf{i}-\mathbf{j}-8\mathbf{k}$ of the common point.

So the common point has coordinates (3, −1, −8).

Plane passing through two intersecting lines Let A, position vector $\mathbf{a}$, be the common point of the two lines and let the directions of the lines be those of the vectors $\mathbf{b}_1$, $\mathbf{b}_2$ (Fig. 38). Let the position vector of any point P of the plane be $\mathbf{r}$. Then the vector $\overline{AP}$ can be resolved into components in the directions of $\mathbf{b}_1$ and $\mathbf{b}_2$, so $\overline{AP} = s\mathbf{b}_1+t\mathbf{b}_2$, where s, t are scalar multiples. Hence $\mathbf{r} = \mathbf{a}+s\mathbf{b}_1+t\mathbf{b}_2$—this is the vector equation of the plane in which a pair of values of the scalar parameters s, t uniquely determines one point of the plane.

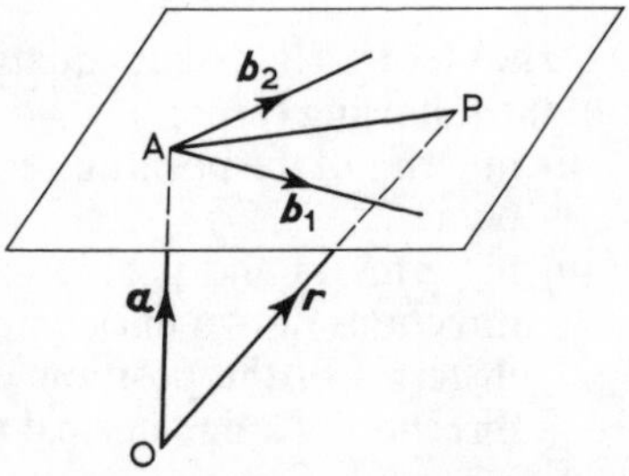

FIG. 38.

Ex. 9 *Find the equation of the plane passing through the point* $3\mathbf{i}+\mathbf{j}-\mathbf{k}$ *and parallel to the vectors* $\mathbf{i}+\mathbf{j}+\mathbf{k}$, $2\mathbf{i}-\mathbf{j}-3\mathbf{k}$. *Also find the unit vectors normal to this plane.*

The plane contains the two lines intersecting at the point $3\mathbf{i}+\mathbf{j}-\mathbf{k}$ and having the directions of the vectors $\mathbf{i}+\mathbf{j}+\mathbf{k}$, $2\mathbf{i}-\mathbf{j}-3\mathbf{k}$. So the equation of the plane is

$$\mathbf{r} = 3\mathbf{i}+\mathbf{j}-\mathbf{k}+s(\mathbf{i}+\mathbf{j}+\mathbf{k})+t(2\mathbf{i}-\mathbf{j}-3\mathbf{k});$$

i.e.
$$\mathbf{r} = \mathbf{i}(3+s+2t)+\mathbf{j}(1+s-t)+\mathbf{k}(-1+s-3t),$$

where s, t are scalar parameters.

As a normal to a plane is perpendicular to all lines in the plane, a normal to this plane will be perpendicular to both the vectors $\mathbf{i}+\mathbf{j}+\mathbf{k}$ and $2\mathbf{i}-\mathbf{j}-3\mathbf{k}$. So a normal to the plane is in one of the directions

$$\pm(\mathbf{i}+\mathbf{j}+\mathbf{k}) \wedge (2\mathbf{i}-\mathbf{j}-3\mathbf{k});\text{ i.e. } \pm(-2\mathbf{i}+5\mathbf{j}-3\mathbf{k}).$$

Hence the unit vectors normal to the plane are $\pm(-2\mathbf{i}+5\mathbf{j}-3\mathbf{k})/\sqrt{38}$.

Plane passing through a given point and perpendicular to a given direction Let the given point A have position vector $\mathbf{a}$ and let the unit vector in the given direction be $\hat{\mathbf{n}}$. In Fig. 39, ON is the perpendicular onto the plane from the origin and assuming $\overline{ON}$ is in the direction of $\hat{\mathbf{n}}$, then $\overline{ON} = n\hat{\mathbf{n}}$, where n is the length of ON. As $\overline{ON}$ is perpendicular to the plane it is perpendicular to $\overline{AP}$.

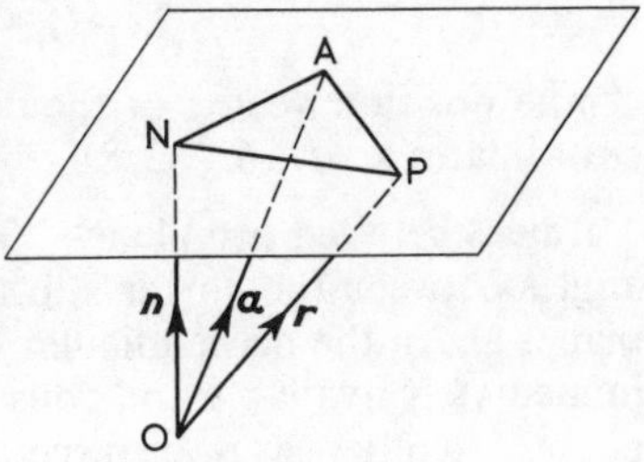

FIG. 39.

$$\therefore \quad (\mathbf{r}-\mathbf{a}).\hat{\mathbf{n}} = 0 \quad \text{or} \quad \mathbf{r}.\hat{\mathbf{n}} = \mathbf{a}.\hat{\mathbf{n}}$$

—the vector equation of the plane.

As $\mathbf{a}.\hat{\mathbf{n}}$ is the projection of $\overline{OA}$ on $\overline{ON}$ it is equal to n, the perpendicular distance of the plane from the origin. So the equation of the plane can be written

$$\mathbf{r}.\hat{\mathbf{n}} = n \text{—} \textit{the perpendicular form.}$$

It is important to notice that in this form of the equation of a plane, the term on the R.H.S., n, must be positive as the scalar product $\mathbf{a}.\hat{\mathbf{n}}$ is positive, the angle between the vectors being acute.

Ex. 10 *Find the direction cosines of the normal to the plane* $\mathbf{r}.(6\mathbf{i}-3\mathbf{j}-2\mathbf{k})+1 = 0$ *from the origin.*

As the vector $6\mathbf{i}-3\mathbf{j}-2\mathbf{k}$ has a modulus of 7, the equation of the plane is first expressed as $\mathbf{r}.(\frac{6}{7}\mathbf{i}-\frac{3}{7}\mathbf{j}-\frac{2}{7}\mathbf{k}) = -\frac{1}{7}$. To get the correct perpendicular form, the term on the R.H.S must be positive, and we have $\mathbf{r}.(-\frac{6}{7}\mathbf{i}+\frac{3}{7}\mathbf{j}+\frac{2}{7}\mathbf{k}) = \frac{1}{7}$. Hence the unit vector normal to the plane from the origin is $-\frac{6}{7}\mathbf{i}+\frac{3}{7}\mathbf{j}+\frac{2}{7}\mathbf{k}$; the direction cosines of this vector are $-\frac{6}{7}, \frac{3}{7}, \frac{2}{7}$.

Ex. 11 *The foot of the perpendicular from the origin to a plane is the point* $(2, -1, 2)$. *Find the vector equation of the plane and the coordinates of its point of intersection with the line* $\mathbf{r} = \lambda\mathbf{i}+(1+\lambda)\mathbf{j}+(2-\lambda)\mathbf{k}$.

If N is the foot of the perpendicular, $\overline{ON} = 2\mathbf{i}-\mathbf{j}+2\mathbf{k}$, $\therefore$ the unit vector in the direction $\overline{ON} = \frac{1}{3}(2\mathbf{i}-\mathbf{j}+2\mathbf{k})$ and the perpendicular $ON = 3$.

So the equation of the plane is

$$\mathbf{r}\,.\,\tfrac{1}{3}(2\mathbf{i}-\mathbf{j}+2\mathbf{k}) = 3;$$

i.e.
$$\mathbf{r}\,.\,(2\mathbf{i}-\mathbf{j}+2\mathbf{k}) = 9.$$

To find the point of intersection of the plane and line, substitute for **r** from the equation of the line into the equation of the plane and get

$$(\lambda\mathbf{i}+(1+\lambda)\mathbf{j}+(2-\lambda)\mathbf{k})\,.\,(2\mathbf{i}-\mathbf{j}+2\mathbf{k}) = 9,$$

i.e.
$$2\lambda-(1+\lambda)+2(2-\lambda) = 9; \quad \lambda = -6.$$

$\therefore$ the position vector of the common point is $-6\mathbf{i}-5\mathbf{j}+8\mathbf{k}$ and its coordinates are $(-6, -5, 8)$.

Angles between two planes The angles between two planes are the angles between the normals to the planes. When the equations of the planes are in the perpendicular form, vectors normal to the planes are immediately available and consequently so are the angles between the planes. In other cases the direction of a normal to a plane is determined by using the vector product of two line vectors in the plane. The following worked examples illustrate the two cases.

Ex. 12 *Find the cosine of the acute angle between the planes* $\mathbf{r}\,.\,(\mathbf{i}+\mathbf{j}+\mathbf{k}) = 3$, $\mathbf{r}\,.\,(2\mathbf{i}+2\mathbf{j}-\mathbf{k}) = 1$.

Unit vectors normal to the planes are $\dfrac{1}{\sqrt{3}}(\mathbf{i}+\mathbf{j}+\mathbf{k})$ and $\tfrac{1}{3}(2\mathbf{i}+2\mathbf{j}-\mathbf{k})$.

So if θ is an angle between the planes,

$$\cos\theta = \frac{1}{\sqrt{3}}(\mathbf{i}+\mathbf{j}+\mathbf{k})\,.\,\tfrac{1}{3}(2\mathbf{i}+2\mathbf{j}-\mathbf{k})$$

$$= \frac{1}{3\sqrt{3}}(2+2-1) = \frac{1}{\sqrt{3}}.$$

Hence the cosine of the acute angle between the planes is $\dfrac{1}{\sqrt{3}}$.

Ex. 13 *Find the acute angle between the plane defined by the points* $A(0, 0, 0)$, $B(1, 2, 3)$, $C(-1, 3, 1)$ *and the plane defined by the points* $P(1, 1, 1)$, $Q(-1, 0, 1)$, $R(0, 1, -1)$.

$$\overline{AB} = \mathbf{i}+2\mathbf{j}+3\mathbf{k}; \quad \overline{BC} = -2\mathbf{i}+\mathbf{j}-2\mathbf{k}.$$

$$\therefore \qquad \overline{AB}\wedge\overline{BC} = \begin{vmatrix} \mathbf{i} & \mathbf{j} & \mathbf{k} \\ 1 & 2 & 3 \\ -2 & 1 & -2 \end{vmatrix} = -7\mathbf{i}-4\mathbf{j}+5\mathbf{k}.$$

So a unit vector $\hat{\mathbf{n}}_1$ normal to plane $ABC = \dfrac{1}{\sqrt{90}}(-7\mathbf{i}-4\mathbf{j}+5\mathbf{k})$.

$$\overline{PQ} = -2\mathbf{i}-\mathbf{j}; \quad \overline{QR} = \mathbf{i}+\mathbf{j}-2\mathbf{k}.$$

$$\therefore \quad \overline{PQ} \wedge \overline{QR} = \begin{vmatrix} \mathbf{i} & \mathbf{j} & \mathbf{k} \\ -2 & -1 & 0 \\ 1 & 1 & -2 \end{vmatrix} = 2\mathbf{i}-4\mathbf{j}-\mathbf{k}.$$

So a unit vector $\hat{\mathbf{n}}_2$ normal to plane $PQR = \dfrac{1}{\sqrt{21}}(2\mathbf{i}-4\mathbf{j}-\mathbf{k})$. If θ is an angle between the planes,

$$\cos\theta = \hat{\mathbf{n}}_1 \cdot \hat{\mathbf{n}}_2 = (-14+16-5)/3\sqrt{210} = -1/\sqrt{210}.$$

Hence the acute angle between the planes is $\cos^{-1} 1/\sqrt{210}$.

Perpendicular distance of a point from a plane First take the case where the plane is given by an equation in the perpendicular form

$$\mathbf{r} \cdot \hat{\mathbf{n}} = n. \qquad \text{(i)}$$

In this equation, $\hat{\mathbf{n}}$ is the unit vector in the direction of the normal from the origin O to the plane and n is the perpendicular distance of the plane from the origin. Suppose that point P' has position vector $\mathbf{r}'$. The equation of a plane parallel to the given one at a distance n' from the origin is

$$\mathbf{r} \cdot \hat{\mathbf{n}} = n'. \qquad \text{(ii)}$$

This plane passes through P' if the position vector of P' satisfies equation (ii), i.e. if

$$\mathbf{r}' \cdot \hat{\mathbf{n}} = n'.$$

$\therefore$ the perpendicular distance from the origin of the plane through P' parallel to the given plane is $\mathbf{r}' \cdot \hat{\mathbf{n}}$ and the distance of P' from the given plane is the difference between n and $\mathbf{r}' \cdot \hat{\mathbf{n}}$, i.e. $n-\mathbf{r}' \cdot \hat{\mathbf{n}}$. This difference will be positive when P' and O lie on the same side of the given plane and negative when they lie on opposite sides.

Ex. 14 *Find the perpendicular distance of the point* $\mathbf{i}+\mathbf{j}+\mathbf{k}$ *from the plane* $\mathbf{r} \cdot (\mathbf{i}-\mathbf{j}-\mathbf{k}) = \sqrt{3}$.

The equation of the plane must first be expressed in the form $\mathbf{r} \cdot \hat{\mathbf{n}} = n$, by replacing the vector $\mathbf{i}-\mathbf{j}-\mathbf{k}$ by $\sqrt{3}\left[\dfrac{1}{\sqrt{3}}(\mathbf{i}-\mathbf{j}-\mathbf{k})\right]$, giving

$$\mathbf{r} \cdot \frac{1}{\sqrt{3}}(\mathbf{i}-\mathbf{j}-\mathbf{k}) = 1.$$

The length of the perpendicular from the given point to this plane

$$= n - \mathbf{r}' \cdot \hat{\mathbf{n}}$$

$$= 1 - (\mathbf{i}+\mathbf{j}+\mathbf{k}) \cdot \frac{1}{\sqrt{3}}(\mathbf{i}-\mathbf{j}-\mathbf{k}) = 1 + \frac{1}{\sqrt{3}}.$$

The positive result indicates that the origin and the given point lie on the same side of the plane.

If the vector equation of the plane is in a form other than the perpendicular one, the determination of the length of the perpendicular from a point to the plane is more laborious—the method is illustrated in the following example.

Ex. 15 *Points B, C, D have coordinates* $(0, 1, -1), (2, 1, 1), (-1, -1, 0)$ *respectively. Find* (i) *the vector equation of the plane BCD*; (ii) *the position vector of the foot of the perpendicular from the point $A(1, -1, -1)$ to the plane BCD*; (iii) *the length of this perpendicular.*
The equation of the plane BCD is

$$\mathbf{r} = \mathbf{j} - \mathbf{k} + s(2\mathbf{i} + 2\mathbf{k}) + t(-\mathbf{i} - 2\mathbf{j} + \mathbf{k})$$

$$= \mathbf{i}(2s - t) + \mathbf{j}(1 - 2t) + \mathbf{k}(-1 + 2s + t).$$

$\therefore$ the vector $\overline{AP}$, where P is the point of the plane corresponding to the values s, t of the scalar parameters, is given by

$$\overline{AP} = \mathbf{i}(2s - t - 1) + \mathbf{j}(2 - 2t) + \mathbf{k}(2s + t).$$

Also $\qquad \overline{BC} = 2\mathbf{i} + 2\mathbf{k}; \quad \overline{BD} = -\mathbf{i} - 2\mathbf{j} + \mathbf{k}.$

Now $\overline{AP}$ is normal to the plane if it is perpendicular to two lines, say $\overline{BC}$, $\overline{BD}$, in the plane; i.e. if $\overline{AP} \cdot \overline{BC} = \overline{AP} \cdot \overline{BD} = 0$. These conditions give

$$2(2s - t - 1) + 2(2s + t) = 0,$$

and $\qquad -1(2s - t - 1) - 2(2 - 2t) + 1(2s + t) = 0,$

with the solution $s = \frac{1}{4}$, $t = \frac{1}{2}$.

$\therefore$ the position vector of the foot of the perpendicular from A to the plane BCD

$$= \mathbf{i}(\tfrac{1}{2} - \tfrac{1}{2}) + \mathbf{j}(1 - 1) + \mathbf{k}(-1 + \tfrac{1}{2} + \tfrac{1}{2}) = \mathbf{0}.$$

$\therefore$ the length of the perpendicular $= \sqrt{[1^2 + (-1)^2 + (-1)^2]} = \sqrt{3}.$

EXAMPLES 4b

1 Find the vector equations of the plane ABC where A, B, C have the following coordinates: (i) $A(0, 0, 0)$, $B(1, 2, 1)$, $C(-2, 1, 2)$; (ii) $A(2, 1, 2)$, $B(0, 3, -1)$, $C(3, 0, 4)$; (iii) $A(-1, 1, 0)$, $B(3, 3, 3)$, $C(2, -1, -2)$; (iv) $A(3, 1, -4)$, $B(2, -1, 2)$, $C(-3, 2, 1)$; (v) $A(a, 0, 0)$, $B(0, a, 0)$, $C(0, 0, a)$.

2 Find the vector equation of the plane passing through the point (1, 1, 1) and parallel to the vectors $2\mathbf{i}+\mathbf{j}$, $\mathbf{i}-\mathbf{j}+2\mathbf{k}$.

3 Find the vector equations of the planes containing the following pairs of intersecting lines : (i) $\mathbf{r} = \lambda(\mathbf{i}+\mathbf{j}+\mathbf{k})$, $\mathbf{r} = \mu(\mathbf{i}-\mathbf{j}-\mathbf{k})$; (ii) $\mathbf{r} = \mathbf{i}-2\mathbf{j}+\lambda(\mathbf{j}-\mathbf{k})$, $\mathbf{r} = \mathbf{i}-2\mathbf{j}+\mu(2\mathbf{i}+3\mathbf{k})$; (iii) $\mathbf{r} = 2\mathbf{i}+\mathbf{j}-3\mathbf{k}+\lambda\mathbf{i}$, $\mathbf{r} = 2\mathbf{i}+\mathbf{j}-3\mathbf{k}+\mu(3\mathbf{i}-\mathbf{j}-2\mathbf{k})$; (iv) $\mathbf{r} = a\mathbf{i}+\lambda(b\mathbf{j}+c\mathbf{k}-a\mathbf{i})$, $\mathbf{r} = a\mathbf{i}+\mu(b\mathbf{j}-c\mathbf{k})$.

4 What is the vector equation of the plane through the point A normal to $\overline{OA}$, where O is the origin, in each of the following cases: (i) $\overline{OA}$ has modulus 6 and direction cosines $\frac{2}{3}, -\frac{1}{3}, \frac{2}{3}$; (ii) $\overline{OA}$ has modulus $2\sqrt{3}$ and is in the direction of $\mathbf{i}+\mathbf{j}+\mathbf{k}$; (iii) A has coordinates $(2, 1, -2)$; (iv) A is the point $p\mathbf{i}+q\mathbf{j}+r\mathbf{k}$?

5 Find the vector equation of the plane through the point A and normal to the vector $\mathbf{v}$ in each of the following cases: (i) $A(1, 1, 1)$, $\mathbf{v} = 2\mathbf{i}-\mathbf{j}+2\mathbf{k}$; (ii) $A(3, -1, 4)$, $\mathbf{v} = 6\mathbf{i}-3\mathbf{j}-2\mathbf{k}$; (iii) $A(1, 3, -4)$, $\mathbf{v} = 2\mathbf{i}+2\mathbf{j}+\mathbf{k}$.

6 Show that the vector equation of the plane passing through the point with position vector $\mathbf{b}$ and normal to the vector $\mathbf{a}$ is $\mathbf{r}\,.\,\mathbf{a} = \mathbf{b}\,.\,\mathbf{a}$.

7 What is the vector equation of the plane containing the axes of x and y? Find the position vector of the point of intersection of this plane and the line $\mathbf{r} = (2+\lambda)\mathbf{i}+(1-\lambda)\mathbf{j}+(3-2\lambda)\mathbf{k}$.

8 Find the vector equation of the plane through the origin perpendicular to the line $\mathbf{r} = (2+3\lambda)\mathbf{i}+(3-2\lambda)\mathbf{j}+(5+2\lambda)\mathbf{k}$.

9 Find (a) the direction cosines, (b) the lengths of the normals from the origin to the following planes: (i) $\mathbf{r}\,.(\mathbf{i}+\mathbf{j}+\mathbf{k}) = 1$; (ii) $\mathbf{r}\,.(-\mathbf{i}+2\mathbf{j}+2\mathbf{k}) = 2$; (iii) $\mathbf{r}\,.(6\mathbf{i}-2\mathbf{j}+3\mathbf{k})+1 = 0$.

10 Obtain the vector equations of (i) the line joining the points $(1, -2, 1)$, $(0, 3, -2)$; (ii) the plane passing through the points (0, 0, 0), (0, 4, 0), (2, 0, 1). Also find the coordinates of the common point of the line and the plane.

11 Show that the planes $\mathbf{r}\,.(2\mathbf{i}+3\mathbf{j}-2\mathbf{k}) = 1$, $\mathbf{r}\,.(4\mathbf{i}-2\mathbf{j}+\mathbf{k}) = 1$ are perpendicular.

12 Prove that the equation of the plane passing through points with position vectors $\mathbf{a}$, $\mathbf{b}$ and parallel to the vector $\mathbf{c}$ can be expressed as $\mathbf{r} = \mathbf{a}+s(\mathbf{b}-\mathbf{a})+t\mathbf{c}$, where s, t are scalar parameters.

13 Find unit vectors normal to each of the following planes: (i) $\mathbf{r} = s(\mathbf{i}+\mathbf{j})+t(\mathbf{j}-\mathbf{k})$; (ii) $\mathbf{r} = s(\mathbf{i}+\mathbf{j}-\mathbf{k})+t(2\mathbf{i}-3\mathbf{j}+\mathbf{k})$; (iii) $\mathbf{r} = 2\mathbf{i}-\mathbf{j}+\mathbf{k}+s(2\mathbf{i}-\mathbf{j}+3\mathbf{k})+t(-\mathbf{i}+\mathbf{j}-\mathbf{k})$; (iv) $\mathbf{r} = \mathbf{i}(3s+2t-1)+\mathbf{j}(s-t+2)+\mathbf{k}(-s+3t+3)$; (v) a plane parallel to the vectors $4\mathbf{i}-2\mathbf{j}+\mathbf{k}$, $\mathbf{i}+3\mathbf{j}+3\mathbf{k}$; (vi) the plane passing through the points $(0, 0, 0)$, $(1, -1, 2)$, $(3, 2, -1)$.

14 What is the position vector of the common point of the line $\mathbf{r} = \mathbf{i}+\mathbf{j}+\mathbf{k}+\lambda(2\mathbf{i}-\mathbf{j})$ and the plane $\mathbf{r} = 3\mathbf{i}+\mathbf{j}-\mathbf{k}+s(2\mathbf{i}+\mathbf{j}-\mathbf{k})+t(\mathbf{j}+\mathbf{k})$?

15 Show that the plane $\mathbf{r} = \mathbf{a}_1+s(\mathbf{a}_2-\mathbf{a}_1)+t\mathbf{b}$ contains the parallel lines $\mathbf{r} = \mathbf{a}_1+\lambda\mathbf{b}$, $\mathbf{r} = \mathbf{a}_2+\mu\mathbf{b}$.

16 Find the distance between the parallel planes $\mathbf{r}.(2\mathbf{i}-\mathbf{j}+2\mathbf{k}) = 6$, $\mathbf{r}.(4\mathbf{i}-2\mathbf{j}+4\mathbf{k})+1 = 0$.

17 Find the cosine of the acute angle between the planes $\mathbf{r}.(\mathbf{i}+\mathbf{j}+\mathbf{k}) = 1$, $\mathbf{r}.(4\mathbf{i}-2\mathbf{j}+\mathbf{k}) = 1$.

18 Show that the vector equation of the plane passing through the point $N(a, b, c)$ and perpendicular to $\overline{ON}$, where O is the origin, is $\mathbf{r}.(a\mathbf{i}+b\mathbf{j}+c\mathbf{k}) = a^2+b^2+c^2$.

19 Find the acute angle between the plane defined by the points (0, 0, 0), (1, 0, 1), (0, 1, 1) and the plane defined by the points (1, −1, 1), (3, 1, −2), (0, 2, −1).

20 Find the perpendicular distance of the point (1, −1, −1) from the plane $\mathbf{r}.(\mathbf{i}+\mathbf{j}+\mathbf{k}) = 1$ and state whether the point and the origin are on the same or opposite sides of the plane.

21 Determine whether the points (1, −2, 1), (−2, 1, 3) are on the same or opposite sides of the plane $\mathbf{r}.(\mathbf{i}+2\mathbf{j}-\mathbf{k}) = 1$.

22 Points A, B have position vectors **a**, **b**. Prove that the equation of the plane which bisects AB at right-angles is $\mathbf{r}.(\mathbf{b}-\mathbf{a}) = \frac{1}{2}(b^2-a^2)$.

23 Find the vector equation of the plane through the point (1, 3, −4) and normal to the vector $2\mathbf{i}+2\mathbf{j}+\mathbf{k}$ and the length of the perpendicular from the point (−2, 0, 1) to this plane.

24 Show that the length of the perpendicular from the origin to the plane passing through the points (3, 0, 3), (1, 3, 1), (−1, 2, 3) is 3 units.

25 Find the equation of the plane passing through the points (1, 1, 1), (3, 2, 2) and perpendicular to a plane which is parallel to the vectors $-\mathbf{i}+\mathbf{j}+\mathbf{k}$, $2\mathbf{i}-\mathbf{j}-\mathbf{k}$.

26 $ABCD$, $A'B'C'D'$ are parallel faces of a cube of side 2 units; X, Y, Z are the mid-points of AD, DD', BC respectively. Taking A as origin and **i**, **j**, **k** as unit vectors in the directions $\overline{AB}$, $\overline{AD}$, $\overline{AA'}$ find (i) the vector equation of the plane ABD'; (ii) the vector equation of the plane $A'ZY$; (iii) the length of the perpendicular from A to the plane $A'ZY$; (iv) the cosine of the acute angle between the planes $AB'X$, $A'ZY$.

27 Find the vector equation of the plane containing the lines $\mathbf{r} = \mathbf{i}\lambda+\mathbf{j}(-2+3\lambda)+\mathbf{k}(1+2\lambda)$, $\mathbf{r} = \mathbf{i}(2-3\mu)+\mathbf{j}(1-3\mu)+\mathbf{k}(4\mu)$.

28 Show that the equations of the planes distance p from the origin and parallel to the vectors **b**, **c** can be expressed in the form $[\mathbf{r}, \mathbf{b}, \mathbf{c}] = \pm pbc$.

29 Show that the equation of the plane passing through the point with position vector **a** and parallel to the vectors **b**, **c** can be expressed in the form $[\mathbf{r}, \mathbf{b}, \mathbf{c}] = [\mathbf{a}, \mathbf{b}, \mathbf{c}]$.

30 A plane meets three mutually perpendicular lines OA, OB, OC at A, B, C, where $OA = OB = OC = a$. Show that the length of the perpendicular from O to the plane ABC is $a/\sqrt{3}$.

31 A point P is equidistant from the vertices of a right-angled triangle ABC and not in the plane of the triangle. Prove that the join of P to the mid-point of the hypotenuse BC is perpendicular to the plane of the triangle.

32 OA, OB, OC are mutually perpendicular edges of a tetrahedron $OABC$; $OA = 4a$, $OB = 4a$, $OC = 3a$. Calculate (i) the cosine of the acute angle between the planes ABC, OAB; (ii) the length of the perpendicular from O to the plane ABC.

33 *ABCD* is a tetrahedron with angles *BDC*, *CDA*, *ADB* each equal to a right angle. Prove that the foot of the perpendicular from *D* to the plane *ABC* is the orthocentre (intersection of the altitudes) of triangle *ABC*.

34 From an external point *O* a perpendicular *ON* is drawn to a plane in which *A*, *B* are two points ; *OM* is drawn perpendicular to *AB* meeting it at *M*. Prove that *MN* is perpendicular to *AB*.

35 Show that the equation of a plane passing through the points **p**, **q** and normal to the plane determined by the intersecting lines $\mathbf{r} = \mathbf{a}+\lambda\mathbf{b}_1$, $\mathbf{r} = \mathbf{a}+\mu\mathbf{b}_2$, can be written $\mathbf{r} = \mathbf{p}(1-s)+\mathbf{q}s+t\mathbf{b}_1 \wedge \mathbf{b}_2$, where s, t are scalar parameters.

36 If vectors **p**, **q**, **r** are coplanar, show that $[\mathbf{p}, \mathbf{q}, \mathbf{r}] = 0$. Deduce that the equation of the plane passing through the points with position vectors **a**, **b**, **c** can be expressed in the form $[\mathbf{r}-\mathbf{a}, \mathbf{a}-\mathbf{b}, \mathbf{b}-\mathbf{c}] = 0$, which simplifies to $[\mathbf{r}, \mathbf{b}, \mathbf{c}]+[\mathbf{r}, \mathbf{c}, \mathbf{a}]+[\mathbf{r}, \mathbf{a}, \mathbf{b}] = [\mathbf{a}, \mathbf{b}, \mathbf{c}]$.

V

PHYSICAL APPLICATIONS OF VECTOR METHODS

Physical vectors Some physical quantities as for example the displacement of a point B from a point A and the velocity of the moving point P, are clearly vector quantities as they have both magnitude and direction. Moreover the straight line $\overline{AB}$ which represents the displacement of B from A is not fixed in position as A can be taken quite arbitrarily nor is the straight line which represents the velocity of P fixed in position as P itself is not fixed. Thus the physical quantities, displacement and velocity and others like them are free vectors and consequently can be compounded by the laws of vectors already established. Some general problems involving the combination of velocity vectors will be considered here.

Sum of two or more velocities An aircraft in flight has two velocities one arising from the propulsion and the other from the wind; similarly a boat in a river or tidal waters will have two velocities and a passenger moving across the deck of the boat will have three velocities, the two velocities of the boat and his or her own velocity relative to the boat. The following examples will serve to illustrate the application of vector methods to the solution of problems involving the sum of two or more velocities.

Ex. 1 *An aircraft pilot sets a course of* 030° *and flies with an airspeed of* 800 *km/h. If there is a wind of* 75 *km/h from the direction* 315°, *find the actual track of the aircraft.*

The aircraft's two velocities can be represented by the vector $\overline{OA}$ with a magnitude proportional to 800 km/h and the vector $\overline{AB}$ with a magnitude proportional to 75 km/h; the proportionality factor being the same in the two cases, the magnitudes of the two vectors can be taken simply as 800 and 75 km/h. Clearly the actual speed and direction of motion (track) of the aircraft is represented by the vector $\overline{OB}$

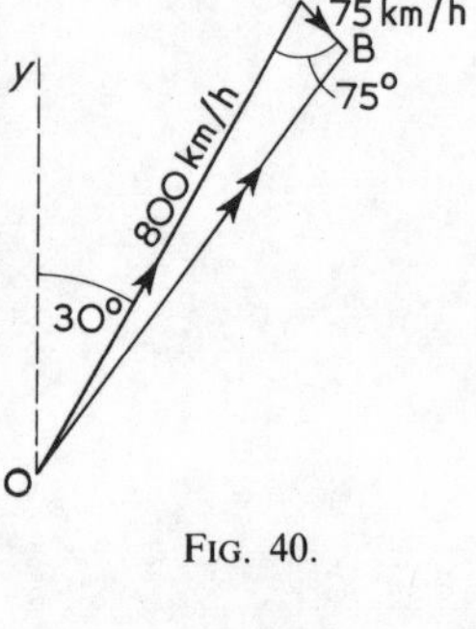

FIG. 40.

Using elementary trigonometry, $OB =$ 784 km/h; angle $AOB = 5° \, 18'$; i.e. the actual track of the aircraft $= 035° \, 18'$.

Ex. 2 *A boat can be rowed in still water at a speed of 8 km/h. In what direction must it be headed in order to travel directly across a river flowing at 5 km/h parallel to the banks?*

The two velocities of the boat can be represented by vectors $\overline{OA}$ of magnitude 8 km/h and $\overline{AB}$ of magnitude 5 km/h which must be such that the vector $\overline{OB}$, representing their sum, is in the direction $\overline{OP}$ directly across the stream (Fig. 41).

Clearly θ, the angle to the upstream bank at which the boat must be headed, is given by $\cos\theta = \frac{5}{8}$; i.e. $\theta = \cos^{-1}\frac{5}{8}$.

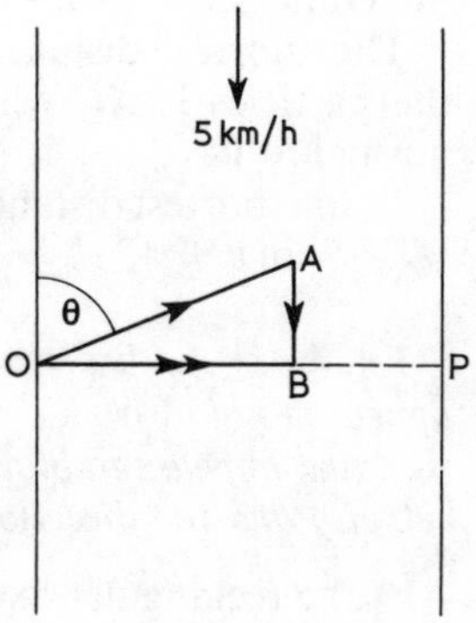

FIG. 41.

Relative velocity Suppose two particles P_1, P_2 have velocities $\mathbf{v}_1, \mathbf{v}_2$ respectively. The relative velocity of P_2 with respect to P_1 is the apparent velocity of P_2 as seen by an observer moving with P_1. To determine the value of this relative velocity $\mathbf{R}$ imagine equal velocities $-\mathbf{v}_1$ to be added to those of P_1 and P_2. The relative motion will be unchanged and the velocities of P_1 and P_2 will become respectively zero and $\mathbf{v}_2 - \mathbf{v}_1$. Clearly then $\mathbf{R} = \mathbf{v}_2 - \mathbf{v}_1$.

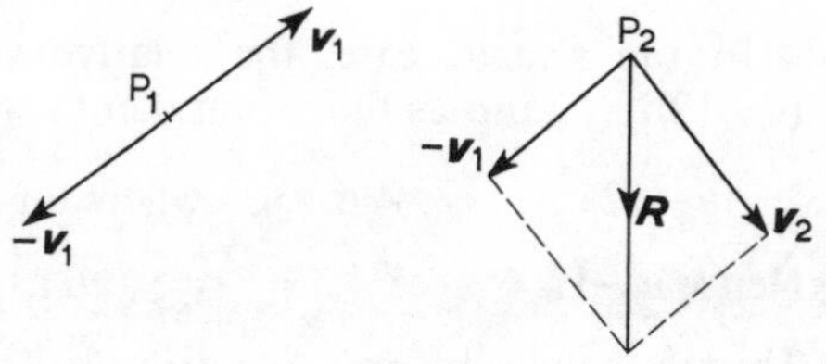

FIG. 42.

Similarly it follows that the relative velocity of P_1 with respect to P_2 is $\mathbf{v}_1 - \mathbf{v}_2$.

So the relative velocity of one moving body with respect to another moving body is the vector difference of their velocities taken in the correct order.

Ex. 3 *Two particles A, B, moving with uniform velocities, the former towards B at 3 m/s and the latter perpendicular to AB at 4 m/s, are instantaneously at points 12 m apart. Find the relative velocity of B with respect to A and the shortest distance apart of the particles in the subsequent motion.*

In the relative motion with A at rest, B will have the relative velocity $\mathbf{R}$ which is the sum of velocities of 4 m/s and 3 m/s in directions at right angles to each other (Fig. 43).

So $R = 5$ m/s and **R** is in a direction $\tan^{-1}\frac{4}{3}$ with $\overline{BA}$.

The shortest distance apart of the particles is AC where $\overline{AC}$ is normal to **R**.

$\therefore$ the shortest distance apart $=$
$12 \sin\theta = 12 \cdot \frac{4}{5} = 9{\cdot}6$ m.

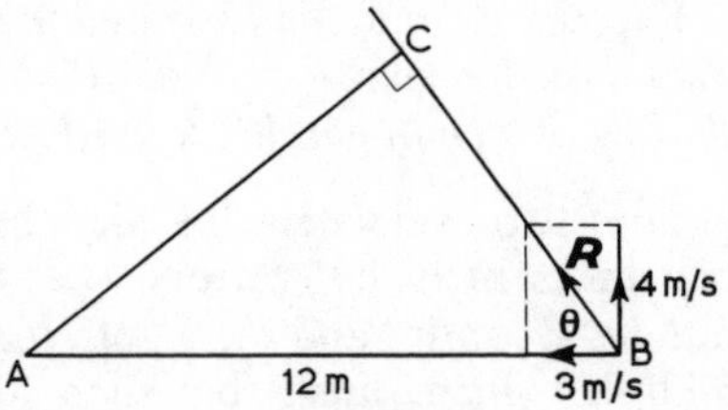

FIG. 43.

Ex. 4 *A cyclist travelling east at 8 km/h notices that the wind appears to blow from the north. When he increases his speed to 12 km/h the wind appears to blow from the north-east. Find the magnitude of the velocity and the direction of the wind.*

Take rectangular axes in the directions E and N and let $\mathbf{i}, \mathbf{j}$ be unit vectors in these directions. Let the velocity of the wind be $u\mathbf{i}+v\mathbf{j}$.

In the first case the velocity of the cyclist is $8\mathbf{i}$ and so the relative velocity of wind to cyclist is $u\mathbf{i}+v\mathbf{j}-8\mathbf{i}$ or $(u-8)\mathbf{i}+v\mathbf{j}$. But this relative velocity is parallel to the vector $-\mathbf{j}$ and hence

$$u-8 = 0; \qquad u = 8 \text{ km/h}.$$

In the second case, the relative velocity of wind to cyclist is $(u-12)\mathbf{i}+v\mathbf{j}$ and as this is parallel to the vector $-(\mathbf{i}+\mathbf{j})$,

$$(u-12)\mathbf{i}+v\mathbf{j} = -c(\mathbf{i}+\mathbf{j}), \quad \text{where } c \text{ is a positive scalar quantity.}$$

Hence $u-12 = -c$; $v = -c$ and as $u = 8$, $v = -4$ km/hr.

Thus the wind velocity $= 8\mathbf{i}-4\mathbf{j}$ km/h—a vector of magnitude $4\sqrt{5}$ km/h in a direction $\tan^{-1}\frac{1}{2}$ south of east.

Forces acting at a point The common physical quantity, force, having both magnitude and direction is a vector. However the effect of a force depends not only on its magnitude and direction but also on its line of action; consequently a force is not a free vector but a *localized or line vector* and as such will require special treatment. The essential difference between a line vector and a free vector is that the latter can be represented by any number of equal parallel lines whereas the former in uniquely represented by one particular line.

Experiment shows that the joint action of two forces acting at a point is the same as that of a single force equal to the vector sum of the two forces and acting through the same point. Consequently forces acting at a point can be compounded by the ordinary laws of free vectors; in particular, the resultant of a set of forces $\mathbf{P}_1, \mathbf{P}_2, \mathbf{P}_3, \ldots$

acting at a point O is the single force **R** acting at O where $\mathbf{R} = \Sigma\mathbf{P}$. Vector components are often useful in dealing with problems involving forces as is illustrated in the following example.

Ex. 5 *Find the magnitudes of the horizontal force* **P** *and the force* **Q** *inclined at* 60° *to the vertical, both acting through a point O, whose resultant is a vertical force through O of* 10 N.

Taking rectangular axes OX, OY in horizontal and vertical directions, then the given forces have a resultant of magnitude 10 N in the direction $\overline{OY}$.

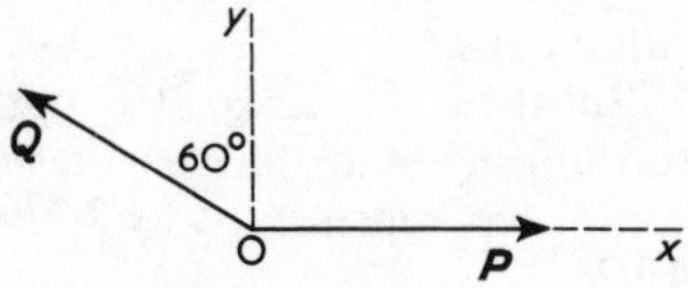

FIG. 44.

If **i**, **j** are unit forces in the directions $\overline{OX}$, $\overline{OY}$, then $\mathbf{P} = P\mathbf{i}$; $\mathbf{Q} = -Q \sin 60° \,\mathbf{i} + Q \cos 60° \,\mathbf{j}$, where P, Q are the magnitudes of the forces.

$$\therefore \quad \text{resultant force} = \mathbf{P}+\mathbf{Q} = (P - Q \sin 60°)\mathbf{i} + Q \cos 60° \,\mathbf{j} \text{ N}.$$

But the resultant $= 10\mathbf{j}$ N, so $P - Q \sin 60° = 0$ and $Q \cos 60° = 10$. Hence $P = 10\sqrt{3}$ N, $Q = 20$ N.

Theorem If two forces acting at a point O are represented by the vectors $\mathbf{m\overline{OA}}$, $\mathbf{n\overline{OB}}$, their resultant is a force through O represented by the vector $\mathbf{(m+n)\overline{OR}}$, where R is the point dividing AB in the ratio n:m.

Through O, draw the line POQ parallel to the line BRA with $OP = AR$ and $OQ = BR$ (Fig. 45).

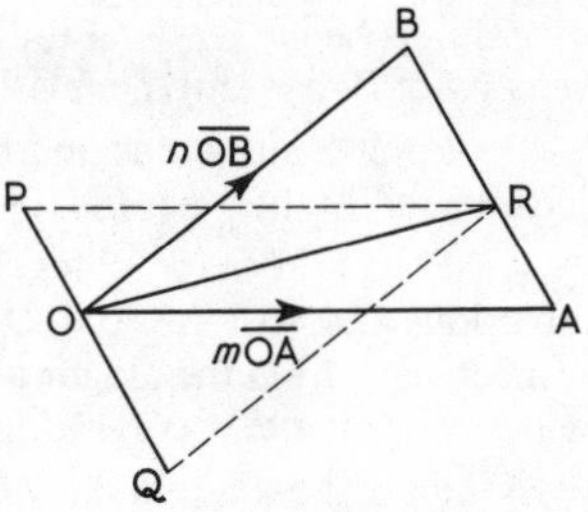

FIG. 45.

Then as $mAR = nBR$, $m\overline{OP} = -n\overline{OQ}$, so the original system of two forces is unaltered by the addition of forces represented completely by $m\overline{OP}$ and $n\overline{OQ}$.

But clearly $OARP$ is a parallelogram and so the resultant of forces represented by $m\overline{OA}$ and $m\overline{OP}$ is a force represented by $m\overline{OR}$.

Similarly the resultant of forces represented by $n\overline{OB}$ and $n\overline{OQ}$ is a force represented by $n\overline{OR}$.

Hence the resultant of the original two forces acting at O is the force completely represented by $(m+n)\overline{OR}$.

Special case Forces represented completely by $\overline{OA}$, $\overline{OB}$ have a resultant represented completely by $2\overline{OM}$, where M is the mid-point of AB.

Ex. 6 *Two forces acting at the vertex A of a quadrilateral ABCD are represented by* $\overline{AB}$, $\overline{AD}$ *and two forces acting at C are represented by* $\overline{CB}$, $\overline{CD}$. *Show that the resultant is completely represented by* $4\overline{PQ}$, *where P, Q are the mid-points of AC, BD respectively.*

Forces $\overline{AB}$, $\overline{AD}$ have a resultant $2\overline{AQ}$ and forces $\overline{CB}$, $\overline{CD}$ have a resultant $2\overline{CQ}$.

But the forces $2\overline{AQ}$, $2\overline{CQ}$ both act through Q and have a resultant completely represented by $2(2\overline{PQ})$ or $4\overline{PQ}$.

So the original system of forces has a resultant completely represented by $4\overline{PQ}$.

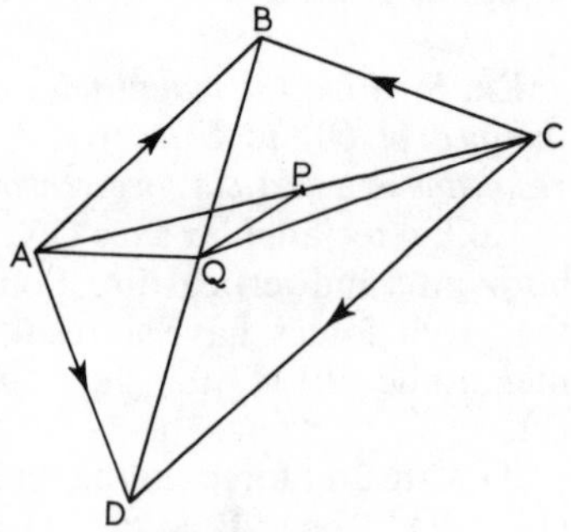

FIG. 46.

EXAMPLES 5a

1 If **i**, **j** are unit vectors in the directions of rectangular axes OX, OY, express each of the following vectors in terms of **i** and **j**: (i) a velocity of 10 cm/s in the direction $\overline{OY}$; (ii) a force of 4 N along $\overline{XO}$; (iii) a velocity of 8 m/s in the direction of the line $3y+4x = 0$; (iv) a force of 39 N in the direction $\overline{OA}$ where A is the point $(-5, 12)$; (v) a force of 20 N at 60° to $\overline{OX}$ and 30° to $\overline{YO}$.

2 Particles A, B have velocities $4\mathbf{i}+3\mathbf{j}$, $3\mathbf{i}-4\mathbf{j}$ respectively the unit of magnitude being km/h. Find the magnitude and direction of (i) the relative velocity of B to A; (ii) the relative velocity of A to B.

3 Find the modulus and direction cosines of the sum of the two velocities represented by the vectors $12\mathbf{i}+3\mathbf{j}-8\mathbf{k}$, $6\mathbf{i}+6\mathbf{j}+2\mathbf{k}$, the unit being cm/s.

4 Forces of magnitudes 25 N and 26 N act through the origin O in the directions $\overline{OA}$, $\overline{OB}$ respectively, where A, B have coordinates (4, 3), (12, -5) respectively. Find the magnitude and direction of a third force acting through O which will maintain equilibrium.

5 Find the magnitudes of a horizontal force **P** and a force **Q** inclined at 30° to the upward vertical, whose resultant is an upward vertical force of 80 N.

6 The relative velocity of A to B is $6\mathbf{i}-4\mathbf{j}+3\mathbf{k}$ and the velocity of A is $4\mathbf{i}-6\mathbf{j}-5\mathbf{k}$, the unit of magnitude being km/h. Find the magnitude and direction cosines of the velocity of B.

7 The resultant of two forces of magnitudes P and $P\sqrt{3}$ is a force of magnitude P. Prove that the two forces are inclined at an angle of 150°.

8 Two points P, Q move along the sides AB, DA respectively of a square $ABCD$, side a, being instantaneously at A and D. If the magnitudes of the velocities of P, Q are respectively v_1, v_2, show that the shortest distance apart of the points is $av_1/\sqrt{(v_1^2+v_2^2)}$.

9 A set of three forces acting at a point O can be represented in magnitude and direction by the vectors $\overline{AB}, \overline{BC}, \overline{CD}$. What vector will represent the resultant in magnitude and direction? If the system is maintained in equilibrium by an additional force acting through a point P, what is the direction of $\overline{PO}$?

10 An aircraft has an airspeed of v km/h; it is required to fly as quickly as possible from a place A to a place B due north of A and distant s km from it. If there is a wind of w km/h from a direction $\varphi°$ east of north, find the course of the aircraft and the time of flight.

11 If $\mathbf{r}_1$ is the relative velocity of Q to P and $\mathbf{r}_2$ is the relative velocity of R to Q, what is the relative velocity of P to R?

12 Forces $\mathbf{P}, \mathbf{Q}$ act at A and forces $\mathbf{R}, \mathbf{S}$ act at B. If the forces are in equilibrium, what is (i) the connection between $\mathbf{P}, \mathbf{Q}, \mathbf{R}, \mathbf{S}$; (ii) the direction of the force $\mathbf{P}+\mathbf{Q}$; (iii) the direction of the force $\mathbf{R}+\mathbf{S}$?

13 Two particles P, Q have respectively velocities of 9000 and 21,000 m/s in the directions of the vectors $2\mathbf{i}-\mathbf{j}+2\mathbf{k}$, $3\mathbf{i}+2\mathbf{j}-6\mathbf{k}$. Find the magnitude and direction cosines of the velocity of Q relative to P.

14 $ABCD$ is a quadrilateral; forces represented in magnitude and direction by vectors $\overline{AB}$, $\overline{BC}$, $\overline{AD}$, $\overline{DC}$ act at the point A. Show that the resultant force is completely represented by the vector $2\overline{AC}$.

15 To a man travelling east at 10 km/h the wind appears to blow from the north. When the man doubles his speed the wind appears to blow from the direction 060°. Find the velocity of the wind.

16 O is any point in the plane of triangle ABC and D, E, F are the mid-points of the sides of the triangle. Show that forces completely represented by $\overline{OA}$, $\overline{OB}$, $\overline{OC}$ are equivalent to forces completely represented by $\overline{OD}$, $\overline{OE}$, $\overline{OF}$.

17 To a cyclist travelling west at 9 km/h the wind appears to blow from the north. When the cyclist travels in a direction 300° at $6\sqrt{3}$ km/h the wind still appears to blow from the north but at double the speed. Find the velocity of the wind.

18 Forces represented by $2\overline{BC}$, $\overline{CA}$, $\overline{BA}$, where ABC is a triangle, act at a point O. Show that the resultant is a force through O represented by $6\overline{DE}$, where D is the mid-point of BC and E the point of CA such that $3CE = CA$.

19 Masses m_1, m_2, m_3 are at points P_1, P_2, P_3. If O is any other point prove that the resultant of forces $m_1\overline{OP}_1$, $m_2\overline{OP}_2$, $m_3\overline{OP}_3$ is the force $(m_1+m_2+m_3)\overline{OG}$, where G is the mass centre of m_1, m_2, m_3.

20 A, B, C are the points $(0, 3, -4)$, $(2, -3, 6)$, $(2, -1, 2)$ respectively and O is the origin. Find the modulus and direction cosines of the resultant of forces 25 N, 21 N, 12 N acting at O in the directions $\overline{OA}$, $\overline{OB}$, $\overline{OC}$ respectively.

21 A cyclist is travelling due east at a speed v along a straight road and to him the wind appears to blow from the south; when he doubles his speed the wind appears to blow from the south-east. Find the direction from which the wind appears to blow when the cyclist trebles his speed.

22 Forces completely represented by $3\overline{BA}$, $7\overline{BC}$, $9\overline{CA}$ act along the sides of triangle ABC; their resultant is $r\overline{PQ}$ acting in a line PQ where P, Q are points on AC, BC respectively. Determine the positions of P and Q and the value of r.

23 If G is the centroid of triangle ABC and O a point not in the plane of the triangle prove that (i) forces completely represented by $\overline{GA}$, $\overline{GB}$, $\overline{GC}$ are in equilibrium; (ii) forces completely represented by $\overline{OA}$, $\overline{OB}$, $\overline{OC}$ have a resultant completely represented by $3\overline{OG}$. Deduce that if $ABCD$ is a tetrahedron and O the point of DG such that $3OG = GD$, then forces completely represented by $\overline{AO}, \overline{BO}, \overline{CO}, \overline{DO}$ are in equilibrium.

24 O is a vertex of a cube and forces of 12 N, 16 N, 8 N act respectively along the diagonals OA, OB, OC of the faces of the cube which contain O. Find the magnitude of the resultant of these forces.

25 Three forces are represented completely by $\overline{AL}, \overline{BM}, \overline{CN}$, where L, M, N are the points in the sides BC, CA, AB of a triangle such that $BL = 2LC$, $2CM = 3MA$, $AN = 2NB$. Show that the resultant force is parallel to $\overline{AC}$.

26 Two forces represented completely by the vectors $\overline{AB}, \overline{BD}$ act at the vertex B of a plane quadrilateral $ABCD$ and two other forces represented completely by $q\overline{CA}$, $r\overline{DC}$, where q, r are scalar multiples, act at the vertex C. If the system is in equilibrium, find (i) the angle between $\overline{AD}$ and $\overline{BC}$; (ii) the values of q and r.

27 The sum of two velocities is in the direction of the vector $6\mathbf{i}-\mathbf{j}+2\mathbf{k}$. If one velocity is 12 cm/s in the direction of the vector $2\mathbf{i}+\mathbf{j}-2\mathbf{k}$, find the direction cosines of the other velocity if its magnitude is 14 cm/s.

28 $ABCD$, $PQRS$ are parallel faces of a cube of which AP, BQ, CR, DS are edges. Forces of 1, 2, 3 and 4 N act at A in the directions of the vectors $\overline{SB}$, $\overline{QD}$, $\overline{AR}$, $\overline{PC}$ respectively, find the magnitude of the resultant force and the cosine of the angle it makes with $\overline{AP}$.

29 A point P starts at the origin O and moves in the direction $\overline{OA}$, where A is the point (3, 2, 6), at a speed of 21 cm/s. Simultaneously a point Q starts from B (3, 4, 0) and moves in the direction $\overline{BC}$, where C is the point (5, 5, 2), at a speed of 18 cm/s. Find the relative velocity of Q to P and the distances the points are apart after 1 s.

30 If $\mathbf{R}$ is the resultant of two forces $\mathbf{F}_1$, $\mathbf{F}_2$ acting on a particle, show that $R = \sqrt{(F_1^2+F_2^2+2\mathbf{F}_1 \cdot \mathbf{F}_2)}$ and more generally, if $\mathbf{R}$ is the resultant of forces $\mathbf{F}_1, \mathbf{F}_2, \mathbf{F}_3, \ldots$ acting on a particle, show that $R = \sqrt{[\Sigma F^2+2\sum_{r\neq s} \mathbf{F}_r \cdot \mathbf{F}_s]}$.

31 Forces of magnitudes F_1, F_2, F_3 acting at a point in the directions of unit vectors $\hat{\mathbf{a}}$, $\hat{\mathbf{b}}$, $\hat{\mathbf{c}}$ are in equilibrium. Establish the following results: (i) $F_1\hat{\mathbf{a}}+F_2\hat{\mathbf{b}}+F_3\hat{\mathbf{c}} = 0$; (ii) $F_2\hat{\mathbf{b}}\wedge\hat{\mathbf{a}}+F_3\hat{\mathbf{c}}\wedge\hat{\mathbf{a}} = 0, F_1\hat{\mathbf{b}}\wedge\hat{\mathbf{a}}+F_3\hat{\mathbf{b}}\wedge\hat{\mathbf{c}} = 0$; (iii) $\hat{\mathbf{b}}\wedge\hat{\mathbf{c}}/F_1 = \hat{\mathbf{c}}\wedge\hat{\mathbf{a}}/F_2 = \hat{\mathbf{a}}\wedge\hat{\mathbf{b}}/F_3$. Deduce that the forces are coplanar and that the magnitude of each force is proportional to the sine of the angle between the other two.

Work done by a constant force The work done by a constant force $\mathbf{F}$ when its point of application is displaced from the point A to the point B, where $\overline{AB} = \mathbf{s}$ (Fig. 47), is equal to the product of the magnitude of $\mathbf{P}$ and the distance moved in the direction of $\mathbf{P}$; this product, $F(s \cos \theta)$, where θ is the angle between $\mathbf{F}$ and $\mathbf{s}$, is the scalar product $\mathbf{s} \cdot \mathbf{F}$.

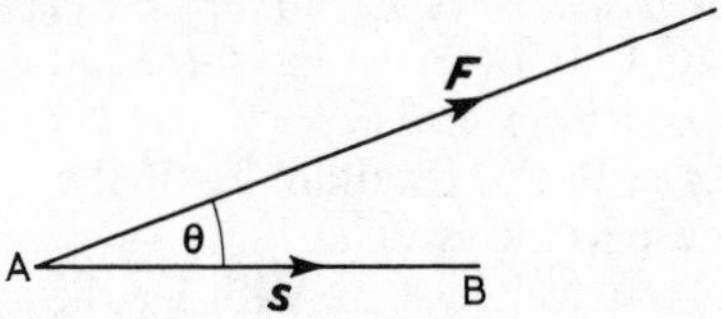

FIG. 47.

So the work done when the point of application of a constant force **F** *is displaced an amount* **s** *is the scalar product* **s . F**.

Ex. 7 *A particle acted upon by forces of 35 N in the direction of the vector* $3\mathbf{i}+2\mathbf{j}-6\mathbf{k}$ *and 24 N in the direction of the vector* $2\mathbf{i}+\mathbf{j}-2\mathbf{k}$ *is displaced from the point A, position vector* $\mathbf{i}+2\mathbf{j}+3\mathbf{k}$, *to the point B, position vector* $5\mathbf{i}+4\mathbf{j}+\mathbf{k}$. *Find the total work done by the forces, the unit of distance being 1 m.*

The force $\mathbf{F}_1$, of magnitude 35 N = 35 (unit vector in direction of $3\mathbf{i}+2\mathbf{j}-6\mathbf{k}$)

$$= 35 \cdot \tfrac{1}{7}(3\mathbf{i}+2\mathbf{j}-6\mathbf{k})$$

$$= 15\mathbf{i}+10\mathbf{j}-30\mathbf{k}\ \text{N}.$$

Similarly, the force $\mathbf{F}_2$ of magnitude 24 N = $24 \cdot \tfrac{1}{3}(2\mathbf{i}+\mathbf{j}-2\mathbf{k}) = 16\mathbf{i}+8\mathbf{j}-16\mathbf{k}$ N.

The displacement $\overline{AB} = 4\mathbf{i}+2\mathbf{j}-2\mathbf{k}$ m.

$\therefore$ Total work done $= \overline{AB} \cdot \mathbf{F}_1 + \overline{AB} \cdot \mathbf{F}_2 = \overline{AB} \cdot (\mathbf{F}_1 + \mathbf{F}_2)$

$$= (4\mathbf{i}+2\mathbf{j}-2\mathbf{k}) \cdot (31\mathbf{i}+18\mathbf{j}-46\mathbf{k})$$

$$= 124+36+92 = 252\ \text{J}.$$

Work done by a set of constant forces acting on a particle Let the forces acting on the particle be $\mathbf{F}_1, \mathbf{F}_2, \mathbf{F}_3, \ldots$ and let the displacement of the particle be **s**.

Then the total work done by the forces $= \mathbf{s} \cdot \mathbf{F}_1 + \mathbf{s} \cdot \mathbf{F}_2 + \mathbf{s} \cdot \mathbf{F}_3 + \ldots$

$$= \mathbf{s} \cdot (\mathbf{F}_1 + \mathbf{F}_2 + \mathbf{F}_3 + \ldots)$$

$$= \mathbf{s} \cdot \mathbf{R},$$

where **R** is the resultant of the set of forces.

So the work done by the set of forces in a displacement of the particle is equal to the work done by the resultant of the forces during the same displacement of the particle.

Ex. 8 *ABCD is a square of side a; a particle at A is acted on by forces* $\lambda\overline{AB}$, $\lambda\overline{BC}$, $\lambda\overline{CA}$, $\lambda\overline{CD}$. *Find the total work done by the forces when the particle moves from A to C.*

As $\overline{AB}+\overline{BC}+\overline{CA} = 0$, the resultant $\mathbf{R}$ of the forces acting on the particle is $\lambda\overline{CD}$.

Taking rectangular axes $\overline{AD}$, $\overline{AB}$ with $\mathbf{i}, \mathbf{j}$ the unit vectors in these directions, then

$$\overline{AC} = a(\mathbf{i}+\mathbf{j}) \quad \text{and} \quad \mathbf{R} = -\lambda a\mathbf{j}$$

$\therefore$ the total work done $= \overline{AC}\cdot\mathbf{R} = -\lambda a^2$ units.

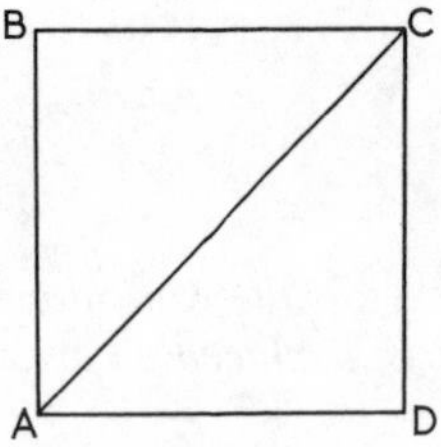

FIG. 48.

Vector moment of a force about a point If P is a point on the line of action of a force $\mathbf{F}$, the scalar moment of $\mathbf{F}$ about a point O is the product $rF\sin\theta$, where $\overline{OP} = \mathbf{r}$ and θ is the angle between $\overline{OP}$ and $\mathbf{F}$. *The vector moment* of $\mathbf{F}$ about O is defined as a vector of modulus $rF\sin\theta$, in a direction $\overline{ON}$ which is normal to the plane containing O and $\mathbf{F}$ and positive in the sense of a right-handed screw rotation from the direction of $\overline{OP}$ to the direction of $\mathbf{F}$; i.e. the vector product $\mathbf{r}\wedge\mathbf{F}$.

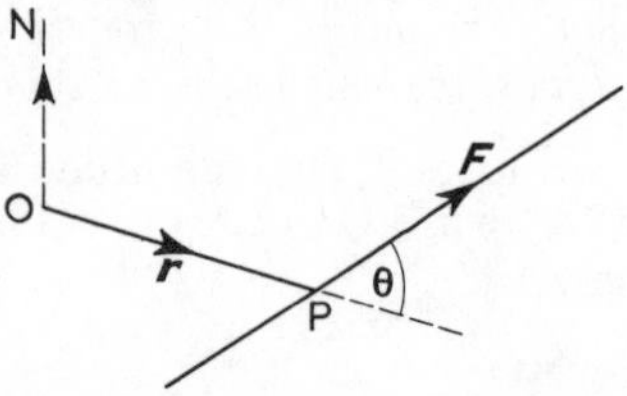

FIG. 49.

So the vector moment of $\mathbf{F}$ *about* $O = \mathbf{r}\wedge\mathbf{F}$, *where* $\mathbf{r}$ *is the position vector, with respect to O, of any point P on the line of action of* $\mathbf{F}$.

Clearly this vector moment is independent of the position of P, for if P' is another point on the line of action of the force, with position vector $\mathbf{r}'$,

$$\mathbf{r}'\wedge\mathbf{F} = (\mathbf{r}+\overline{PP'})\wedge\mathbf{F} = \mathbf{r}\wedge\mathbf{F}, \quad \text{as} \quad \overline{PP'}\wedge\mathbf{F} = 0.$$

Ex. 9 *A force of magnitude 27 N in the direction of the vector* $-2\mathbf{i}+\mathbf{j}+2\mathbf{k}$ *acts through the point P* (1, 3, −1). *Find the vector moment of the force about the origin, the length unit being 1 m.*

$$\text{The force } \mathbf{F} = 27\,.\tfrac{1}{3}(-2\mathbf{i}+\mathbf{j}+2\mathbf{k}) = -18\mathbf{i}+9\mathbf{j}+18\mathbf{k}\text{ N}.$$

$$\overline{OP} = \mathbf{r} = \mathbf{i}+3\mathbf{j}-\mathbf{k}.$$

$$\therefore \quad \text{moment of } \mathbf{F} \text{ about } O = \mathbf{r}\wedge\mathbf{F} = (\mathbf{i}+3\mathbf{j}-\mathbf{k})\wedge(-18\mathbf{i}+9\mathbf{j}+18\mathbf{k})$$

$$= \begin{vmatrix} \mathbf{i} & \mathbf{j} & \mathbf{k} \\ 1 & 3 & -1 \\ -18 & 9 & 18 \end{vmatrix} = 63(\mathbf{i}+\mathbf{k})\text{ N m}.$$

Ex. 10 *Forces* $\mathbf{F}_1$, $\mathbf{F}_2$, $\mathbf{F}_3 \ldots$ *act through a point P. Show that the sum of their vector moments about any point O is equal to the vector moment of their resultant about O.*

Taking $\overline{OP}$ as **r**, then the sum of the vector moments of the forces about O

$$= \mathbf{r} \wedge \mathbf{F}_1 + \mathbf{r} \wedge \mathbf{F}_2 + \mathbf{r} \wedge \mathbf{F}_3 + \ldots$$
$$= \mathbf{r} \wedge (\mathbf{F}_1 + \mathbf{F}_2 + \mathbf{F}_3 + \ldots)$$
$$= \mathbf{r} \wedge \mathbf{R}, \quad \text{where } \mathbf{R} \text{ is the resultant force,}$$
$$= \text{vector moment of the resultant about } O.$$

Moment of a force about a line The moment of a force **F** about a non-intersecting line through a point O parallel to a unit vector $\hat{\mathbf{b}}$ is the component of the vector moment of the force about O in the direction of the line. So it is equal to the scalar quantity $(\mathbf{r} \wedge \mathbf{F}) \cdot \hat{\mathbf{b}}$, i.e. the triple product $[\mathbf{r}, \mathbf{F}, \hat{\mathbf{b}}]$, where **r** is the position vector with respect to O of any point P on the line of action of the force (Fig. 50).

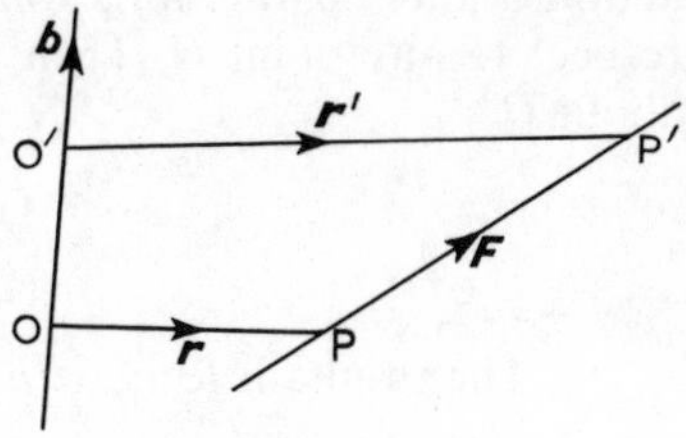

FIG. 50.

To show that this scalar quantity is independent of the choice of the points O, P, take other points O', P' as shown in Fig. 50. Then if $\hat{\mathbf{f}}$ is a unit vector in the direction of **F**,

$$\overline{OO'} = \lambda \hat{\mathbf{b}}; \quad \overline{PP'} = \mu \hat{\mathbf{f}}, \quad \text{where } \lambda, \mu \text{ are scalars.}$$

But $$\overline{O'P'} = \overline{O'O} + \overline{OP} + \overline{PP'},$$

i.e. $$\mathbf{r}' = \mathbf{r} + \mu \hat{\mathbf{f}} - \lambda \hat{\mathbf{b}}.$$

So $$(\mathbf{r}' \wedge \mathbf{F}) \cdot \hat{\mathbf{b}} = (\mathbf{r} \wedge \mathbf{F}) \cdot \hat{\mathbf{b}} + \mu(\hat{\mathbf{f}} \wedge \mathbf{F}) \cdot \hat{\mathbf{b}} - \lambda(\hat{\mathbf{b}} \wedge \mathbf{F}) \cdot \hat{\mathbf{b}}.$$

But $$\hat{\mathbf{f}} \wedge \mathbf{F} = 0 \quad \text{and} \quad (\hat{\mathbf{b}} \wedge \mathbf{F}) \cdot \hat{\mathbf{b}} = 0,$$

$$\therefore \quad (\mathbf{r}' \wedge \mathbf{F}) \cdot \hat{\mathbf{b}} = (\mathbf{r} \wedge \mathbf{F}) \cdot \hat{\mathbf{b}}.$$

Ex. 11 *Find the moment about the line through the point A* $(-1, 0, 2)$ *parallel to the vector* $-\mathbf{i} - 2\mathbf{j} + 2\mathbf{k}$, *of a force of* 28 *N acting through the point P* (3, 1, 3) *in the direction of the vector* $2\mathbf{i} - 3\mathbf{j} + 6\mathbf{k}$, *the unit of length being the m.*

$$\text{Force } \mathbf{F} = 28 \cdot \tfrac{1}{7}(2\mathbf{i} - 3\mathbf{j} + 6\mathbf{k}) = 8\mathbf{i} - 12\mathbf{j} + 24\mathbf{k} \text{ N}.$$

$$\text{Moment of } \mathbf{F} \text{ about } A = \overline{AP} \wedge \mathbf{F} = (4\mathbf{i} + \mathbf{j} + \mathbf{k}) \wedge (8\mathbf{i} - 12\mathbf{j} + 24\mathbf{k})$$
$$= 4(9\mathbf{i} - 22\mathbf{j} - 14\mathbf{k}) \text{ N m}.$$

The unit vector in the direction of the given line is $\frac{1}{3}(-\mathbf{i}-2\mathbf{j}+2\mathbf{k})$.

$$\therefore \quad \text{moment of } \mathbf{F} \text{ about this line} = 4(9\mathbf{i}-22\mathbf{j}-14\mathbf{k}) \cdot \tfrac{1}{3}(-\mathbf{i}-2\mathbf{j}+2\mathbf{k})$$
$$= \tfrac{28}{3}\text{ N m}$$

Non-concurrent forces Some consideration will now be given to the applications of vector methods in statical problems involving sets of forces which do not act through a point.

Resultant of a set of parallel forces Let the forces act in the direction of the unit vector $\hat{\mathbf{a}}$ and have magnitudes $F_1, F_2, F_3, \ldots$, so they are $F_1\hat{\mathbf{a}}, F_2\hat{\mathbf{a}}, F_3\hat{\mathbf{a}} \ldots$. Now let points $P_1, P_2, P_3, \ldots$, on the lines of action of the separate forces have position vectors $\mathbf{r}_1, \mathbf{r}_2, \mathbf{r}_3, \ldots$, with respect to any point O. Then the sum of the moments of the forces about O

$$= \mathbf{r}_1 \wedge F_1\hat{\mathbf{a}} + \mathbf{r}_2 \wedge F_2\hat{\mathbf{a}} + \mathbf{r}_3 \wedge F_3\hat{\mathbf{a}} + \ldots$$
$$= (\Sigma F\mathbf{r}) \wedge \hat{\mathbf{a}}.$$

$$\text{The resultant force} = F_1\hat{\mathbf{a}} + F_2\hat{\mathbf{a}} + F_3\hat{\mathbf{a}} + \ldots = \hat{\mathbf{a}}\Sigma F.$$

The line of action of this resultant must be such that the moment of the resultant about O is the same as that of the original system, so if the position vector of some point P on the line of action of the resultant is $\mathbf{r}$,

$$\mathbf{r} \wedge \hat{\mathbf{a}}\Sigma F = (\Sigma F\mathbf{r}) \wedge \hat{\mathbf{a}},$$

or

$$\mathbf{r} \wedge \hat{\mathbf{a}} = \frac{\Sigma F\mathbf{r}}{\Sigma F} \wedge \hat{\mathbf{a}}.$$

$$\therefore \quad \mathbf{r} = \frac{\Sigma F\mathbf{r}}{\Sigma F} + \lambda\hat{\mathbf{a}}, \quad \text{where } \lambda \text{ is a scalar parameter.}$$

This is the vector equation of the line of action of the resultant; showing that the resultant passes through the point with position vector $(\Sigma F\mathbf{r})/\Sigma F$, the case $\Sigma F = 0$ being excluded.

In the special case where $\Sigma F = 0$, the system of parallel forces will be equivalent to a pair of equal and opposite forces not acting in the same line, unless of course the system is in equilibrium; such a pair of forces constitute *a couple*.

Vector moment of a couple Suppose the couple is made up of equal and parallel forces $\pm\mathbf{F}$ whose lines of action are at a perpendicular distance apart of p.

The vector moment of the couple about any point O not necessarily in its plane

$$= \overline{OP} \wedge \mathbf{F} + \overline{OQ} \wedge (-\mathbf{F}), \quad \text{(Fig. 51)},$$
$$= (\overline{OP} - \overline{OQ}) \wedge \mathbf{F}$$
$$= \overline{QP} \wedge \mathbf{F}.$$

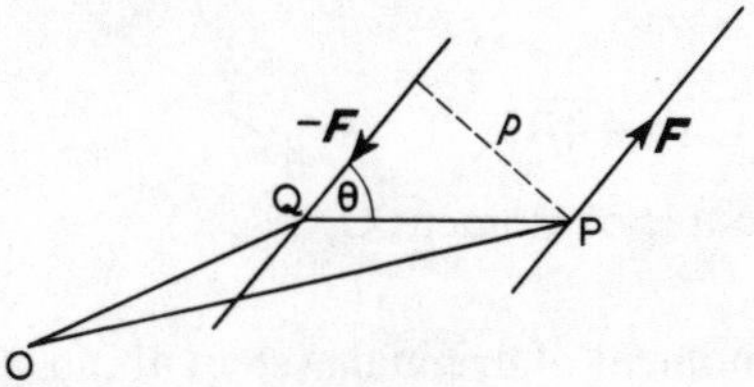

FIG. 51.

This vector moment $\mathbf{G}$ has a direction normal to the plane of the couple and a modulus or magnitude of $(QP)F \sin\theta$ or pF, which is independent of the position of O. *Consequently the vector moment of a couple is constant.*

Resultant of a set of couples Suppose the vector moments of the couples are $\mathbf{G}_1, \mathbf{G}_2, \mathbf{G}_3, \ldots$. Then the total moment of the set of couples about every point is $\Sigma\mathbf{G}$, so the set must be equivalent to a single couple of vector moment $\Sigma\mathbf{G}$.

Reduction of a general system of forces Let the general system be made up of forces $\mathbf{F}_1, \mathbf{F}_2, \mathbf{F}_3, \ldots$, acting respectively through points $P_1, P_2, P_3, \ldots$.

With respect to any point O, let the position vectors of $P_1, P_2, P_3, \ldots$ be $\mathbf{r}_1, \mathbf{r}_2, \mathbf{r}_3, \ldots$. At O, introduce equal and opposite forces $\pm\mathbf{F}_1$ (Fig. 52); then the forces $\mathbf{F}_1$ at P_1 and $-\mathbf{F}_1$ at O constitute a couple of moment $\mathbf{r}_1 \wedge \mathbf{F}_1$. So the original force $\mathbf{F}_1$ acting at P_1 is equivalent to an equal forces $\mathbf{F}_1$ at O together with a couple of moment $\mathbf{r}_1 \wedge \mathbf{F}_1$.

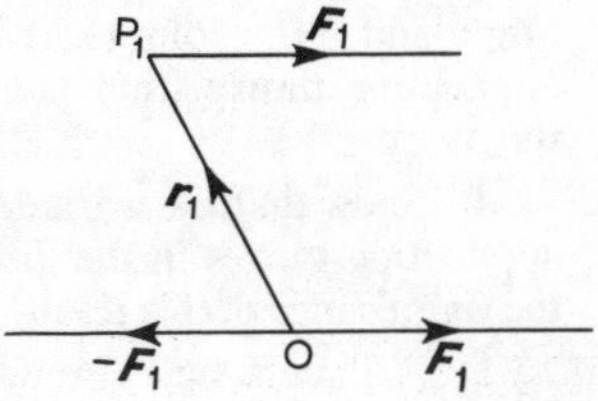

FIG. 52.

Similarly the forces $\mathbf{F}_2, \mathbf{F}_3, \ldots$ acting respectively at $P_2, P_3, \ldots$ are equivalent to forces $\mathbf{F}_2, \mathbf{F}_3, \ldots$ at O together with couples of moments $\mathbf{r}_2 \wedge \mathbf{F}_2, \mathbf{r}_3 \wedge \mathbf{F}_3, \ldots$.

Hence the original system is reducible to a single force $\mathbf{R}$ *acting at a specified point* O *together with a couple of moment* $\mathbf{G}$ *where* $\mathbf{R} = \Sigma\mathbf{F}$ *and* $\mathbf{G} = \Sigma\mathbf{r} \wedge \mathbf{F}$, *the moment of the original system about* O.

Ex. 12 *Forces represented completely by the vectors* $k\overline{BC}$, $k\overline{CA}$, $k\overline{AB}$, *where k is a scalar constant, act along the sides of triangle ABC. Show that the forces are equivalent to a couple of vector moment* $2k\mathbf{\Delta}$, *where* $\mathbf{\Delta}$ *is the vector area of the triangle.*

The given system reduces to a single force **R** acting at any one of the vertices, say A, of the triangle, where

$$\mathbf{R} = k\overline{BC}+k\overline{CA}+k\overline{AB} = 0,$$

together with a couple of moment **G**, where

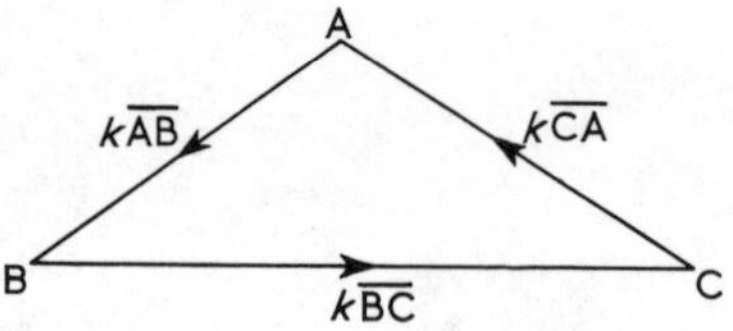

FIG. 53.

$$\mathbf{G} = \text{vector moment of original system about } A = \overline{AB}\wedge k\overline{BC}.$$

But $\frac{1}{2}\overline{AB}\wedge\overline{BC} = \frac{1}{2}\overline{BC}\wedge\overline{CA} = \frac{1}{2}\overline{CA}\wedge\overline{AB} = \mathbf{\Delta}$, the vector area of triangle ABC. Hence the given system of forces is equivalent to a couple of vector moment $2k\mathbf{\Delta}$.

EXAMPLES 5b

1 Find the work done by a force **F** during a displacement **s** of its point of application in each of the following cases, the unit of force being the newton and the unit of distance the metre: (i) $\mathbf{F} = 5\mathbf{i}+\mathbf{j}$, $\mathbf{s} = 2\mathbf{i}-3\mathbf{j}$; (ii) $\mathbf{F} = \mathbf{i}-\mathbf{j}+3\mathbf{k}$, $\mathbf{s} = 3\mathbf{i}-4\mathbf{j}-2\mathbf{k}$; (iii) $\mathbf{F} = 3\mathbf{i}+4\mathbf{j}+\mathbf{k}$; $\mathbf{s} = -\mathbf{i}-3\mathbf{j}+2\mathbf{k}$; (iv) $\mathbf{F} = 4\mathbf{i}-\mathbf{j}+3\mathbf{k}$, $\mathbf{s} = \mathbf{i}+\mathbf{j}-\mathbf{k}$; (v) $\mathbf{F} = X\mathbf{i}+Y\mathbf{j}+Z\mathbf{k}$, $\mathbf{s} = x\mathbf{i}+y\mathbf{j}+z\mathbf{k}$.

2 The line of action of a force of magnitude 5 N is inclined at angles of 30° and 60° respectively to the axes $\overline{OX}$, $\overline{OY}$. Find the work done by the force when its point of application moves from the point (0, 1) to the point (4, −1), the length unit being the metre.

3 A force of magnitude of 15 N acts in the direction $\overline{OP}$ where O is the origin and P the point (3, 4). Find the work done by the force when its point of application moves from the origin to the point (−3, 2), the length unit being the metre.

4 Show that the work done by the force $10(3\mathbf{i}-\mathbf{j}+\mathbf{k})$ units when its point of application moves in the direction of the vector $2\mathbf{i}+5\mathbf{j}-\mathbf{k}$ is zero and explain the significance of this result.

5 A force **F** acts through a point P; find the vector moment of **F** about the origin O in each of the following cases: (i) $\mathbf{F} = 3\mathbf{i}+2\mathbf{j}$, P is the point (2, 1); (ii) $\mathbf{F} = 3(\mathbf{i}+2\mathbf{j}-\mathbf{k})$, $\overline{OP} = 4\mathbf{i}-\mathbf{j}+\mathbf{k}$; (iii) $\mathbf{F} = 10(\mathbf{i}-\mathbf{j}+\mathbf{k})$, P is the point (−1, −2, 3); (iv) **F** has a magnitude of 56 units and is in the direction of $\overline{OA}$ where A is the point (−3, 6, 2), P is the point (0, 3, 3); (v) $\mathbf{F} = X\mathbf{i}+Y\mathbf{j}+Z\mathbf{k}$, P is the point (x, y, z).

6 A force having components 10 N, 6 N, −4 N respectively in the directions of the axes $\overline{OX}$, $\overline{OY}$, $\overline{OZ}$, acts through the point (−1, 2, −3). Find the vector moment of the force about the origin and the moment of the force about the axis $\overline{OZ}$; the length unit is the metre.

7 A force of 140 N acts parallel to the vector joining the origin to the point (6, −3, 2). Find the work done by the force when its point of application moves from the point (1, −1, 2) to the point (4, −2, 3); the unit of length being the metre.

8 A force of magnitude 60 N acts in the line $\overline{AB}$ where A, B are the points (3, −1, 4), (7, −3, 8) respectively. Taking the length unit as a metre, find the vector moment of the force about (i) the origin; (ii) the point (1, 4, 3).

9 A particle acted on by forces $2\mathbf{i}+\mathbf{j}-2\mathbf{k}$, $3\mathbf{i}+2\mathbf{j}+\mathbf{k}$, $\mathbf{i}-3\mathbf{j}+\mathbf{k}$ units is displaced from the point (1, 4, −1) to the point (4, 1, −3). Find the total work done by the forces.

10 A force of 42 units acts along the line $\overline{AB}$ where A, B are respectively the points (2, 3, 6), (1, 1, 8). Find (i) the vector moment of the force about the point (0, −1, 10), explaining the significance of the result; (ii) the moment of the force about the line joining the origin to the point (1, 1, 1).

11 $OABC$ is a square; O is the origin and B the point (3, 4). A particle at O is acted on by forces represented in magnitude and direction by the vectors $\overline{OA}$, $\overline{AB}$; the unit of force being represented by unit length. Find the work done by the forces when the particle is displaced from O to B.

12 A force of 25 N acts in the line $\overline{AB}$ where A, B are the points (2, −1), (5, 3) respectively; a second force acts in the line $\overline{CD}$ where C, D are the points (5, 0), (3, −1) respectively. If the sum of the moments of the forces about the origin is zero, find the magnitude of the second force.

13 A particle is acted on by forces represented completely by $\overline{OA}$, $\overline{OB}$, $\overline{OC}$, $\overline{OD}$, where A, B, C, D have coordinates (−2, 1, −2), (3, 4, 0), (6, −2, 3), (12, 0, −5) respectively, unit force being represented by unit length. Find (i) the magnitudes of the four forces; (ii) the total work done by the forces when the particle is moved from O to A and then from A to C.

14 Find the moment about the line through the point A(3, 2, −1) parallel to the vector $\mathbf{i}+2\mathbf{j}-2\mathbf{k}$ of a force of 56 N acting in the line $\overline{PQ}$ where P, Q are respectively the points (1, 1, 1), (4, −1, 7); the length unit being one metre.

15 Forces acting in the sides of a quadrilateral $ABCD$ are completely represented by the vectors $\overline{AB}$, $\overline{BC}$, $\overline{AD}$, $\overline{DC}$; show that their resultant is a force represented by the vector $2\overline{AC}$ and acting through the mid-point of BD.

16 $ABCD$, $PQRS$ are parallel faces of a cube of side 10 cm of which AP, BQ, CR, DS are edges. Forces of magnitudes $4\sqrt{2}$, $6\sqrt{2}$, $8\sqrt{3}$ N respectively act in the lines $\overline{BR}$, $\overline{RD}$, $\overline{QD}$. Find (i) the vector moment of the system about A; (ii) the moment of the system about the edge $\overline{AP}$. Take axes along $\overline{AB}$, $\overline{AD}$ and $\overline{AP}$.

17 A particle acted upon by forces of 36 N in the direction of the vector $\mathbf{i}-2\mathbf{j}-2\mathbf{k}$ and 49 N in the direction of the vector $-2\mathbf{i}+3\mathbf{j}+6\mathbf{k}$ is displaced from the point with position vector $\mathbf{i}+\mathbf{j}+\mathbf{k}$ to the point with position vector $3\mathbf{i}-4\mathbf{j}+2\mathbf{k}$. If the unit of length is 1 m, find the total work done by the forces.

18 Forces represented completely by the vectors $\overline{BC}$, $\overline{AC}$, $\overline{AB}$ act in the sides of triangle ABC. Show that the resultant of the system is a force represented in magnitude and direction by the vector $2\overline{AC}$ and state where its line of action cuts AB.

19 A force of magnitude F acts in the line $\mathbf{r} = \mathbf{a} + \lambda\hat{\mathbf{b}}$, where $\hat{\mathbf{b}}$ is a unit vector and λ a scalar parameter. Show that the vector moment of the force about the origin is $F(\mathbf{a} \wedge \hat{\mathbf{b}})$.

20 Show that forces acting along the sides of a triangle in the same sense and with magnitudes proportional to the sides are equivalent to a couple of magnitude proportional to the area of the triangle. Deduce a similar result in the case of a plane quadrilateral.

21 $ABCD$, $PQRS$ are parallel faces of a rectangular parallelepiped in which $AB = AP = 1$ cm, $BC = 2$ cm. Forces of magnitudes 6, 3, 2, N act respectively in the edges $\overline{QR}$, $\overline{RS}$, $\overline{CR}$. If the system is reduced to a force acting at A together with a couple, find the magnitudes of the force and the couple.

22 A, B, C have coordinates $(1, 1, 1)$, $(3, -1, 2)$, $(-5, 3, -2)$ respectively. Forces of magnitudes 12 N and 14 N in the lines $\overline{AB}$, $\overline{AC}$ respectively act on a particle at A. Find the total work done by the forces when the particle is displaced from A to B to C and back to A.

23 $ABCD$, $PQRS$ are parallel faces of a cube of side a. Find the moment about the line $\overline{AS}$ of forces of magnitudes $\sqrt{3}F$, $\sqrt{2}F$ respectively acting in the lines $\overline{BS}$ and $\overline{RD}$.

24 Forces $l\overline{BC}$, $m\overline{CA}$, $n\overline{AB}$ where l, m, n are positive constants act along the sides of a triangle ABC. Show that the line of action of their resultant divides BC, CA, AB respectively, externally in the ratios m/n, n/l, l/m. What happens if $l = m = n$?

25 X, Y, Z are points on the sides of triangle ABC such that $BX:XC = CY:YA = AZ:ZB = c:1$. Prove that forces represented completely by vectors $\overline{AX}$, $\overline{BY}$, $\overline{CZ}$ are equivalent to a couple of moment $2\Delta(1-c)/(1+c)$ where Δ is the area of triangle ABC.

26 A general system of forces is reduced to a force $\mathbf{R}$ at the origin O together with a couple of moment $\mathbf{G}$. What will be the moment of the couple if the system is reduced to a force at the point A together with a couple, A being the point with position vector $\mathbf{a}$?

27 Prove that a force $\mathbf{R}$ acting at a point O together with a couple of moment $\mathbf{G}$ is equivalent to a single force $\mathbf{R}$ whose perpendicular distance from O is G/R. Deduce that a general system of forces is equivalent either to a force or a couple.

28 Prove that a system of forces which has equal moments about three non-collinear points must be equivalent to a couple.

29 $ABCD$, $PQRS$ are parallel faces of a rectangular parallelepiped of which AP, BQ, CR, DS are edges; $AB = a$, $BC = b$, $AP = c$. Forces of magnitudes X, Y, Z respectively act along the edges $\overline{PQ}$, $\overline{BC}$, $\overline{DS}$. Prove that the perpendicular distance of the line of action of the resultant of the system from A is $\sqrt{(c^2X^2 + a^2Y^2 + b^2Z^2)}/\sqrt{(X^2+Y^2+Z^2)}$.

30 A system of forces is equivalent to a force $\mathbf{R}$ acting at the origin O together with a couple of moment $\mathbf{G}$. If $\mathbf{s}$ is the position vector of a point on the line of action of the resultant of the system, show that $\mathbf{G} - \mathbf{s} \wedge \mathbf{R} = 0$.

31 Forces $\mathbf{F}_1$, $\mathbf{F}_2$, $\mathbf{F}_3$, $\mathbf{F}_4$ acting at the origin O are in equilibrium and $\mathbf{P}$ is any other force. If M_1, M_2, M_3, M_4 are the moments of $\mathbf{P}$ about the respective lines of action of the given forces, prove that $M_1F_1 + M_2F_2 + M_3F_3 + M_4F_4 = 0$.

VI

DIFFERENTIATION AND INTEGRATION OF VECTOR FUNCTIONS

Vector functions of a scalar variable If for every value of a scalar parameter t in a given interval, there exists a vector quantity $\mathbf{a}(t)$, or more simply $\mathbf{a}$, whose value depends on the value of t, then $\mathbf{a}$ is said to be a vector function of t. As an example of a vector function consider a point P on a plane curve, whose position is determined by the arc length AP, or s, measured from a fixed point A on the curve (Fig. 54). The position vector, $\mathbf{r}$, of P with respect to some origin O, will have a value dependent on the location of P, that is, on the value of the scalar quantity s. So $\mathbf{r}$ is a vector function of s. In addition the unit vectors $\hat{\boldsymbol{\tau}}$, $\hat{\mathbf{n}}$, in the directions of the tangent and inward normal to the curve at P, are also vector functions of s.

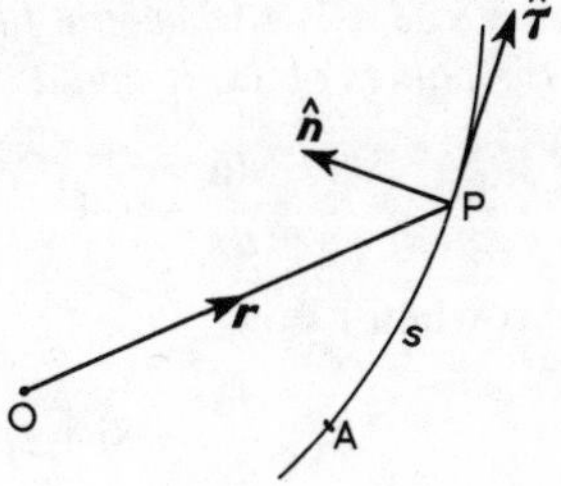

FIG. 54.

As further instances of vector functions, consider a point P moving in space; clearly $\mathbf{r}$, the position vector of P, $\mathbf{v}$, the velocity of P, and $\mathbf{a}$, the acceleration of P, are each vector functions of the scalar variable t, the time.

Derivative of a vector function Suppose $\mathbf{a}$ is a vector function of the scalar variable t. Then when t increases by a small quantity δt, the corresponding increase in $\mathbf{a}$, $\delta\mathbf{a}$, can be expressed as $\delta\mathbf{a} = \mathbf{a}(t+\delta t)-\mathbf{a}(t)$.

The derivative of $\mathbf{a}$ with respect to t is defined as

$$\frac{d\mathbf{a}}{dt} = \lim_{\delta t\to 0}\frac{\delta\mathbf{a}}{\delta t} = \lim_{\delta t\to 0}\left\{\frac{\mathbf{a}(t+\delta t)-\mathbf{a}(t)}{\delta t}\right\},$$

assuming this limit exists.

The derivative of $\mathbf{a}$ is in general also a function of t and its derivative is the second derivative of $\mathbf{a}$ with respect to t and is written $d^2\mathbf{a}/dt^2$. There are similar definitions for higher derivatives.

If a_x, a_y, a_z are the components of $\mathbf{a}$ in the directions of rectangular axes, the derivative of $\mathbf{a}$ with respect to t can be expressed in terms of the derivatives of the scalar functions a_x, a_y, a_z.

For $$\mathbf{a}(t) = a_x\mathbf{i}+a_y\mathbf{j}+a_z\mathbf{k},$$

$$\therefore\quad \mathbf{a}(t+\delta t) = (a_x+\delta a_x)\mathbf{i}+(a_y+\delta a_y)\mathbf{j}+(a_z+\delta a_z)\mathbf{k}.$$

So $$\delta\mathbf{a} = \delta a_x\mathbf{i}+\delta a_y\mathbf{j}+\delta a_z\mathbf{k}$$

and $$\frac{\delta\mathbf{a}}{\delta t} = \frac{\delta a_x}{\delta t}\mathbf{i}+\frac{\delta a_y}{\delta t}\mathbf{j}+\frac{\delta a_z}{\delta t}\mathbf{k}.$$

In the limit as $\delta t \to 0$,

$$\frac{d\mathbf{a}}{dt} = \frac{da_x}{dt}\mathbf{i}+\frac{da_y}{dt}\mathbf{j}+\frac{da_z}{dt}\mathbf{k}.$$

Ex. 1 *If the vector function* $\mathbf{a} = (3t^3-t)\mathbf{i}+(2t+1)\mathbf{j}+(1-t^2)\mathbf{k}$, *find the values of* $d\mathbf{a}/dt$ *and* $d^2\mathbf{a}/dt^2$ *when* $t = 1$.

$$\frac{d\mathbf{a}}{dt} = (9t^2-1)\mathbf{i}+2\mathbf{j}-2t\mathbf{k}\,; \qquad \frac{d^2\mathbf{a}}{dt^2} = 18t\mathbf{i}-2\mathbf{k}.$$

So when $t = 1$,

$$\frac{d\mathbf{a}}{dt} = 8\mathbf{i}+2\mathbf{j}-2\mathbf{k}\,; \qquad \frac{d^2\mathbf{a}}{dt^2} = 18\mathbf{i}-2\mathbf{k}.$$

Important differentiation results In the following results, **a**, **b** are vector functions and u a scalar function of the scalar variable t; **c** is a constant vector, that is constant in magnitude and direction, and c is a constant scalar. In result (iv), the function of a function rule, s a second scalar variable is a function of t.

(i) $$\frac{d\mathbf{c}}{dt} = 0\,;$$

(ii) $$\frac{d}{dt}(c\mathbf{a}) = c\frac{d\mathbf{a}}{dt}\,;$$

(iii) $$\frac{d}{dt}(\mathbf{a}+\mathbf{b}) = \frac{d\mathbf{a}}{dt}+\frac{d\mathbf{b}}{dt}\,;$$

(iv) $$\frac{d\mathbf{a}}{dt} = \frac{d\mathbf{a}}{ds}\cdot\frac{ds}{dt}\,;$$

(v) $$\frac{d}{dt}(u\mathbf{a}) = \frac{du}{dt}\mathbf{a}+u\frac{d\mathbf{a}}{dt}\,;$$

$$\frac{d}{dt}(\mathbf{a}\,.\,\mathbf{b}) = \frac{d\mathbf{a}}{dt}\,.\,\mathbf{b}+\mathbf{a}\,.\,\frac{d\mathbf{b}}{dt}\,;$$

$$\frac{d}{dt}(\mathbf{a}\wedge\mathbf{b}) = \frac{d\mathbf{a}}{dt}\wedge\mathbf{b}+\mathbf{a}\wedge\frac{d\mathbf{b}}{dt}.$$

These results are proved from first principles; the method is illustrated by the following proof of the product rule in the case of the scalar product.

Suppose $$\mathbf{v} = \mathbf{a} \cdot \mathbf{b}.$$

Let t increase by a small amount δt and let the corresponding increases in **a**, **b**, and **v** be $\delta\mathbf{a}$, $\delta\mathbf{b}$ and $\delta\mathbf{v}$ respectively.

Then
$$\mathbf{v}+\delta\mathbf{v} = (\mathbf{a}+\delta\mathbf{a}) \cdot (\mathbf{b}+\delta\mathbf{b})$$
$$= \mathbf{a} \cdot \mathbf{b}+\delta\mathbf{a} \cdot \mathbf{b}+\mathbf{a} \cdot \delta\mathbf{b}+\delta\mathbf{a} \cdot \delta\mathbf{b}.$$
$$\therefore \quad \delta\mathbf{v} = \delta\mathbf{a} \cdot \mathbf{b}+\mathbf{a} \cdot \delta\mathbf{b}+\delta\mathbf{a} \cdot \delta\mathbf{b}$$
and
$$\frac{\delta\mathbf{v}}{\delta t} = \frac{\delta\mathbf{a}}{\delta t} \cdot \mathbf{b}+\mathbf{a} \cdot \frac{\delta\mathbf{b}}{\delta t}+\frac{\delta\mathbf{a}}{\delta t} \cdot \delta\mathbf{b}.$$

In the limit as $\delta t \to 0$, this becomes
$$\frac{d\mathbf{v}}{dt} = \frac{d\mathbf{a}}{dt} \cdot \mathbf{b}+\mathbf{a} \cdot \frac{d\mathbf{b}}{dt}.$$

As an example of the use of this product rule consider the derivative of $\mathbf{a}^2$.
$$\frac{d}{dt}(\mathbf{a}^2) = \frac{d}{dt}(\mathbf{a} \cdot \mathbf{a}) = \frac{d\mathbf{a}}{dt} \cdot \mathbf{a}+\mathbf{a} \cdot \frac{d\mathbf{a}}{dt} = 2\mathbf{a} \cdot \frac{d\mathbf{a}}{dt}.$$

Similarly it will be found that
$$\frac{d}{dt}(\mathbf{a}^3) = \left(2\mathbf{a} \cdot \frac{d\mathbf{a}}{dt}\right)\mathbf{a}+\mathbf{a}^2\frac{d\mathbf{a}}{dt}.$$

Derivative of a vector function of constant magnitude Suppose $\mathbf{a}(t)$ has a constant magnitude but a direction changing with t. Then as $\mathbf{a}^2 = a^2 =$ constant, it follows that the derivative of $\mathbf{a}^2$ with respect to t is zero.

So $$2\mathbf{a} \cdot \frac{d\mathbf{a}}{dt} = 0; \quad \text{i.e.} \quad \mathbf{a} \cdot \frac{d\mathbf{a}}{dt} = 0.$$

Consequently **a** and its derivative $d\mathbf{a}/dt$ are perpendicular vectors.

Ex. 2 *If* **a** *is a constant vector and* **r** *a vector function of t, find the second derivative of the product* **a . r**.

$$\frac{d}{dt}(\mathbf{a} \cdot \mathbf{r}) = \frac{d\mathbf{a}}{dt} \cdot \mathbf{r}+\mathbf{a} \cdot \frac{d\mathbf{r}}{dt} = \mathbf{a} \cdot \frac{d\mathbf{r}}{dt}, \quad \text{as} \quad \frac{d\mathbf{a}}{dt} = 0.$$
$$\therefore \quad \frac{d^2}{dt^2}(\mathbf{a} \cdot \mathbf{r}) = \frac{d}{dt}\left(\mathbf{a} \cdot \frac{d\mathbf{r}}{dt}\right) = \mathbf{a} \cdot \frac{d^2\mathbf{r}}{dt^2}.$$

Ex. 3 *If* $n, \mathbf{a}, \mathbf{b}$ *are constants and* $\mathbf{r} = \cos nt\mathbf{a} + \sin nt\mathbf{b}$, *prove* (i) $\dfrac{d^2\mathbf{r}}{dt^2} + n^2\mathbf{r} = 0$; (ii) $\mathbf{r} \wedge \dfrac{d\mathbf{r}}{dt} = n\mathbf{a} \wedge \mathbf{b}$.

(i) $$\frac{d\mathbf{r}}{dt} = -n \sin nt\mathbf{a} + n \cos nt\mathbf{b}, \quad \text{as} \quad \frac{d\mathbf{a}}{dt} = \frac{d\mathbf{b}}{dt} = 0.$$

$$\therefore \quad \frac{d^2\mathbf{r}}{dt^2} = -n^2 \cos nt\mathbf{a} - n^2 \sin nt\mathbf{b} = -n^2\mathbf{r}.$$

I.e. $$\frac{d^2\mathbf{r}}{dt^2} + n^2\mathbf{r} = 0.$$

(ii) $$\mathbf{r} \wedge \frac{d\mathbf{r}}{dt} = (\cos nt\mathbf{a} + \sin nt\mathbf{b}) \wedge (-n \sin nt\mathbf{a} + n \cos nt\mathbf{b})$$
$$= n(\cos^2 nt\mathbf{a} \wedge \mathbf{b} - \sin^2 nt\mathbf{b} \wedge \mathbf{a}), \quad \text{as} \quad \mathbf{a} \wedge \mathbf{a} = \mathbf{b} \wedge \mathbf{b} = 0,$$
$$= n\mathbf{a} \wedge \mathbf{b}(\cos^2 nt + \sin^2 nt) = n\mathbf{a} \wedge \mathbf{b}.$$

Integration The operation of vector integration is defined as in the scalar calculus; the process consists of being given a vector function say $\mathbf{a}(t)$ and finding another function $\mathbf{A}(t)$ such that $d\mathbf{A}/dt = \mathbf{a}$. In this event the result is written as

$$\int \mathbf{a}\, dt = \mathbf{A}.$$

As however $d(\mathbf{A} + \mathbf{c})/dt$, where $\mathbf{c}$ is an arbitrary constant vector, will also equal $\mathbf{a}$, the general result is

$$\int \mathbf{a}\, dt = \mathbf{A} + \mathbf{c},$$

where $\mathbf{c}$ is an arbitrary vector constant.

Ex. 4 *Evaluate* (i) $\int \{(3t^2 - 1)\mathbf{i} + 4t\mathbf{j}\}\, dt$; (ii) $\int \mathbf{u} \cos 3t\, dt$, *where* $\mathbf{u}$ *is a constant vector.*

(i) $\int \{(3t^2 - 1)\mathbf{i} + 4t\mathbf{j}\}\, dt = (t^3 - t)\mathbf{i} + 2t^2\mathbf{j} + \mathbf{c}$, where $\mathbf{c}$ is a constant vector of the form $a\mathbf{i} + b\mathbf{j}$, where a, b are scalar constants.

(ii) $\int \mathbf{u} \cos 3t\, dt = \frac{1}{3}\mathbf{u} \sin 3t + \mathbf{c}$, where $\mathbf{c}$ is a constant vector.

Integrals of products of vectors Integrals of the forms $\int \mathbf{a} \,.\, \mathbf{b}\, dt$, $\int \mathbf{a} \wedge \mathbf{b}\, dt$ where $\mathbf{a}$, $\mathbf{b}$ are vector functions of t can usually be evaluated by expressing the vector functions in terms of their components along rectangular axes; the products being evaluated prior to integration.

Ex. 5 *Evaluate* $\int \mathbf{a} \,.\, \mathbf{b}\, dt$ *and* $\int \mathbf{a} \wedge \mathbf{b}\, dt$ *where* $\mathbf{a} = t\mathbf{i} + t^2\mathbf{j} + 3\mathbf{k}$, $\mathbf{b} = -\mathbf{i} + t\mathbf{j} + t^2\mathbf{k}$.

$$\mathbf{a} \,.\, \mathbf{b} = -t + t^3 + 3t^2; \quad \mathbf{a} \wedge \mathbf{b} = (t^4 - 3t)\mathbf{i} + (-3 - t^3)\mathbf{j} + 2t^2\mathbf{k}.$$

$$\therefore \quad \int \mathbf{a}\,.\,\mathbf{b}\,dt = \int (-t+t^3+3t^2)\,dt = -\tfrac{1}{2}t^2+\tfrac{1}{4}t^4+t^3+c,$$

where in this case, c is a scalar arbitrary constant.

Also $\displaystyle\int \mathbf{a}\wedge\mathbf{b}\,dt = \int \{(t^4-3t)\mathbf{i}+(-3-t^3)\mathbf{j}+2t^2\mathbf{k}\}\,dt$

$$= (\tfrac{1}{5}t^5-\tfrac{3}{2}t^2)\mathbf{i}-(3t+\tfrac{1}{4}t^4)\mathbf{j}+\tfrac{2}{3}t^3\mathbf{k}+\mathbf{c},$$

where **c** is an arbitrary vector constant.

Ex. 6 *Evaluate* $\int \mathbf{F}\,.\,d\mathbf{s}$ *where* $\mathbf{F} = \cos^2 t\mathbf{i}+\sin^2 t\mathbf{j}$, $\mathbf{s} = \cos t\mathbf{i}+\sin t\mathbf{j}$, *over the range* $t = 0$ *to* $t = \frac{1}{2}\pi$.

As $\quad \mathbf{s} = \cos t\mathbf{i}+\sin t\mathbf{j}, \quad d\mathbf{s} = (-\sin t\mathbf{i}+\cos t\mathbf{j})\,dt.$

So $\quad \mathbf{F}\,.\,d\mathbf{s} = (-\cos^2 t\sin t+\sin^2 t\cos t)\,dt.$

$$\text{Required integral} = \int_0^{\frac{1}{2}\pi} (-\cos^2 t\sin t+\sin^2 t\cos t)\,dt$$

$$= [\tfrac{1}{3}\cos^3 t+\tfrac{1}{3}\sin^3 t]_0^{\frac{1}{2}\pi} = 0.$$

Vector differential equations Certain vector differential equations of common occurrence can be solved by using methods similar to those of the scalar calculus. Two of the methods are illustrated in the worked examples which follow.

Ex. 7 *If* $d^2\mathbf{r}/dt^2 = -n^2\mathbf{r}$, *where* n *is a scalar constant, and* $d\mathbf{r}/dt = 0$ *when* $\mathbf{r} = \mathbf{a}$, *find the value of* $|d\mathbf{r}/dt|^2$.

Taking the scalar product of both sides of the equation with $2\dfrac{d\mathbf{r}}{dt}$, the L.H.S. becomes $\dfrac{d}{dt}[d\mathbf{r}/dt]^2$ and the R.H.S. becomes $-\dfrac{d}{dt}(n^2\mathbf{r}^2)$.

So integration with respect to t gives

$$\left(\frac{d\mathbf{r}}{dt}\right)^2 = -n^2\mathbf{r}^2+c,$$

where the arbitrary constant c is scalar as the other terms in the equation are scalar.

As $\dfrac{d\mathbf{r}}{dt} = 0$ when $\mathbf{r} = \mathbf{a}$, then $c = n^2\mathbf{a}^2$.

$$\therefore \quad \left(\frac{d\mathbf{r}}{dt}\right)^2 = -n^2\mathbf{r}^2+n^2\mathbf{a}^2.$$

But $\quad \left(\dfrac{d\mathbf{r}}{dt}\right)^2 = \left|\dfrac{d\mathbf{r}}{dt}\right|^2, \quad \mathbf{r}^2 = r^2 \quad \text{and} \quad \mathbf{a}^2 = a^2.$

$$\therefore \quad \left|\frac{d\mathbf{r}}{dt}\right|^2 = n^2a^2 - n^2r^2 = n^2(a^2 - r^2).$$

Ex. 8 *Find the general solutions of the equation* $a\dfrac{d^2\mathbf{r}}{dt^2} + b\dfrac{d\mathbf{r}}{dt} + c\mathbf{r} = 0$, *where* a, b, c *are scalar constants.*

Following the method used in the solution of scalar equations of the same form, the general solution of the given equation depends on the nature and value of the roots of the auxiliary equation

$$am^2 + bm + c = 0.$$

Case (i). If the roots of the auxiliary equation are real and different, say $m = m_1, m_2$, the general solution is

$$\mathbf{r} = \mathbf{A}\,e^{m_1 t} + \mathbf{B}\,e^{m_2 t},$$

where **A**, **B** are arbitrary vector constants.

Case (ii). If the roots of the auxiliary equation are real and equal, say $m = m_1, m_1$, the general solution is

$$\mathbf{r} = e^{m_1 t}(\mathbf{A} + \mathbf{B}t).$$

Case (iii). If the roots of the auxiliary equation are complex, say $m = p \pm iq$, the general solution is

$$\mathbf{r} = e^{pt}(\mathbf{A}\cos qt + \mathbf{B}\sin qt).$$

EXAMPLES 6a

1 A vector function $\mathbf{a}(u)$ of a scalar variable u is given by the relationship $\mathbf{a}(u) = (3u - u^3)\mathbf{i} + 3u^2\mathbf{j} + (3u + u^3)\mathbf{k}$. Find the value $\mathbf{a}(0)$ of $\mathbf{a}$ when $u = 0$ and the value of $\mathbf{a}(1)$.

2 The velocity $\mathbf{v}$ of a moving point is given by $\mathbf{v} = (4t^3 - t + 2)\mathbf{i} + (2t^2 - 1)\mathbf{j}$, where t is the time. Find (i) the initial velocity; (ii) the positive value of t for which the velocity is parallel to the axis of x.

3 The position vector $\mathbf{r}$ of a point is given by $\mathbf{r} = a\cos\theta\mathbf{i} + a\sin\theta\mathbf{j} + a\theta\mathbf{k}$, where θ is a scalar parameter and a is a constant. Find the distance between the points corresponding to $\theta = 0$ and $\theta = \frac{1}{2}\pi$.

4 If $\mathbf{v} = \boldsymbol{\omega} \wedge \mathbf{r}$ where $\boldsymbol{\omega} = t\mathbf{k}$ and $\mathbf{r} = t^2\mathbf{i} + 2t\mathbf{j}$, where t is a scalar variable, find the value of $\mathbf{v}$ when $t = 2$.

5 Find $d\mathbf{a}/dt$ in each of the following cases: (i) $\mathbf{a} = 3t\mathbf{i} + (2t^2 - 1)\mathbf{j}$; (ii) $\mathbf{a} = 4\sin t\mathbf{i} + 3\cos t\mathbf{j}$; (iii) $\mathbf{a} = e^t\mathbf{i} + e^{-t}\mathbf{j} + t\mathbf{k}$; (iv) $\mathbf{a} = b\cos\omega t\mathbf{i} + b\sin\omega t\mathbf{j} - g\mathbf{k}$, where b, ω, g are constants.

6 If $\mathbf{a} = 2t\mathbf{i} + t^2\mathbf{j} + 2\mathbf{k}$, $\mathbf{b} = t^2\mathbf{i} - 2\mathbf{j} + t\mathbf{k}$, find the derivatives with respect to t of (i) $\mathbf{a} + \mathbf{b}$; (ii) $\mathbf{a} \cdot \mathbf{b}$; (iii) $\mathbf{a} \wedge \mathbf{b}$; (iv) $\mathbf{a}^2$.

7 If $\mathbf{v} = 2t\mathbf{i} + t^2\mathbf{j} - t\mathbf{k}$, find the values when $t = 1$ of (i) v, the modulus of $\mathbf{v}$; (ii) dv/dt; (iii) $|d\mathbf{v}/dt|$.

8 Given that $\mathbf{F}(t) = m(t)\mathbf{a}(t)$, where $\mathbf{F}(t) = F(\cos 2t\mathbf{i} + \sin 2t\mathbf{j})$, $m(t) = m_0(1 + \alpha t)$, the scalars F, m_0, α being constants, find the value of $d\mathbf{a}/dt$.

9 If $\mathbf{r}$ is a vector function of s, express (i) $\dfrac{d}{ds}(\mathbf{r}^2)$; (ii) $\dfrac{d}{ds}\left\{\left(\dfrac{d\mathbf{r}}{ds}\right)^2\right\}$; (iii) $\dfrac{d}{ds}\left(\mathbf{r}^2\dfrac{d\mathbf{r}}{ds}\right)$; (iv) $\dfrac{d}{ds}\left(\mathbf{r}\,.\,\dfrac{d\mathbf{r}}{ds}\right)$; (v) $\dfrac{d}{ds}\left(\mathbf{r}\wedge\dfrac{d\mathbf{r}}{ds}\right)$, in terms of $\mathbf{r}$ and its derivatives.

10 If $\mathbf{u}$ is a constant vector and $\mathbf{a}$ is a vector function of t, find the derivatives with respect to t of (i) $\mathbf{a}\,.\,\mathbf{u}$; (ii) $a\mathbf{a}$; (iii) $a^2\mathbf{a}+\mathbf{u}\wedge\dfrac{d\mathbf{a}}{dt}$.

11 If $\mathbf{v} = 2s^3\mathbf{i}+e^s\mathbf{j}+\sqrt{(s^2+1)}\mathbf{k}$, where $s = e^{-t}+2\sin t$, find the value of $d\mathbf{v}/dt$ when $t = 0$.

12 Given that $\mathbf{a} = d^2\mathbf{r}/dt^2$, find $\mathbf{a}$ when (i) $\mathbf{r} = t^2\mathbf{i}+t^3\mathbf{j}+t^4\mathbf{k}$; (ii) $\mathbf{r} = \cos t\mathbf{i}+\sin t\mathbf{j}+\sin 2t\mathbf{k}$; (iii) $\mathbf{r} = \sin 2t\mathbf{i}+\cos 3t\mathbf{j}+e^t\mathbf{k}$.

13 If $\mathbf{a}$ is a vector function of t, prove that $\dfrac{d}{dt}\left(\mathbf{a}\wedge\dfrac{d\mathbf{a}}{dt}\right) = \mathbf{a}\wedge\dfrac{d^2\mathbf{a}}{dt^2}$.

14 Given that $\mathbf{p}, \mathbf{q}$ are constant vectors and $\mathbf{r} = \cos 4t\mathbf{p}+\sin 4t\mathbf{q}$, prove that $\mathbf{r}\wedge\dfrac{d\mathbf{r}}{dt} = 4\mathbf{p}\wedge\mathbf{q}$.

15 By writing $\mathbf{r}^3$ as $\mathbf{r}^2\mathbf{r}$, show that if $\hat{\mathbf{r}}$ is constant, $d(\mathbf{r}^3)/dt = 3\mathbf{r}^2 d\mathbf{r}/dt$.

16 If $\mathbf{a} = t\mathbf{p}+t^{-1}\mathbf{q}$, $\mathbf{b} = t^{-1}\mathbf{p}+t\mathbf{q}$, where $\mathbf{p}, \mathbf{q}$ are constant vectors, show that $d(\mathbf{a}\wedge\mathbf{b})/dt = 2(t+t^{-3})\mathbf{p}\wedge\mathbf{q}$.

17 If $\hat{\mathbf{r}}$ is a unit vector making an angle θ with the axis $\overline{OX}$, show that $\hat{\mathbf{r}} = \cos\theta\mathbf{i}+\sin\theta\mathbf{j}$. Find $d\mathbf{r}/dt$ and deduce that it is a vector of magnitude $d\theta/dt$ in a direction normal to that of $\hat{\mathbf{r}}$.

18 P is the point with position vector $\mathbf{r} = a\cos\omega t\mathbf{i}+b\sin\omega t\mathbf{j}$, where a, b, ω are constants. Show that the vector $d^2\mathbf{r}/dt^2$ is in the direction $\overline{PO}$ where O is the origin and that the vector $\mathbf{r}\wedge d\mathbf{r}/dt$ is constant.

19 Evaluate $\int \mathbf{a}(t)\,dt$ in the cases where (i) $\mathbf{a}(t) = 3t^2\mathbf{i}-4t\mathbf{j}+\mathbf{k}$; (ii) $\mathbf{a}(t) = \sin t\mathbf{i}+\cos t\mathbf{j}+2t\mathbf{k}$; (iii) $\mathbf{a}(t) = e^t\mathbf{i}+e^{-t}\mathbf{j}$.

20 Evaluate $\int \mathbf{a}\,.\,\mathbf{b}\,dt$ where $\mathbf{a} = t\mathbf{i}-t^2\mathbf{j}+t^{-1}\mathbf{k}$, $\mathbf{b} = \mathbf{i}+t\mathbf{j}+\log t\mathbf{k}$.

21 If $\mathbf{p}, \mathbf{q}$ are constant vectors, evaluate $\int_0^{\frac{1}{4}\pi}(\sin t\mathbf{p}+\cos t\mathbf{q})\wedge(\cos t\mathbf{p}+\sin t\mathbf{q})\,dt$.

22 Given that $d\mathbf{v}/dt = (4-3t^2)\mathbf{i}+(1-2t)\mathbf{j}-\mathbf{k}$ and $\mathbf{v} = \mathbf{i}$ when $t = 0$, find the modulus of $\mathbf{v}$ when $t = 2$.

23 If $d^2\mathbf{r}/dt^2 = n^2\mathbf{r}$ where n is a constant, show that $[d\mathbf{r}/dt]^2 = c+n^2\mathbf{r}^2$, where c is an arbitrary constant.

24 Evaluate $\int \mathbf{F}\,.\,d\mathbf{s}$ with $\mathbf{F} = \sin t\mathbf{i}+\cos t\mathbf{j}$, $\mathbf{s} = t\mathbf{i}+2\mathbf{j}$ over the range $t = 0$ to $t = \frac{1}{4}\pi$.

25 Find the general solutions of the equations (i) $\dfrac{d^2\mathbf{r}}{dt^2}-\dfrac{d\mathbf{r}}{dt}-2\mathbf{r} = 0$; (ii) $\dfrac{d^2\mathbf{r}}{dt^2}-\dfrac{d\mathbf{r}}{dt} = 0$; (iii) $\dfrac{d^2\mathbf{r}}{dt^2}-4\dfrac{d\mathbf{r}}{dt}+4\mathbf{r} = 0$; (iv) $\dfrac{d^2\mathbf{r}}{dt^2}-2\dfrac{d\mathbf{r}}{dt}+2\mathbf{r} = 0$.

26 A vector function $\mathbf{a}(t)$ has a constant magnitude and a variable direction. Representing $\mathbf{a}(t)$ by the vector $\overline{OP}$ and $\mathbf{a}(t+\delta t)$ by the vector $\overline{OQ}$ where $OP = OQ$, show that in the limit as $\delta t \to 0$, angle $OPQ \to \frac{1}{2}\pi$. Deduce that the direction of the derivative of $\mathbf{a}(t)$ is perpendicular to the direction of $\mathbf{a}(t)$.

27 If $\hat{\mathbf{r}}$ is a unit vector in the direction of the vector $\mathbf{r}$ so $\mathbf{r} = r\hat{\mathbf{r}}$, prove that $\hat{\mathbf{r}}\,.\,d\mathbf{r}/dt = dr/dt$.

28 With the notation of the previous example, let $d^2\mathbf{r}/dt^2 = -\mu\hat{\mathbf{r}}/r^2$, where μ is a constant. By taking the scalar product of both sides of the equation with $2d\mathbf{r}/dt$, show that $[d\mathbf{r}/dt]^2 = 2\mu/r + c$, where c is an arbitrary constant.

29 P is a point on a plane curve with position vector $\mathbf{r}$; the arc length AP, where A is a fixed point on the curve, is s; Q is a neighbouring point on the curve with position vector $\mathbf{r}+\delta\mathbf{r}$ and arc length AQ equal to $s+\delta s$. Show that $\overline{PQ} = \delta\mathbf{r}$ and arc $PQ = \delta s$. Deduce that $d\mathbf{r}/ds$ is equal to the unit vector $\hat{\mathbf{t}}$ along the tangent at P in the direction s increasing (Fig. 54).

30 If the tangent at P to the plane curve makes an angle ψ with a fixed direction, show that, with the notation of the previous example, $d\hat{\mathbf{t}}/ds$ is a vector along the inward normal at P with a magnitude equal to $d\psi/ds$ or κ, the curvature at P.

Vector functions of more than one scalar variable If t_1, t_2, t_3 are independent scalar variables, the vector function $\mathbf{u}(t_1, t_2, t_3) = t_1^2t_2t_3\mathbf{i} + t_1t_2^2t_3\mathbf{j} + t_1t_2t_3^2\mathbf{k}$ for example is a function of three scalar variables. In physical sciences there are many important vector functions of more than one scalar variable as for example, the velocity at a point in a moving fluid at any instant; in general this will be a function of the coordinates of the point and the time.

Partial derivatives If $\mathbf{u}(t_1, t_2, t_3)$ is a vector function of the independent scalar variables t_1, t_2, t_3, the partial derivatives $\dfrac{\partial \mathbf{u}}{\partial t_1}, \dfrac{\partial \mathbf{u}}{\partial t_2}, \dfrac{\partial \mathbf{u}}{\partial t_3}$ are defined as in the scalar calculus.

So $\dfrac{\partial \mathbf{u}}{\partial t_1} = \lim\limits_{\delta t_1 \to 0} \dfrac{\mathbf{u}(t_1+\delta t_1, t_2, t_3) - \mathbf{u}(t_1, t_2, t_3)}{\delta t_1}$, assuming the limit exists; with similar definitions for $\dfrac{\partial \mathbf{u}}{\partial t_2}$ and $\dfrac{\partial \mathbf{u}}{\partial t_3}$.

As in the scalar calculus, it is clear that the process of partial differentiation of a vector function $\mathbf{u}(t_1, t_2, \ldots)$ with respect to one of the scalar variables, say t_1, is identical with that of the ordinary differentiation of the same function in which only t_1 is treated as variable.

E.g. if
$$\mathbf{u} = t_1^2t_2t_3\mathbf{i} + t_1t_2^2t_3\mathbf{j} + t_1t_2t_3^2\mathbf{k},$$
then
$$\frac{\partial \mathbf{u}}{\partial t_1} = 2t_1t_2t_3\mathbf{i} + t_2^2t_3\mathbf{j} + t_2t_3^2\mathbf{k};$$
$$\frac{\partial \mathbf{u}}{\partial t_2} = t_1^2t_3\mathbf{i} + 2t_1t_2t_3\mathbf{j} + t_1t_3^2\mathbf{k};$$
$$\frac{\partial \mathbf{u}}{\partial t_3} = t_1^2t_2\mathbf{i} + t_1t_2^2\mathbf{j} + 2t_1t_2t_3\mathbf{k}.$$

Higher partial derivatives In general the partial derivatives $\frac{\partial \mathbf{u}}{\partial t_1}, \frac{\partial \mathbf{u}}{\partial t_2}, \frac{\partial \mathbf{u}}{\partial t_3}$ will be vector functions of the same variables and consequently they can each be differentiated partially with respect to t_1, t_2, t_3 to give second order partial derivatives denoted as follows:

$$\frac{\partial}{\partial t_1}\left(\frac{\partial \mathbf{u}}{\partial t_1}\right) = \frac{\partial^2 \mathbf{u}}{\partial t_1^2}; \quad \frac{\partial}{\partial t_2}\left(\frac{\partial \mathbf{u}}{\partial t_1}\right) = \frac{\partial^2 \mathbf{u}}{\partial t_2\, \partial t_1}; \quad \frac{\partial}{\partial t_3}\left(\frac{\partial \mathbf{u}}{\partial t_1}\right) = \frac{\partial^2 \mathbf{u}}{\partial t_3\, \partial t_1};$$

and similarly for the other second order derivatives. As in the scalar calculus it can be shown that the order of partial differentiation is immaterial so

$$\frac{\partial^2 \mathbf{u}}{\partial t_2\, \partial t_1} = \frac{\partial^2 \mathbf{u}}{\partial t_1\, \partial t_2}; \quad \frac{\partial^2 \mathbf{u}}{\partial t_3\, \partial t_2} = \frac{\partial^2 \mathbf{u}}{\partial t_2\, \partial t_3}; \quad \frac{\partial^2 \mathbf{u}}{\partial t_1\, \partial t_3} = \frac{\partial^2 \mathbf{u}}{\partial t_3\, \partial t_1}.$$

Ex. 9 *If* $\mathbf{u} = t_1 t_2 t_3(t_1^2\mathbf{i} + t_2^2\mathbf{j} + t_3^2\mathbf{k})$, *verify that* $\frac{\partial^2 \mathbf{u}}{\partial t_1\, \partial t_2} = \frac{\partial^2 \mathbf{u}}{\partial t_2\, \partial t_1}$ *and evaluate* $\frac{\partial^2 \mathbf{u}}{\partial t_1^2} + \frac{\partial^2 \mathbf{u}}{\partial t_2^2} + \frac{\partial^2 \mathbf{u}}{\partial t_3^2}$.

$$\frac{\partial \mathbf{u}}{\partial t_1} = 3t_1^2 t_2 t_3\mathbf{i} + t_2^3 t_3\mathbf{j} + t_2 t_3^3\mathbf{k}; \quad \frac{\partial \mathbf{u}}{\partial t_2} = t_1^3 t_3\mathbf{i} + 3t_1 t_2^2 t_3\mathbf{j} + t_1 t_3^3\mathbf{k}.$$

$$\therefore \quad \frac{\partial^2 \mathbf{u}}{\partial t_2\, \partial t_1} = 3t_1^2 t_3\mathbf{i} + 3t_2^2 t_3\mathbf{j} + t_3^3\mathbf{k}; \quad \frac{\partial^2 \mathbf{u}}{\partial t_1\, \partial t_2} = 3t_1^2 t_3\mathbf{i} + 3t_2^2 t_3\mathbf{j} + t_3^3\mathbf{k},$$

and so the two second order partial derivatives are equal.

Also
$$\frac{\partial^2 \mathbf{u}}{\partial t_1^2} + \frac{\partial^2 \mathbf{u}}{\partial t_2^2} + \frac{\partial^2 \mathbf{u}}{\partial t_3^2} = 6t_1 t_2 t_3\mathbf{i} + 6t_1 t_2 t_3\mathbf{j} + 6t_1 t_2 t_3\mathbf{k}$$
$$= 6t_1 t_2 t_3(\mathbf{i} + \mathbf{j} + \mathbf{k}).$$

Differential operators Certain differential operators which are of great importance in the more advanced physical applications of vectors will now be defined although the full treatment of them is far beyond the scope of this book.

If $\varphi(x, y, z)$ is a scalar function of position, that is, a function of the variables x, y, z where (x, y, z) are the coordinates of a point in space, the vector function

$$\frac{\partial \varphi}{\partial x}\mathbf{i} + \frac{\partial \varphi}{\partial y}\mathbf{j} + \frac{\partial \varphi}{\partial z}\mathbf{k},$$

is called the *vector gradient of* φ and spoken of as *grad* φ; it is denoted symbolically by

$$\nabla\varphi,$$

where ∇ is the vector differential operator $\mathbf{i}\frac{\partial}{\partial x}+\mathbf{j}\frac{\partial}{\partial y}+\mathbf{k}\frac{\partial}{\partial z}$. For example, if

$$\varphi = x^2yz+x^3,$$

$$\text{grad } \varphi = (2xyz+3x^2)\mathbf{i}+x^2z\mathbf{j}+x^2y\mathbf{k}.$$

If $\mathbf{a}(x, y, z)$ is a vector function of position, the scalar function

$$\frac{\partial a_x}{\partial x}+\frac{\partial a_y}{\partial y}+\frac{\partial a_z}{\partial z},$$

where a_x, a_y, a_z are the magnitudes of the components of $\mathbf{a}$ in the directions of the coordinate axes, is called *the divergence of* $\mathbf{a}$ and spoken of as div $\mathbf{a}$; it can be denoted symbolically by

$$\nabla . \mathbf{a}.$$

For
$$\nabla . \mathbf{a} = \left(\mathbf{i}\frac{\partial}{\partial x}+\mathbf{j}\frac{\partial}{\partial y}+\mathbf{k}\frac{\partial}{\partial z}\right) . \left(a_x\mathbf{i}+a_y\mathbf{j}+a_z\mathbf{k}\right)$$
$$= \frac{\partial a_x}{\partial x}+\frac{\partial a_y}{\partial y}+\frac{\partial a_z}{\partial z}.$$

Finally, the vector function

$$\left(\frac{\partial a_z}{\partial y}-\frac{\partial a_y}{\partial z}\right)\mathbf{i}+\left(\frac{\partial a_x}{\partial z}-\frac{\partial a_z}{\partial x}\right)\mathbf{j}+\left(\frac{\partial a_y}{\partial x}-\frac{\partial a_x}{\partial y}\right)\mathbf{k},$$

is called *the curl of* $\mathbf{a}$ and spoken of as curl $\mathbf{a}$; it can be denoted symbolically by

$$\nabla \wedge \mathbf{a}.$$

For
$$\nabla \wedge \mathbf{a} = \left(\mathbf{i}\frac{\partial}{\partial x}+\mathbf{j}\frac{\partial}{\partial y}+\mathbf{k}\frac{\partial}{\partial z}\right) \wedge \left(a_x\mathbf{i}+a_y\mathbf{j}+a_z\mathbf{k}\right)$$
$$= \begin{vmatrix} \mathbf{i} & \mathbf{j} & \mathbf{k} \\ \frac{\partial}{\partial x} & \frac{\partial}{\partial y} & \frac{\partial}{\partial z} \\ a_x & a_y & a_z \end{vmatrix}$$
$$= \left(\frac{\partial a_z}{\partial y}-\frac{\partial a_y}{\partial z}\right)\mathbf{i}+\left(\frac{\partial a_x}{\partial z}-\frac{\partial a_z}{\partial x}\right)\mathbf{j}+\left(\frac{\partial a_y}{\partial x}-\frac{\partial a_x}{\partial y}\right)\mathbf{k}.$$

For example, if $\mathbf{a} = xy\mathbf{i}+yz\mathbf{j}+zx\mathbf{k}$,

$$\text{div}\,\mathbf{a} = y+z+x,$$

and $\text{curl}\,\mathbf{a} = -y\mathbf{i}-z\mathbf{j}-x\mathbf{k}$.

Ex. 10 *If $r = OP$, where P is the point (x, y, z), show that* grad $r = \hat{\mathbf{r}}$, *the unit vector in the direction $\overline{OP}$.*

So $$r = \sqrt{(x^2+y^2+z^2)}.$$

$$\frac{\partial r}{\partial x} = \frac{x}{\sqrt{(x^2+y^2+z^2)}};\quad \frac{\partial r}{\partial y} = \frac{y}{\sqrt{(x^2+y^2+z^2)}};\quad \frac{\partial r}{\partial z} = \frac{z}{\sqrt{(x^2+y^2+z^2)}}.$$

$$\therefore\quad \text{grad}\,r = \frac{1}{r}(x\mathbf{i}+y\mathbf{j}+z\mathbf{k}) = \frac{\mathbf{r}}{r}$$

$$= \hat{\mathbf{r}},\quad \text{the unit vector in the direction } \overline{OP}.$$

Ex. 11 *If* $\mathbf{a}$ *is a vector function of position, prove that* div (curl $\mathbf{a}$) = 0.

The components A_x, A_y, A_z of curl $\mathbf{a}$ parallel to the coordinate axes are

$$A_x = \frac{\partial a_z}{\partial y}-\frac{\partial a_y}{\partial z};\quad A_y = \frac{\partial a_x}{\partial z}-\frac{\partial a_z}{\partial x};\quad A_z = \frac{\partial a_y}{\partial x}-\frac{\partial a_x}{\partial y}.$$

$$\therefore\quad \text{div}\,(\text{curl}\,\mathbf{a}) = \frac{\partial A_x}{\partial x}+\frac{\partial A_y}{\partial y}+\frac{\partial A_z}{\partial z}$$

$$= \frac{\partial^2 a_z}{\partial x\,\partial y}-\frac{\partial^2 a_y}{\partial x\,\partial z}+\frac{\partial^2 a_x}{\partial y\,\partial z}-\frac{\partial^2 a_z}{\partial y\,\partial x}+\frac{\partial^2 a_y}{\partial z\,\partial x}-\frac{\partial^2 a_x}{\partial z\,\partial y}$$

$$= 0,\quad \text{as } \frac{\partial^2 a_z}{\partial x\,\partial y} = \frac{\partial^2 a_z}{\partial y\,\partial x} \text{ etc.}$$

EXAMPLES 6b

1 If $\mathbf{u}(t_1, t_2)$ is a vector function of the scalar variables t_1, t_2 given by $\mathbf{u}(t_1, t_2) = 2(t_1+t_2)\mathbf{i}+2(t_1-t_2)\mathbf{j}+t_1t_2\mathbf{k}$, find $\mathbf{u}(2, 1)$ the value of $\mathbf{u}$ when $t_1 = 2$, $t_2 = 1$. Also find the value of $|\mathbf{u}(1, -1)|$.

2 Find $\dfrac{\partial \mathbf{a}}{\partial u}, \dfrac{\partial \mathbf{a}}{\partial v}, \dfrac{\partial \mathbf{a}}{\partial w}$ when (i) $\mathbf{a} = u^2\mathbf{i}+v^2\mathbf{j}+w^2\mathbf{k}$; (ii) $\mathbf{a} = uvw(\mathbf{i}+\mathbf{j}+\mathbf{k})$; (iii) $\mathbf{a} = v\sin w\mathbf{i}+w\sin u\mathbf{j}+u\sin v\mathbf{k}$; (iv) $\mathbf{a} = e^{vw}\mathbf{i}+e^{wu}\mathbf{j}+e^{uv}\mathbf{k}$.

3 If $u(\theta, \varphi) = c\cos\theta\cos\varphi\mathbf{i} + c\cos\theta\sin\varphi\mathbf{j} + c\sin\varphi\mathbf{k}$, where θ, φ are scalar parameters and c is a constant, find the values of (i) $\frac{\partial \mathbf{u}}{\partial \theta}$; (ii) $\frac{\partial \mathbf{u}}{\partial \varphi}$ when $\theta = \frac{1}{2}\pi$, $\varphi = \frac{1}{4}\pi$.

4 If $\mathbf{r}$ is the position vector with respect to the origin of the point with coordinates (x, y, z), show that $\frac{\partial \mathbf{r}}{\partial x} = \mathbf{i}$ and $\frac{\partial r}{\partial x} = \frac{x}{r}$, where r is the modulus of $\mathbf{r}$.

5 Verify that $\frac{\partial^2 \mathbf{u}}{\partial x\, \partial y} = \frac{\partial^2 \mathbf{u}}{\partial y\, \partial x}$ in the following cases: (i) $\mathbf{u} = y^3z^3\mathbf{i} + z^3x^3\mathbf{j} + x^3y^3\mathbf{k}$; (ii) $\mathbf{u} = y\sin z\mathbf{i} + z\sin x\mathbf{j} + x\sin y\mathbf{k}$; (iii) $\mathbf{u} = \sin(yz)\mathbf{i} + \sin(zx)\mathbf{j} + \sin(xy)\mathbf{k}$.

6 If $\mathbf{r}(u, v) = u\cos v\mathbf{i} + u\sin v\mathbf{j} + u^2\mathbf{k}$, show that $\frac{\partial \mathbf{r}}{\partial u} \cdot \frac{\partial \mathbf{r}}{\partial v} = 0$.

7 Find the values of $\frac{\partial \mathbf{u}}{\partial x}$ and $\frac{\partial \mathbf{u}}{\partial y}$ in the case where $\mathbf{u} = (x^2+y^2)^{-\frac{1}{2}}(x\mathbf{i}+y\mathbf{j})$.

8 The position vector of a point on a curve is given by $\mathbf{r} = u\cos v\mathbf{i} + u\sin v\mathbf{j} + cv\mathbf{k}$, where u, v are scalar parameters and c is a constant. Find the values of (i) $\frac{\partial \mathbf{r}}{\partial u}$; (ii) $\frac{\partial \mathbf{r}}{\partial v}$; (iii) $\frac{\partial^2 \mathbf{r}}{\partial u^2}$; (iv) $\frac{\partial^2 \mathbf{r}}{\partial u\, \partial v}$; (v) $\frac{\partial^2 \mathbf{r}}{\partial v^2}$; (vi) $\frac{\partial \mathbf{r}}{\partial u} \cdot \frac{\partial \mathbf{r}}{\partial v}$; (vii) $\frac{\partial \mathbf{r}}{\partial u} \wedge \frac{\partial \mathbf{r}}{\partial v}$.

9 Obtain the vector gradients of the following scalar functions of the coordinates x, y, z of a point in space: (i) $x+y+z$; (ii) $x^2+y^2+z^2$; (iii) $y^2z^2 + x^2y^2 + z^2x^2$.

10 If $\mathbf{r}$ is the position vector with respect to the origin of the point (x, y, z), prove (i) $\operatorname{div}\mathbf{r} = 3$; (ii) $\operatorname{curl}\mathbf{r} = 0$.

11 If φ_1, φ_2 are two scalar functions of position show that (i) $\operatorname{grad}(\varphi_1+\varphi_2) = \operatorname{grad}\varphi_1 + \operatorname{grad}\varphi_2$; (ii) $\operatorname{grad}(\varphi_1\varphi_2) = \varphi_1\operatorname{grad}\varphi_2 + \varphi_2\operatorname{grad}\varphi_1$.

12 If $\mathbf{u}_1$, $\mathbf{u}_2$ are two vector functions of position show that (i) $\operatorname{div}(\mathbf{u}_1+\mathbf{u}_2) = \operatorname{div}\mathbf{u}_1 + \operatorname{div}\mathbf{u}_2$; (ii) $\operatorname{curl}(\mathbf{u}_1+\mathbf{u}_2) = \operatorname{curl}\mathbf{u}_1 + \operatorname{curl}\mathbf{u}_2$.

13 Obtain (i) the divergence; (ii) the curl of the vector function of position $\sin y\mathbf{i} + x(1+\cos y)\mathbf{j}$.

14 If $\mathbf{r}$ is the position vector of the point (x, y, z) with respect to the origin prove that $\nabla\left(\frac{1}{r}\right) = -\frac{1}{r^3}\mathbf{r}$, where r is the modulus of $\mathbf{r}$.

15 With the notation of the previous example show that $\nabla \cdot (\mathbf{r}/r^3) = 0$.

16 Find a function of position $\varphi(x, y, z)$, such that $\operatorname{grad}\varphi = \mathbf{r}$, the position vector of the point (x, y, z) with respect to the origin.

17 If $\mathbf{a}$ is a constant vector and $\mathbf{r}$ is the position vector of the point (x, y, z) with respect to the origin, show that (i) $\operatorname{grad}(\mathbf{a}\cdot\mathbf{r}) = \mathbf{a}$; (ii) $\operatorname{div}(\mathbf{a}\wedge\mathbf{r}) = 0$.

18 Defining the operator ∇^2 as $\nabla \cdot \nabla$ where $\nabla = \mathbf{i}\frac{\partial}{\partial x} + \mathbf{j}\frac{\partial}{\partial y} + \mathbf{k}\frac{\partial}{\partial z}$, show that if φ is a scalar function of position, $\nabla^2\varphi$ is equal to $\frac{\partial^2\varphi}{\partial x^2} + \frac{\partial^2\varphi}{\partial y^2} + \frac{\partial^2\varphi}{\partial z^2}$.

19 Find $\nabla^2\varphi$ in the case where $\varphi = 1/\sqrt{(x^2+y^2+z^2)}$.

20 Verify that $\operatorname{curl}(\operatorname{grad}\varphi) = 0$, where φ is a scalar function of position.

21 If $\mathbf{u} = \mathbf{r}(\mathbf{a} \cdot \mathbf{r})$ where $\mathbf{a}$ is a constant vector and $\mathbf{r}$ is the position vector of the point (x, y, z) with respect to the origin, prove that (i) $\operatorname{div} \mathbf{u} = 4(\mathbf{a} \cdot \mathbf{r})$; (ii) $\operatorname{curl} \mathbf{u} = \mathbf{a} \wedge \mathbf{r}$.

22 Show that (i) $\operatorname{div}(u\mathbf{v}) = \nabla u \cdot \mathbf{v} + u \operatorname{div} \mathbf{v}$; (ii) $\operatorname{curl}(u\mathbf{v}) = \nabla u \wedge \mathbf{v} + u \operatorname{curl} \mathbf{v}$, where u, $\mathbf{v}$ are respectively scalar and vector functions of position.

23 If r is the modulus of $\mathbf{r}$, the position vector of the point (x, y, z) with respect to the origin, show that (i) $\nabla r^m = m r^{m-2}\mathbf{r}$; (ii) $\nabla^2 r^m = m \operatorname{div}(r^{m-2}\mathbf{r}) = m(m+1)r^{m-2}$, using the result in example 22(i) and that in example 10(i).

VII

RATES OF CHANGE OF VECTORS AND APPLICATIONS IN KINEMATICS

Rate of change of a vector The rate of change of a vector $\mathbf{u}$ which is a function of the time t is the derivative $\dfrac{d\mathbf{u}}{dt}$ or $\dot{\mathbf{u}}$. So, for example, if $\mathbf{u} = (2t^2 - t^3)\mathbf{i} + (t^3 - t)\mathbf{j} + 2\mathbf{k}$, where t is the time, the rate of change of $\mathbf{u}$ is given by

$$\dot{\mathbf{u}} = (4t - 3t^2)\mathbf{i} + (3t^2 - 1)\mathbf{j}.$$

Ex. 1 *If* $\mathbf{H} = \mathbf{r} \wedge (m\dot{\mathbf{r}})$, *where m is a constant, show that the rate of change of* $\mathbf{H}$ *is equal to* $\mathbf{r} \wedge (m\ddot{\mathbf{r}})$.

As $\mathbf{H} = \mathbf{r} \wedge (m\dot{\mathbf{r}})$, the rate of change of $\mathbf{H}$ is given by

$$\dot{\mathbf{H}} = \frac{d}{dt}[\mathbf{r} \wedge (m\dot{\mathbf{r}})]$$

$$= \dot{\mathbf{r}} \wedge (m\dot{\mathbf{r}}) + \mathbf{r} \wedge (m\ddot{\mathbf{r}}),$$

where $\ddot{\mathbf{r}}$ is the second derivative of $\mathbf{r}$ with respect to the time t.

$$\therefore \quad \dot{\mathbf{H}} = \mathbf{r} \wedge (m\ddot{\mathbf{r}}), \quad \text{as} \quad \dot{\mathbf{r}} \wedge (m\dot{\mathbf{r}}) = m\dot{\mathbf{r}} \wedge \dot{\mathbf{r}} = 0.$$

Rate of change of a two-dimensional unit vector If $\hat{\mathbf{r}}$ is a two-dimensional unit vector whose direction is a function of the time, its values $\hat{\mathbf{r}}_1, \hat{\mathbf{r}}_2, \hat{\mathbf{r}}_3, \ldots$ at times $t_1, t_2, t_3, \ldots$ can be represented by coplanar vectors $\overline{OP_1}, \overline{OP_2}, \overline{OP_3}, \ldots$ all of unit magnitude (Fig. 55).

Now suppose at time t the unit vector $\hat{\mathbf{r}}$ is represented by the vector $\overline{OP}$ which makes an angle θ radians with a fixed direction $\overline{OX}$ in in the plane of $\hat{\mathbf{r}}$ (Fig. 56). Let t increase by a small amount δt and let the corresponding increases in $\hat{\mathbf{r}}$ and θ be $\delta\hat{\mathbf{r}}$, $\delta\theta$ respectively. Then at time $t + \delta t$, we will have a unit vector $\hat{\mathbf{r}} + \delta\hat{\mathbf{r}}$ represented by a vector $\overline{OP'}$ which makes an angle $\theta + \delta\theta$ with $\overline{OX}$. Clearly $\delta\hat{\mathbf{r}}$ is represented by the vector $\overline{PP'}$.

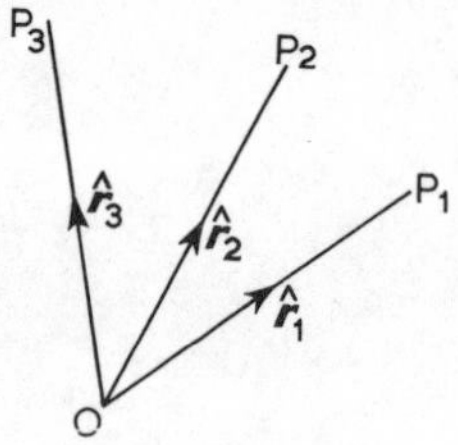

FIG. 55.

So the vector $\dfrac{\delta\hat{\mathbf{r}}}{\delta t}$ will have the direction of $\overline{PP'}$; this direction in the

limit as $\delta t \to 0$, i.e. $P' \to P$, becomes perpendicular to $\overline{OP}$ in the direction of θ increasing, as triangle OPP' is isosceles. Consequently the vector $\frac{d\hat{\mathbf{r}}}{dt}$ is perpendicular to $\overline{OP}$ in the direction of θ increasing.

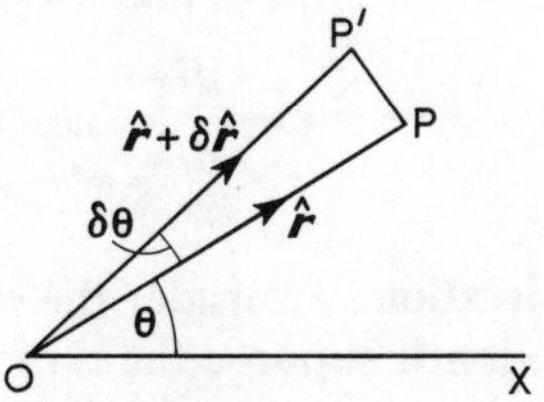

FIG. 56.

Also as angle $P'OP = \delta\theta$ and $OP = OP' = 1$, it follows that the length $PP' \simeq \delta\theta$; i.e. $|\delta\hat{\mathbf{r}}| \simeq \delta\theta$.

$$\therefore \quad \left|\frac{d\hat{\mathbf{r}}}{dt}\right| = \lim_{\delta t\to 0}\frac{|\delta\hat{\mathbf{r}}|}{\delta t} = \lim_{\delta t\to 0}\frac{\delta\theta}{\delta t} = \frac{d\theta}{dt}.$$

So the rate of change of the two-dimensional unit vector $\hat{\mathbf{r}}$, *is given by*

$$\frac{d\hat{\mathbf{r}}}{dt} = \frac{d\theta}{dt}\hat{\mathbf{n}} = \omega\hat{\mathbf{n}},$$

where ω *is the angular velocity of* $\hat{\mathbf{r}}$ *measured in radians per unit time, and* $\hat{\mathbf{n}}$ *is a unit vector normal to* $\hat{\mathbf{r}}$ *in the direction of rotation of* $\hat{\mathbf{r}}$.

Ex. 2 *Perpendicular axes OP, OQ are rotating in their own plane in the direction* $\overline{OP}$ *to* $\overline{OQ}$ *with an angular velocity* ω. *If* $\hat{\mathbf{p}}$, $\hat{\mathbf{q}}$ *are unit vectors in the directions* $\overline{OP}$, $\overline{OQ}$, *show that the rate of change of* $\hat{\mathbf{p}}$ *is equal to* $\omega\hat{\mathbf{q}}$ *and find the rate of change of* $\hat{\mathbf{q}}$.

As $\hat{\mathbf{p}}$ is a two-dimensional unit vector rotating at an angular velocity ω, its rate of change is a vector of magnitude ω in a direction normal to $\hat{\mathbf{p}}$ in the sense of its rotation, i.e. in the direction of $\hat{\mathbf{q}}$. So the rate of change of $\hat{\mathbf{p}}$ is equal to $\omega\hat{\mathbf{q}}$.

Similarly, the rate of change of $\hat{\mathbf{q}}$ being a vector of magnitude ω in the direction of $-\hat{\mathbf{p}}$, is equal to $-\omega\hat{\mathbf{p}}$.

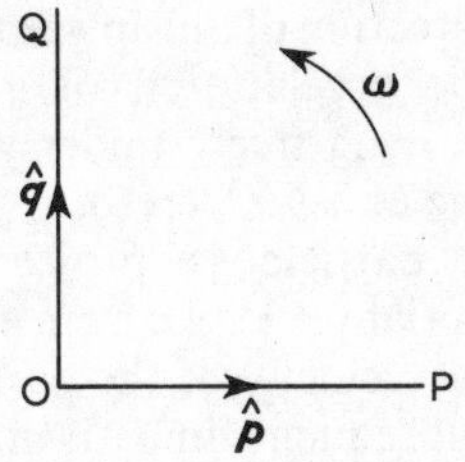

FIG. 57.

Velocity and acceleration Suppose at time t, the position vector of a moving point P relative to a fixed origin O is $\mathbf{r}$. Then the instantaneous velocity $\mathbf{v}$ of P at time t is equal to the rate of change of $\mathbf{r}$ with respect to t.

So
$$\mathbf{v} = \frac{d\mathbf{r}}{dt} \quad \text{or} \quad \dot{\mathbf{r}}.$$

Also as the instantaneous acceleration **a** of P is equal to the rate of change of **v** with respect to t, it follows that

$$\mathbf{a} = \frac{d\mathbf{v}}{dt} \quad \text{i.e.} \quad \dot{\mathbf{v}} = \frac{d^2\mathbf{r}}{dt^2} \quad \text{i.e.} \quad \ddot{\mathbf{r}}.$$

Case of constant acceleration Consider the case of a point moving with a constant acceleration **f**; suppose the initial velocity of the point is **u** and let the initial position of the point be taken as the origin.

Then as $\dot{\mathbf{v}} = \mathbf{f}$, $\mathbf{v} = \mathbf{f}t+\mathbf{c}$ where **c** is an arbitrary constant vector.

But when $t = 0$, $\mathbf{v} = \mathbf{u}$, therefore $\mathbf{c} = \mathbf{u}$.

Hence
$$\mathbf{v} = \mathbf{u}+\mathbf{f}t. \qquad \text{(i)}$$

Writing **v** as $\dot{\mathbf{r}}$, where **r** is the position vector of the point with respect to the origin at time t, and integrating,

$$\mathbf{r} = \mathbf{u}t+\tfrac{1}{2}\mathbf{f}t^2+\mathbf{d},$$

where the constant of integration **d** is zero as $\mathbf{r} = 0$ when $t = 0$.

So
$$\mathbf{r} = \mathbf{u}t+\tfrac{1}{2}\mathbf{f}t^2. \qquad \text{(ii)}$$

Also
$$2\mathbf{f}\,.\,\mathbf{r} = 2t\mathbf{f}\,.\,\mathbf{u}+\mathbf{f}^2t^2,$$
$$= (\mathbf{u}+\mathbf{f}t)^2-\mathbf{u}^2 = \mathbf{v}^2-\mathbf{u}^2.$$

Hence
$$\mathbf{v}^2 = \mathbf{u}^2+2\mathbf{f}\,.\,\mathbf{r}. \qquad \text{(iii)}$$

The similarity of the results (i), (ii), (iii) to those applicable in the case of constantly accelerated motion in a straight line will be noted.

Motion of a projectile under gravity If $\hat{\mathbf{d}}$ is a unit vector in the direction of the upward vertical, the acceleration of a particle moving freely under gravity is the constant vector $-g\hat{\mathbf{d}}$. So if a particle is projected with initial velocity **u** from a point O, the velocity of the particle at a subsequent time t is given by

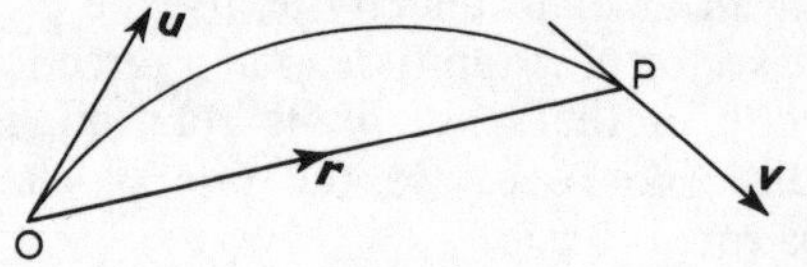

FIG. 58.

$$\mathbf{v} = \mathbf{u}-gt\hat{\mathbf{d}},$$

and the position vector $\overline{OP}$, or **r**, of P relative to O is given by

$$\mathbf{r} = \mathbf{u}t-\tfrac{1}{2}gt^2\hat{\mathbf{d}}.$$

Ex. 3 *Show that the relative velocity of two particles projected simultaneously under gravity remains constant.*

Using suffixes 1, 2 for the two particles; at time t from the start

$$\mathbf{v}_1 = \mathbf{u}_1 - gt\hat{\mathbf{d}}; \quad \mathbf{v}_2 = \mathbf{u}_2 - gt\hat{\mathbf{d}}.$$

$$\therefore \quad \text{the relative velocity } \mathbf{v}_2 - \mathbf{v}_1 = \mathbf{u}_2 - \mathbf{u}_1 = \text{constant.}$$

Ex. 4 *The direction of motion of a projectile at a point P of its path is normal to the line joining the point of projection to P. Show that, in general, there are two possible positions of P.*

With the notation used previously, $\mathbf{v}$ and $\mathbf{r}$ are perpendicular.

$$\therefore \quad (\mathbf{u} - gt\hat{\mathbf{d}}) \cdot (\mathbf{u}t - \tfrac{1}{2}gt^2\hat{\mathbf{d}}) = 0.$$

Removing the factor t as the solution $t = 0$ does not apply and expanding gives $\quad \mathbf{u}^2 - \frac{3}{2}gt\mathbf{u} \cdot \hat{\mathbf{d}} + \frac{1}{2}g^2t^2 = 0$—a quadratic equation in t.

Hence, in general, there are two possible points P on the trajectory.

Circular motion Suppose that a point P is describing a circle centre O, radius r and that at time t the angular velocity of OP is ω radians per unit time.

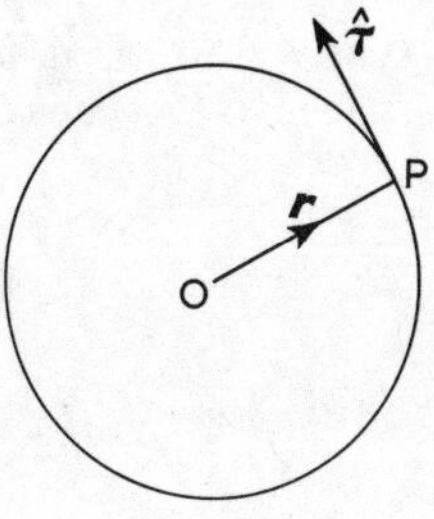

FIG. 59.

Then $\mathbf{r}$, the position vector of P relative to O, is given by

$$\mathbf{r} = r\hat{\mathbf{r}},$$

where $\hat{\mathbf{r}}$ is a unit vector in the direction $\overline{OP}$.

So the velocity of P,

$$\mathbf{v} = \dot{\mathbf{r}} = r\dot{\hat{\mathbf{r}}}, \quad \text{as } \dot{r} = 0.$$

But $\dot{\hat{\mathbf{r}}} = \omega\hat{\boldsymbol{\tau}}$, where $\hat{\boldsymbol{\tau}}$ is a unit vector normal to $\mathbf{r}$ and in the direction of its rotation; i.e. $\hat{\boldsymbol{\tau}}$ is a unit vector along the tangent at P.

$$\therefore \quad \mathbf{v} = r\omega\hat{\boldsymbol{\tau}},$$

showing that *the velocity of P is along the tangent and of magnitude $r\omega$.*

The acceleration of P, $\quad \dot{\mathbf{v}} = \dfrac{d}{dt}(r\omega\hat{\boldsymbol{\tau}}),$

$$= r\dot{\omega}\hat{\boldsymbol{\tau}} + r\omega\dot{\hat{\boldsymbol{\tau}}}.$$

But $\dot{\hat{\boldsymbol{\tau}}} = -\omega\hat{\mathbf{r}}$, since $\hat{\boldsymbol{\tau}}$ is a two-dimensional unit vector.

So $$\dot{\mathbf{v}} = r\dot{\omega}\hat{\boldsymbol{\tau}} - r\omega^2\hat{\mathbf{r}}.$$

Hence the acceleration of P has two components, $r\dot{\omega}$ along the tangent and $r\omega^2$ along the inward radius.

Motion of a particle along a plane curve When a particle P is moving along a plane curve its motion can be considered in three ways by taking component velocities and accelerations in the directions of

(i) rectangular axes;
(ii) the tangent and inward normal to the curve at P;
(iii) the position vector $\overline{OP}$ and the normal to it in the direction of the rotation of $\overline{OP}$.

In case (i), we speak of rectangular components of velocity and acceleration, in case (ii) of tangential and normal components and in case (iii) of radial and transverse components. All three cases will now be dealt with by vector methods.

Rectangular components of velocity and acceleration Consider a particle P moving along a plane curve and let the coordinates of P at time t be (x, y). Then $\mathbf{r}$, the position vector of P relative to the origin O is given by

$$\mathbf{r} = x\mathbf{i}+y\mathbf{j}.$$

$$\therefore \quad \text{velocity } \dot{\mathbf{r}} = \dot{x}\mathbf{i}+\dot{y}\mathbf{j} \quad \text{and} \quad \text{acceleration } \ddot{\mathbf{r}} = \ddot{x}\mathbf{i}+\ddot{y}\mathbf{j}.$$

Hence P has velocity components $\dot{x}$, $\dot{y}$ and acceleration components $\ddot{x}$, $\ddot{y}$ parallel to the coordinate axes.

Ex. 5 *The coordinates of a moving point P at time t are $(a\cos\omega t, b\sin\omega t)$ where a, b, ω are constants. Prove that the acceleration of P is $-\omega^2\overline{OP}$, where O is the origin.*

$$\overline{OP} = \mathbf{r} = a\cos\omega t\mathbf{i}+b\sin\omega t\mathbf{j}.$$

$$\begin{aligned}\therefore \quad \text{acceleration } \ddot{\mathbf{r}} &= -a\omega^2\cos\omega t\mathbf{i}-b\omega^2\sin\omega t\mathbf{j}\\ &= -\omega^2(a\cos\omega t\mathbf{i}+b\sin\omega t\mathbf{j})\\ &= -\omega^2\overline{OP}.\end{aligned}$$

Tangential and normal components of velocity and acceleration Consider a particle moving along a plane curve and let P be its position at at time t, where $\overline{OP} = \mathbf{r}$ and arc length $AP = s$ (Fig. 60). Then the velocity of the particle at P

$$= \dot{\mathbf{r}} = \frac{d\mathbf{r}}{ds}\frac{ds}{dt} = \dot{s}\frac{d\mathbf{r}}{ds}.$$

To evaluate $\dfrac{d\mathbf{r}}{ds}$, let the particle move from P to a neighbouring point Q on the curve in the time interval δt. Then $\overline{OQ} = \mathbf{r}+\delta\mathbf{r}$; $\overline{PQ} = \delta\mathbf{r}$ and arc $PQ = \delta s$.

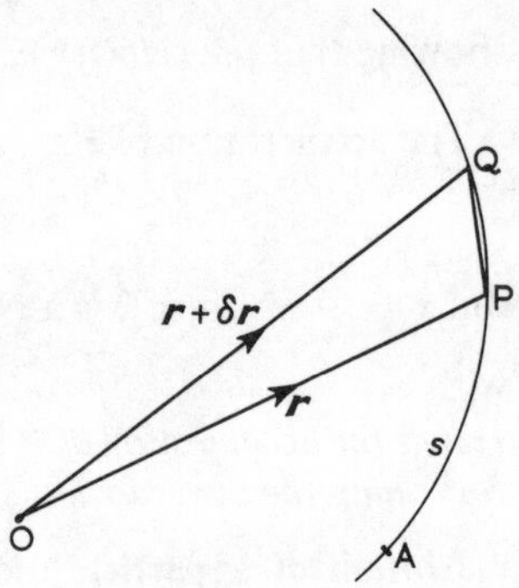

FIG. 60.

So $\left|\frac{\delta\mathbf{r}}{\delta s}\right|$, which equals the ratio of the lengths of chord PQ and arc PQ, tends to 1 as $Q \to P$, i.e. as $\delta s \to 0$.

$$\therefore \quad \left|\frac{d\mathbf{r}}{ds}\right| = 1.$$

Also the direction of $\frac{\delta\mathbf{r}}{\delta s}$ is that of $\overline{PQ}$ which tends in the limit as $\delta s \to 0$ to the direction of the tangent to the curve at P in the sense of s increasing.

$$\therefore \quad \frac{d\mathbf{r}}{ds} = \hat{\boldsymbol{\tau}},$$

where $\hat{\boldsymbol{\tau}}$ is a unit vector along the tangent at P in the sense of s increasing.

Hence $\dot{\mathbf{r}} = \dot{s}\hat{\boldsymbol{\tau}}$ or $v\hat{\boldsymbol{\tau}}$, where v is the speed of the particle at time t.

$\therefore$ *at P, the particle has a velocity of magnitude v in the direction of the tangent to the curve.*

The acceleration of the particle at $P = \frac{d}{dt}(v\hat{\boldsymbol{\tau}})$

$$= \dot{v}\hat{\boldsymbol{\tau}} + v\dot{\hat{\boldsymbol{\tau}}}.$$

But $\dot{\hat{\boldsymbol{\tau}}} = \dot{\psi}\hat{\mathbf{n}}$, where $\hat{\mathbf{n}}$ is a unit vector along the inward normal to the curve at P and ψ is the angle the tangent at P makes with a fixed direction (Fig. 61).

So the acceleration of the particle

at $P \qquad = \dot{v}\hat{\boldsymbol{\tau}} + v\dot{\psi}\hat{\mathbf{n}}.$

But

$$v\dot{\psi} = v\frac{d\psi}{ds}\frac{ds}{dt} = \frac{v^2}{\rho},$$

where $\qquad \rho = \frac{ds}{d\psi}$

is the radius of curvature of the curve at P.

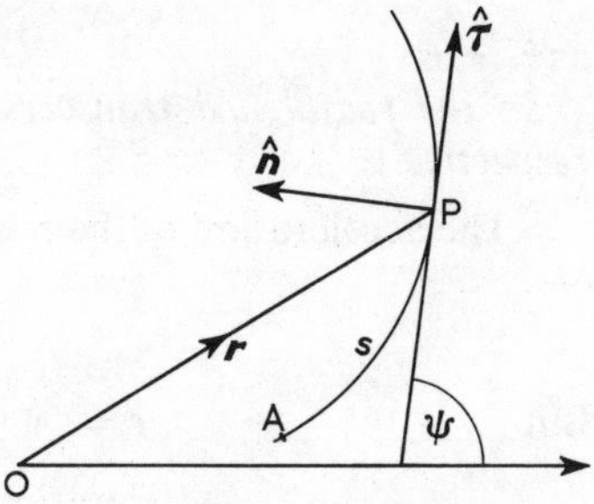

FIG. 61.

Hence the acceleration at $P = \dot{v}\hat{\boldsymbol{\tau}} + \frac{v^2}{\rho}\hat{\mathbf{n}}$, and consequently *the acceleration components of the particle at P are* $\dot{v}$ *or* $v\frac{dv}{ds}$ *along the tangent and* v^2/ρ *along the inward normal.*

Ex. 6 *A particle describes the curve $s = 4a \sin \psi$ in such a way that the rate of change of ψ is constant and equal to ω. Show that the direction of the acceleration of the particle at any point P on the curve makes an angle ψ with the inward normal to the curve at P.*

$$\text{Acceleration of the particle} = \dot{v}\hat{\mathbf{t}} + v\dot{\psi}\hat{\mathbf{n}}.$$

But $v = \dot{s} = 4a\omega \cos \psi$ and $\dot{v} = -4a\omega^2 \sin \psi$, as $\dot{\psi} = \omega$.

$$\therefore \quad \text{acceleration} = -4a\omega^2 \sin \psi\hat{\mathbf{t}} + 4a\omega^2 \cos \psi\hat{\mathbf{n}}.$$

Clearly this is a vector of magnitude $4a\omega^2$ making an angle ψ with the vector $\hat{\mathbf{n}}$.

Radial and transverse components of velocity and acceleration Consider a particle moving along a plane curve and let P be its position at time t where the radius vector $\overline{OP}$ $(=\mathbf{r})$ makes an angle θ with a direction fixed in the plane of the curve.

Let $\hat{\mathbf{r}}$, $\hat{\mathbf{s}}$ be unit vectors in the direction $\overline{OP}$ and in the direction normal to $\overline{OP}$ in the sense of θ increasing (Fig. 62). Then

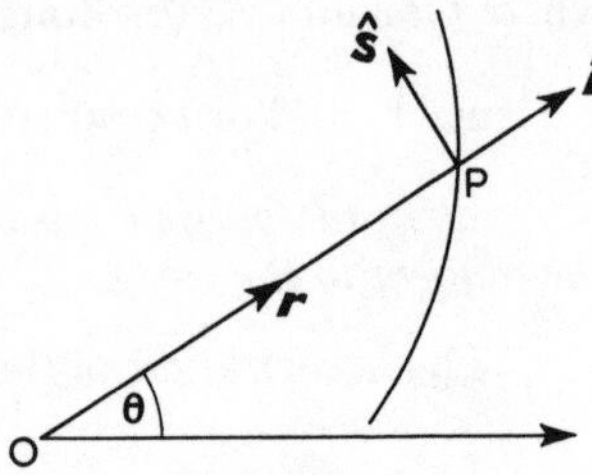

FIG. 62.

$$\overline{OP} = \mathbf{r} = r\hat{\mathbf{r}} \quad \text{where} \quad r = OP.$$

$$\therefore \quad \text{the velocity of the particle at } P, \quad \dot{\mathbf{r}} = \dot{r}\hat{\mathbf{r}} + r\dot{\hat{\mathbf{r}}} = \dot{r}\hat{\mathbf{r}} + r\dot{\theta}\hat{\mathbf{s}},$$

as $\dot{\hat{\mathbf{r}}} = \dot{\theta}\hat{\mathbf{s}}$.

So the radial and transverse components of velocity are $\dot{r}$ and $r\dot{\theta}$ respectively.

$$\text{The acceleration of the particle at } P = \frac{d}{dt}(\dot{r}\hat{\mathbf{r}} + r\dot{\theta}\hat{\mathbf{s}})$$

$$= \ddot{r}\hat{\mathbf{r}} + \dot{r}\dot{\hat{\mathbf{r}}} + \dot{r}\dot{\theta}\hat{\mathbf{s}} + r\ddot{\theta}\hat{\mathbf{s}} + r\dot{\theta}\dot{\hat{\mathbf{s}}}.$$

But $\qquad \dot{\hat{\mathbf{r}}} = \dot{\theta}\hat{\mathbf{s}} \quad \text{and} \quad \dot{\hat{\mathbf{s}}} = -\dot{\theta}\hat{\mathbf{r}}.$

$$\therefore \quad \text{acceleration} = (\ddot{r} - r\dot{\theta}^2)\hat{\mathbf{r}} + (r\ddot{\theta} + 2\dot{r}\dot{\theta})\hat{\mathbf{s}}.$$

So the radial and transverse components of acceleration are $\ddot{r} - r\dot{\theta}^2$ and $r\ddot{\theta} + 2\dot{r}\dot{\theta}$ respectively.

In applications of this result the term $r\ddot{\theta} + 2\dot{r}\dot{\theta}$ can conveniently be expressed in the form $\dfrac{1}{r}\dfrac{d}{dt}(r^2\dot{\theta})$.

Ex. 7 *A particle moves in a plane so that its velocity at any instant is the sum of a velocity of constant magnitude V in a direction perpendicular* *to the radius vector joining the origin to the particle and a velocity of constant magnitude U in a fixed direction. Prove that the acceleration of the particle is towards the origin.*

Suppose $\overline{OP}$ makes an angle θ with the fixed direction of **U** and let $\hat{\mathbf{r}}$, $\hat{\mathbf{s}}$ be unit vectors along and perpendicular to $\overline{OP}$, the latter in the direction of θ increasing. Then resolving **V** and **U** in the directions of $\hat{\mathbf{r}}$, $\hat{\mathbf{s}}$, it follows that the velocity of P is given by

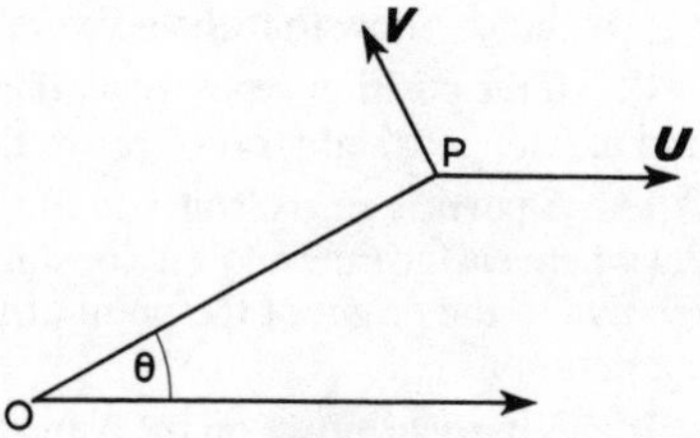

FIG. 63.

$$\mathbf{v} = U\cos\theta\hat{\mathbf{r}} + (V - U\sin\theta)\hat{\mathbf{s}}.$$

$$\therefore \quad \text{acceleration } \dot{\mathbf{v}} = -U\sin\theta\dot{\theta}\hat{\mathbf{r}} + U\cos\theta(\dot{\theta}\hat{\mathbf{s}}) - U\cos\theta\dot{\theta}\hat{\mathbf{s}} + (V - U\sin\theta)(-\dot{\theta}\hat{\mathbf{r}})$$

$$= -V\dot{\theta}\hat{\mathbf{r}}.$$

So the acceleration of P is in the direction of $-\hat{\mathbf{r}}$, i.e. the direction $\overline{PO}$.

EXAMPLES 7a

1 Find the rate of change of the vector **u** in each of the following cases: (i) $\mathbf{u} = t^2\mathbf{i} + t^3\mathbf{j}$; (ii) $\mathbf{u} = 2t\mathbf{i} + (3t^2 - 1)\mathbf{j} + t^4\mathbf{k}$; (iii) $\mathbf{u} = e^t\mathbf{i} + e^{-t}\mathbf{j} + t\mathbf{k}$; (iv) $\mathbf{u} = \sin t\mathbf{i} + \cos t\mathbf{j} + \sin 2t\mathbf{k}$, t being the time.

2 If $\mathbf{F} = a\cos\omega t\mathbf{i} + b\sin\omega t\mathbf{j}$ where a, b, ω are constants, find the rate of change of **F** when (i) $t = 0$; (ii) $t = \pi/2\omega$.

3 A vector **v** is a function of the time t and is given by $\mathbf{v} = 2\cos 2t\mathbf{i} - 3\sin 3t\mathbf{j} + e^t\mathbf{k}$. Find the modulus of the rate of increase of **v** when $t = 0$.

4 Given that $\mathbf{r} = \mathbf{i} + t\mathbf{j} + t^2\mathbf{k}$, $\mathbf{P} = (t^2 - 1)\mathbf{i} + t^2\mathbf{j} + \mathbf{k}$, find the rate of change of $\mathbf{r} \wedge \mathbf{P}$ when $t = 1$.

5 If $\mathbf{r} = 2\cos t\mathbf{i} + 3\sin t\mathbf{j} + \sin 2t\mathbf{k}$, find an expression for the rate of change of the product $\mathbf{r} \wedge \dot{\mathbf{r}}$.

6 The position vector of a moving point with respect to the origin is **r**. Find the velocity and acceleration of the point at time t in each of the following cases: (i) $\mathbf{r} = t^2\mathbf{i} + t^3\mathbf{j} + t^4\mathbf{k}$; (ii) $\mathbf{r} = \sin t\mathbf{i} + \cos t\mathbf{j} + t\mathbf{k}$; (iii) $\mathbf{r} = \mathbf{a}e^{-t}$, where **a** is a constant vector; (iv) $\mathbf{r} = \mathbf{a}\sin 2t + \mathbf{b}\cos 2t$, where **a**, **b** are constant vectors.

7 At time t a particle has a velocity equal to $\mathbf{a}t^2 + \mathbf{b}t + \mathbf{c}$ where **a**, **b**, **c** are constant vectors. Show that the rate of increase of the acceleration is constant.

8 A particle P starts from rest at O and moves with a constant acceleration of $2\mathbf{f}$, show that at time t, $\overline{OP} = \mathbf{f}t^2$.

9 The position vector of a particle at time t is $(4t^2 - 1)\mathbf{i} + t^3\mathbf{j}$. Find the magnitude and direction of its acceleration when $t = 2$.

10 Find the magnitudes of the component velocities in the directions of the axes for a moving point whose position vectors at time t relative to the origin are given by (i) $\mathbf{r} = t\mathbf{i}+t^2\mathbf{j}$; (ii) $\mathbf{r} = e^t\mathbf{i}+e^{-t}\mathbf{j}$; (iii) $\mathbf{r} = \sin \omega t\mathbf{i} - \cos \omega t\mathbf{j}$, where ω is a constant.

11 The coordinates of a moving point are $(at^2, 2at)$ where a is a constant and t is the time. Show that the acceleration of the point is parallel to the axis of x.

12 If the position vector of a point is given by $\mathbf{r} = \mathbf{u}t+\frac{1}{2}\mathbf{f}t^2$ where t is the time and $\mathbf{u}$, $\mathbf{f}$ are constant vectors, prove that the acceleration of the point is constant.

13 A particle starts from rest at the origin and moves with an acceleration of $2t\mathbf{a}$ where t is the time and $\mathbf{a}$ is constant. If $\mathbf{v}$, $\mathbf{r}$ are the velocity and position vector relative to the origin of the point at time t, show that $2\mathbf{v}^2 = 3\mathbf{r}\,.\,\mathbf{f}$, where $\mathbf{f}$ is the acceleration.

14 A particle moves on the plane curve $r = a \sin \theta$ such that the rate of change of θ is constant and equal to ω. Find the radial and transverse components of (i) its velocity; (ii) its acceleration when $\theta = 0$.

15 Find the radial and transverse components of the acceleration of a particle which moves on the curve $r\theta = a$, where $\theta = \frac{1}{2}t$ and t is the time.

16 If $\mathbf{a}$, $\mathbf{b}$ are constant vectors and t is the time, show that the point whose position vector is given by $\mathbf{r} = e^{nt}\mathbf{a}+e^{-nt}\mathbf{b}$ where n is constant, has an acceleration proportional to $\mathbf{r}$.

17 If the angular velocity of a particle about a fixed origin in its plane is constant, prove that the transverse component of its acceleration is proportional to the radial component of its velocity.

18 Unit vectors $\hat{\mathbf{a}}$, $\hat{\mathbf{b}}$ are perpendicular to each other and are rotating in their own plane at a constant angular velocity ω in the sense $\hat{\mathbf{a}}$ to $\hat{\mathbf{b}}$. Show that $\dot{\hat{\mathbf{a}}} = \omega\hat{\mathbf{b}}$ and $\ddot{\hat{\mathbf{a}}} = -\omega^2\hat{\mathbf{a}}$.

19 A particle is projected in a vertical plane with a velocity of magnitude $\sqrt{(2ga)}$ of which the vertical component is of magnitude u. If $\mathbf{v}$ is the velocity of projection and $\hat{\mathbf{d}}$ a unit vector in the upward vertical direction show that (i) $u = \mathbf{v}\,.\,\hat{\mathbf{d}}$; (ii) the direction of motion of the particle is perpendicular to its direction of projection after a time $2a/u$.

20 A particle moving in a plane has radial and transverse components of velocity equal to λr^2, $\mu\theta^2$ respectively where λ, μ are constants. Find the radial and transverse components of its acceleration in terms of r, θ the polar coordinates of its instantaneous position.

21 The acceleration of a moving point is $-cu\mathbf{i}-(g+cv)\mathbf{j}$ where c, g are constants and u, v are the magnitudes of the component velocities of the point parallel to the axes at time t. Show that $\dot{u} = -cu$, $\dot{v} = -(g+cv)$ and by solving these equations to give u and v in terms of t, deduce that the acceleration of the point is in a fixed direction.

22 A particle moves on the curve $r = ae^{\theta \cot \alpha}$, a and α being constants, such that the radius vector has a constant angular velocity ω. Show that the acceleration of the particle makes a constant angle 2α with the radius vector and is of magnitude v^2/r where v is the speed of the particle and r its distance from the origin.

23 The coordinates of a moving point are $x = a(\cos \theta+\theta \sin \theta)$, $y = a(\sin \theta - \theta \cos \theta)$, where θ increases at a uniform rate ω. Prove that the point has a velocity of magnitude $a\theta\omega$ and find its direction.

24 A particle moves in a plane with an acceleration $\mathbf{f}$ given by $\mathbf{f} = c\mathbf{V}+a\mathbf{i}$ where $\mathbf{V}$ is its velocity, $\mathbf{i}$ is a unit vector parallel to the axis of x and c and a are constants. If u, v are the components of the speed parallel to the axes and φ is the angle which the direction of $\mathbf{f}$ makes with the axis of x, show that $\tan\varphi = \dot{v}/\dot{u} = cv/(cu+a)$. Deduce by integration that $cv = A(cu+a)$ where A is a constant, and hence that φ is constant.

25 A rod AB is in motion with its ends A, B constrained to move on rectangular axes OX, OY respectively. If A moves towards O with constant velocity, prove that the acceleration of any point of the rod is perpendicular to OX and inversely proportional to the cube of its distance from it.

26 A point P moves in a circle of radius a such that its angular velocity about a point O on the circumference is constant and equal to ω. By using the polar equation of the circle with respect to O as origin, show that the acceleration of P has a constant magnitude of $4a\omega^2$.

27 Two particles are simultaneously projected under gravity one from O with a speed v_1 in the direction $\overline{OA}$ and the other from A with a speed v_2 in the direction $\overline{AO}$. Show that the relative velocity of the particles in the subsequent motion is constant and that the particles collide after a time $OA/(v_1+v_2)$.

28 In terms of unit vectors $\mathbf{i}$, $\mathbf{j}$ along rectangular axes OX, OY, the position vector of a point is given by $\mathbf{r} = x\mathbf{i}+y\mathbf{j}$. If the axes are rotating with constant angular velocity ω in a positive sense, prove that the velocity $\dot{\mathbf{r}}$ of the point is $(\dot{x}-y\omega)\mathbf{i}+(\dot{y}+x\omega)\mathbf{j}$ and obtain an expression for its acceleration.

29 A particle is projected from the origin O with velocity $\mathbf{u}$ and moves under a uniform acceleration $\mathbf{f}$, show that its position vector at time t is given by $\mathbf{r} = \mathbf{u}t+\frac{1}{2}\mathbf{f}t^2$. If three particles are projected simultaneously from O with velocities $\mathbf{u}_1$, $\mathbf{u}_2$, $\mathbf{u}_3$ and move in a plane under the uniform acceleration $\mathbf{f}$, prove that the area of the triangle which they form at time t is proportional to t^2.

30 A particle projected under gravity from a point O is at a point P after time t. If $\mathbf{r}$ is the position vector $\overline{OP}$, $\mathbf{u}$ the initial velocity, $\hat{\mathbf{d}}$ a unit vector in the direction of the upward vertical and λ a scalar parameter, show that (i) $\mathbf{r} = \mathbf{u}t-\frac{1}{2}gt^2\hat{\mathbf{d}}$; (ii) the position vector of any point on the tangent at P to the trajectory is equal to $\mathbf{u}(t+\lambda)-\frac{1}{2}gt\hat{\mathbf{d}}(t+2\lambda)$. Deduce that the tangent to the trajectory at time t passes through a point whose position vector is independent of $\mathbf{u}$.

31 A particle P moves in a plane with constant angular velocity ω about O. If the rate of increase of its acceleration is parallel to $\overline{PO}$, prove that $\ddot{r} = \frac{1}{3}r\omega^2$ where $r = OP$.

32 Three particles are projected simultaneously from the same point under gravity with velocities $\mathbf{u}_1$, $\mathbf{u}_2$, $\mathbf{u}_3$, show that the particles will be collinear at all subsequent times if $\mathbf{u}_2\wedge\mathbf{u}_3+\mathbf{u}_3\wedge\mathbf{u}_1+\mathbf{u}_1\wedge\mathbf{u}_2 = 0$.

Vector angular velocity Suppose that a particle P is rotating about a fixed axis OA with an angular velocity ω and let PN be drawn perpendicular to OA (Fig. 64). Then as P is moving in a circular path with centre N and radius NP its velocity $\mathbf{v}$ has a magnitude $NP\omega$, i.e. $OP\omega\sin\theta$ and a direction which is perpendicular to the plane OPN in the sense of the rotation.

$$\therefore \quad \mathbf{v} = \omega\hat{\mathbf{a}} \wedge \mathbf{r},$$

where $\mathbf{r}$ is the position vector of P relative to O and $\hat{\mathbf{a}}$ is the unit vector in the direction $\overline{OA}$.

The vector $\omega\hat{\mathbf{a}}$ is defined as *the vector angular velocity* of the particle P about O; it is a vector of magnitude ω localised in the line, OA, its direction being that of a right-handed screw turning in the direction of ω.

Writing $\omega\hat{\mathbf{a}}$ as $\boldsymbol{\omega}$, the vector angular velocity, then

$$\mathbf{v} = \boldsymbol{\omega} \wedge \mathbf{r}.$$

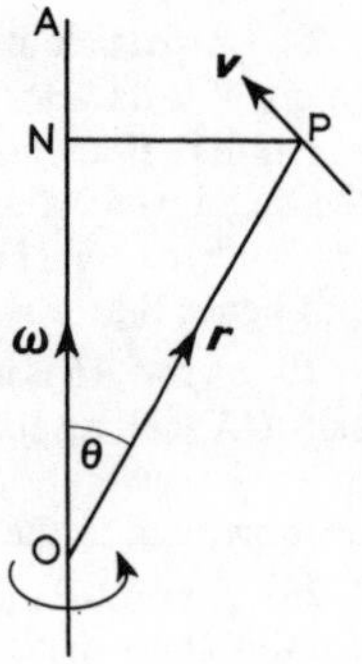

FIG. 64.

If the origin O has a velocity $\mathbf{u}$ whilst the direction of $\overline{OA}$ remains fixed, then clearly the velocity $\mathbf{v}$ of the particle P is given by

$$\mathbf{v} = \mathbf{u} + \boldsymbol{\omega} \wedge \mathbf{r}.$$

Ex. 8 *A particle P with position vector* $3\mathbf{i} - \mathbf{j} + 2\mathbf{k}$ *relative to a fixed origin O is rotating about an axis through O in the direction of the vector* $2\mathbf{i} + 2\mathbf{j} - \mathbf{k}$ *with an angular velocity of* 12 rad/s. *Find the speed of P, the length unit being* 1 cm.

The unit vector $\hat{\mathbf{a}}$ in the direction of the axis of rotation $= \frac{1}{3}(2\mathbf{i} + 2\mathbf{j} - \mathbf{k})$.

$\therefore$ the vector angular velocity $\boldsymbol{\omega} = \omega\hat{\mathbf{a}} = 4(2\mathbf{i} + 2\mathbf{j} - \mathbf{k})$.

So the velocity of P, $\mathbf{v} = \boldsymbol{\omega} \wedge \mathbf{r}$

$$= 4(2\mathbf{i} + 2\mathbf{j} - \mathbf{k}) \wedge (3\mathbf{i} - \mathbf{j} + 2\mathbf{k})$$

$$= 4(3\mathbf{i} - 7\mathbf{j} - 8\mathbf{k}),$$

i.e. the speed of P, $\quad v = 4\sqrt{122}$ cm/s.

Ex. 9 *A point A has position vector* $\mathbf{i} + \mathbf{j} + \mathbf{k}$ *and velocity* $\mathbf{u} = 3\mathbf{i} - \mathbf{j} + \mathbf{k}$ cm/s. *A particle P with position vector* $4\mathbf{i} + 2\mathbf{j} - \mathbf{k}$ *is rotating about A with angular velocity* $\boldsymbol{\omega} = 6\mathbf{i} - 2\mathbf{j} + 3\mathbf{k}$ rad/s. *Find the velocity* $\mathbf{v}$ *of P, the unit of length being* 1 cm.

We have $\mathbf{v} = \mathbf{u} + \boldsymbol{\omega} \wedge \mathbf{r}$, where $\mathbf{r}$, the position vector of P relative to A, is given by $\mathbf{r} = \overline{AP} = 3\mathbf{i} + \mathbf{j} - 2\mathbf{k}$.

$$\therefore \quad \mathbf{v} = 3\mathbf{i} - \mathbf{j} + \mathbf{k} + (6\mathbf{i} - 2\mathbf{j} + 3\mathbf{k}) \wedge (3\mathbf{i} + \mathbf{j} - 2\mathbf{k})$$

$$= 3\mathbf{i} - \mathbf{j} + \mathbf{k} + \mathbf{i} + 21\mathbf{j} + 12\mathbf{k}$$

$$= 4\mathbf{i} + 20\mathbf{j} + 13\mathbf{k} \text{ cm/s}.$$

Coplanar motion If a particle P is moving in a plane with velocity $\mathbf{v}$, its vector angular velocity $\boldsymbol{\omega}$ about a fixed point O in the plane has a magnitude ω equal to the rate of rotation of OP and a direction parallel to the unit vector $\hat{\mathbf{n}}$ which is normal to the plane in the direction of the motion of a right-handed screw rotating with OP (Fig. 65).

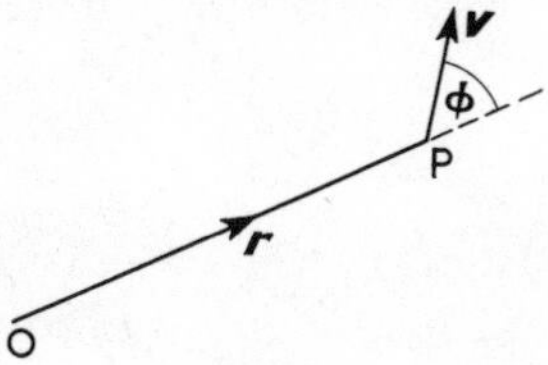

FIG. 65.

Clearly $$\omega = \frac{v \sin \varphi}{r} = \frac{1}{r^2}|\mathbf{r} \wedge \mathbf{v}|.$$

But the direction of $\hat{\mathbf{n}}$ is also the direction of $\mathbf{r} \wedge \mathbf{v}$.

$\therefore$ the vector angular velocity of P about O is given by

$$\boldsymbol{\omega} = \omega\hat{\mathbf{n}} = \frac{1}{r^2}\mathbf{r} \wedge \mathbf{v}.$$

If O, instead of being at rest, has a velocity $\mathbf{u}$ in the plane, then

$$\boldsymbol{\omega} = \frac{1}{r^2}\mathbf{r} \wedge (\mathbf{v} - \mathbf{u}).$$

Ex. 10 *Particles A, B moving in the XOY plane have at a particular instant, coordinates* $(1, -2)$, $(3, 1)$ *and velocities with components parallel to the axes of* $(2, -3)$, $(-1, 2)$ *respectively. Find the vector angular velocity of B about A.*

Angular velocity of B about A,

$$\boldsymbol{\omega} = \frac{1}{r^2}\mathbf{r} \wedge (\mathbf{v} - \mathbf{u}),$$

where $\mathbf{r} = \overline{AB} = 2\mathbf{i} + 3\mathbf{j}$; $r = \sqrt{13}$; $\mathbf{v} = -\mathbf{i} + 2\mathbf{j}$; $\mathbf{u} = 2\mathbf{i} - 3\mathbf{j}$.

$$\therefore \quad \boldsymbol{\omega} = \tfrac{1}{13}(2\mathbf{i} + 3\mathbf{j}) \wedge (-3\mathbf{i} + 5\mathbf{j})$$
$$= \tfrac{19}{13}\mathbf{k}.$$

i.e. a vector in the positive direction of the z-axis with magnitude $\frac{19}{13}$ units.

Angular velocity of a rigid body Suppose a rigid body is rotating about a fixed axis OA in three dimensions at an angular rate of ω. Then the velocity $\mathbf{v}$ of any point P of the body has a magnitude ωPN, where PN is perpendicular to OA, and a direction normal to the plane OPN (Fig. 66). Treating the angular velocity of the body as a vector $\boldsymbol{\omega}$ of magnitude ω localised in the line OA, its direction being that arising from a right-handed screw rotation in the direction of the body's rotation, then the velocity of P can be completely expressed

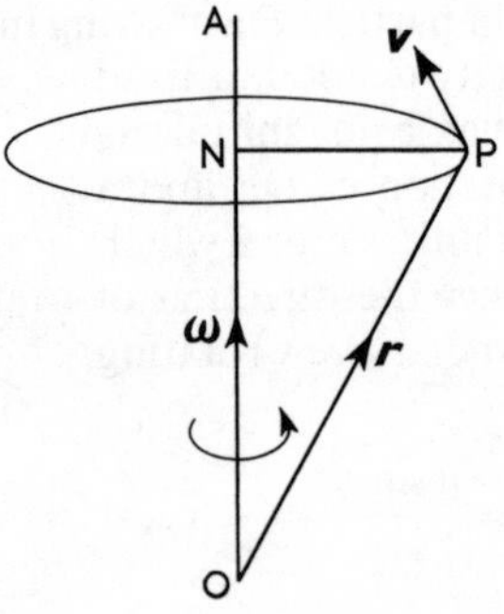

FIG. 66.

as

$$\mathbf{v} = \boldsymbol{\omega} \wedge \overline{NP} = \boldsymbol{\omega} \wedge (\overline{OP} - \overline{ON})$$

$$= \boldsymbol{\omega} \wedge \overline{OP} \quad \text{or} \quad \boldsymbol{\omega} \wedge \mathbf{r}, \quad \text{as} \quad \boldsymbol{\omega} \wedge \overline{ON} = 0.$$

I.e. the velocity $\mathbf{v}$ of a point P of a rigid body rotating about a fixed axis with angular velocity $\boldsymbol{\omega}$ is given by

$$\mathbf{v} = \boldsymbol{\omega} \wedge \mathbf{r},$$

where $\mathbf{r}$ is the position vector of the point with respect to a point on the axis of rotation.

If the axis of rotation is moving parallel to itself at a velocity $\mathbf{u}$, the velocity of the point P is given by

$$\mathbf{v} = \mathbf{u} + \boldsymbol{\omega} \wedge \mathbf{r}.$$

Two-dimensional motion of a lamina The vector angular velocity $\boldsymbol{\omega}$ of a lamina moving in its own plane is equal to $\omega\hat{\mathbf{n}}$, where ω is the rate of rotation of every line fixed in the lamina and $\hat{\mathbf{n}}$ is a unit vector normal to the plane of the lamina in the direction of motion of a right-handed screw rotating in the same sense as the lamina.

Relative to an origin O fixed in the lamina, the velocity $\mathbf{v}$ of any point P of the lamina has a magnitude of ωOP and a direction in the plane of the lamina normal to $\overline{OP}$. So the velocity of P relative to O is given by

$$\mathbf{v} = \boldsymbol{\omega} \wedge \mathbf{r},$$

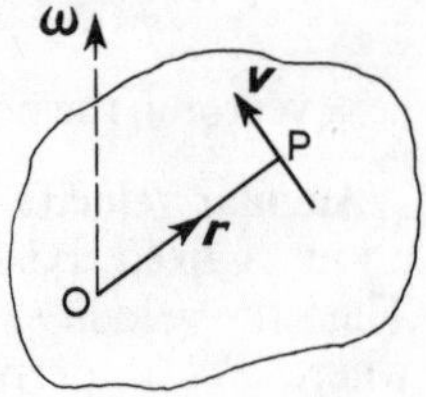

FIG. 67.

where $\mathbf{r}$ is the position vector of P relative to O. Consequently if O has a velocity $\mathbf{u}$, the actual velocity of the point P is given by

$$\mathbf{v} = \mathbf{u} + \boldsymbol{\omega} \wedge \mathbf{r}.$$

Ex. 11 *A lamina is rotating in its own plane with angular speed* 12 rad/s. *Relative to perpendicular axes fixed in direction and intersecting at a point O of the lamina, the instantaneous coordinates of a point P of the lamina are* (3, −4). *If O has a velocity with components* (2, −11) *parallel to the axes and the unit of length is the cm, find the velocity of P.*

Velocity of P, $\mathbf{v} = \mathbf{u} + \boldsymbol{\omega} \wedge \mathbf{r}$,

where $\mathbf{u} = 2\mathbf{i} - 11\mathbf{j}$; $\boldsymbol{\omega} = 12\mathbf{k}$; $\mathbf{r} = 3\mathbf{i} - 4\mathbf{j}$.

Here it is assumed that the unit vectors **i**, **j**, **k** have their usual definitions and that the lamina's rotation is in a counterclockwise direction.

Hence

$$\begin{aligned}\mathbf{v} &= 2\mathbf{i} - 11\mathbf{j} + 12\mathbf{k} \wedge (3\mathbf{i} - 4\mathbf{j}) \\ &= 2\mathbf{i} - 11\mathbf{j} + 36\mathbf{j} + 48\mathbf{i} \\ &= 50\mathbf{i} + 25\mathbf{j},\end{aligned}$$

i.e. the velocity of P has a magnitude of $25\sqrt{5}$ cm/s and a direction making an angle $\tan^{-1}\frac{1}{2}$ with the positive x-axis.

Instantaneous centre of rotation As the velocity of a point P in a lamina is given by

$$\mathbf{v} = \mathbf{u} + \boldsymbol{\omega} \wedge \mathbf{r},$$

it follows that P is instantaneously at rest if

$$\mathbf{u} + \boldsymbol{\omega} \wedge \mathbf{r} = 0.$$

To solve this equation for **r**, take the vector product with respect to $\boldsymbol{\omega}$, giving

$$\boldsymbol{\omega} \wedge \mathbf{u} + \boldsymbol{\omega} \wedge (\boldsymbol{\omega} \wedge \mathbf{r}) = 0.$$

But

$$\begin{aligned}\boldsymbol{\omega} \wedge (\boldsymbol{\omega} \wedge \mathbf{r}) &= (\boldsymbol{\omega} . \mathbf{r})\boldsymbol{\omega} - (\boldsymbol{\omega} . \boldsymbol{\omega})\mathbf{r}, \\ &= -\omega^2 \mathbf{r}, \quad \text{as} \quad \boldsymbol{\omega} . \mathbf{r} = 0.\end{aligned}$$

$$\therefore \quad \boldsymbol{\omega} \wedge \mathbf{u} - \omega^2 \mathbf{r} = 0; \quad \mathbf{r} = \frac{1}{\omega^2}(\boldsymbol{\omega} \wedge \mathbf{u}).$$

Consequently the point with position vector $(\boldsymbol{\omega} \wedge \mathbf{u})/\omega^2$ *is instantaneously at rest; it is called the instantaneous centre of rotation of the lamina and usually denoted by I.*

The position of I can also be determined by using vector components.

For if $\mathbf{u} = u_1\mathbf{i}+u_2\mathbf{j}$, $\boldsymbol{\omega} = \omega\mathbf{k}$ and $\mathbf{r} = x\mathbf{i}+y\mathbf{j}$,

$$\begin{aligned}\mathbf{v} &= u_1\mathbf{i}+u_2\mathbf{j}+\omega\mathbf{k}\wedge(x\mathbf{i}+y\mathbf{j})\\ &= u_1\mathbf{i}+u_2\mathbf{j}+x\omega\mathbf{j}-y\omega\mathbf{i}\\ &= (u_1-y\omega)\mathbf{i}+(u_2+x\omega)\mathbf{j}.\end{aligned}$$

For the point I, $\mathbf{v} = 0$, and consequently

$$u_1-y\omega = 0 \quad\text{and}\quad u_2+x\omega = 0.$$

Hence the coordinates of the instantaneous centre I are $(-u_2/\omega, u_1/\omega)$ where u_1, u_2 are the components along the axes of the velocity of the origin and ω is the angular speed of the lamina.

Ex. 12 *Show that the velocity of any point P of a lamina moving in its own plane is normal to the line joining P to the instantaneous centre of rotation.*

If (x, y) are the coordinates of P, its velocity is given by

$$\mathbf{v} = (u_1-y\omega)\mathbf{i}+(u_2+x\omega)\mathbf{j}, \quad \text{where } u_1, u_2, \omega \text{ are}$$

as previously defined.

Also I is the point $(-u_2/\omega, u_1/\omega)$ and so

$$\overline{IP} = (x+u_2/\omega)\mathbf{i}+(y-u_1/\omega)\mathbf{j},$$

$$\begin{aligned}\therefore\quad \mathbf{v}\cdot\overline{IP} &= (u_1-y\omega)(x+u_2/\omega)+(u_2+x\omega)(y-u_1/\omega)\\ &= 0,\end{aligned}$$

i.e. $\mathbf{v}$ is normal to $\overline{IP}$.

EXAMPLES 7b

[*When required, assume the unit of length is* 1 *cm*]

1 The vector angular velocity of a point about the origin which is fixed is $2(6\mathbf{i}-2\mathbf{j}+3\mathbf{k})$ rad/s. Find (i) the angular speed; (ii) the velocity of the point at the instant when its coordinates are (0, 1, 0).

2 A rigid body is rotating about the axis AB with an angular speed of 15 rad/s. Find the vector angular velocity of the body if the coordinates of A, B are $(1, -1, 2)$, $(2, 1, 0)$ respectively.

3 A particle P has instantaneous coordinates $(3, -2, 1)$. Find the speed of P if it is rotating about the origin which is fixed at an angular velocity of $2\mathbf{i}+4\mathbf{j}-6\mathbf{k}$ rad/s.

4 A particle is rotating about a fixed origin with an angular velocity of magnitude 28 rad/s in the direction of the vector $3\mathbf{i}-2\mathbf{j}+6\mathbf{k}$. Find the velocity of the particle at the instant when its position vector relative to the origin is $4\mathbf{i}+\mathbf{j}-\mathbf{k}$.

5 Relative to an origin O the vector angular velocity of a particle P is $2\mathbf{i}+3\mathbf{j}-\mathbf{k}$ rad/s. If O has a velocity with components $(4, -3, 2)$ parallel to the axes, find the speed of P at the instant when its coordinates are $(0, 2, 1)$.

6 The angular velocity of a body rotating about a fixed origin has components of magnitudes $(3, -1, 4)$ parallel to the axes. Find the velocity of the particle of the body instantaneously at the point $(2, 2, -2)$.

7 At the instant when a particle P moving in the XOY plane has coordinates $(5, 12)$ its velocity components in the directions of the axes $\overline{OX}$, $\overline{OY}$ are $(6, -1)$. Find the angular speed of P about O.

8 A particle P is moving in a plane containing a fixed point O. If the velocity of P has a magnitude v and a direction inclined at an angle α to $\overline{OP}$, show that the angular speed of P about O is $v \sin \alpha/r$, where $r = OP$.

9 A lamina is rotating with angular speed of 12 rad/s in a counterclockwise direction about an axis normal to its plane passing through a point O fixed in it. If O has velocity components $(4, 5)$ cm/s parallel to rectangular axes $\overline{OX}$, $\overline{OY}$ fixed in direction, find the components of the velocity of the point of the lamina with instantaneous coordinates $(-3, 2)$. Also find the coordinates of the point of the lamina which is instantaneously at rest.

10 A rigid body is rotating with an angular speed of 15 rad/s about a fixed axis parallel to $3\mathbf{j}-4\mathbf{k}$ passing through the point $(1, 3, -1)$. Find the velocity of the particle of the body with instantaneous coordinates $(4, -2, 1)$.

11 O is a point fixed in a lamina which moves in its own plane and O', P are two other points fixed in the lamina with position vectors $\mathbf{s}, \mathbf{r}$ relative to O. If the lamina has an angular velocity $\boldsymbol{\omega}$ about O and $\mathbf{u}, \mathbf{w}, \mathbf{v}$ are the velocities of O, O', P respectively show that $\mathbf{v} = \mathbf{w}+\boldsymbol{\omega}\wedge(\mathbf{r}-\mathbf{s})$ and deduce that the angular velocity of the lamina about O' is also $\boldsymbol{\omega}$.

12 If O is a fixed point on the circumference of a circle radius a and P is a particle which describes the circle at a uniform speed u, show that the angular speed of P about O is $u/2a$.

13 If two particles describe the same circle, radius a, in the same direction with the same speed u, show that at any instant their relative angular speed is u/a.

14 Particles A, B move in a plane such that the distance between them is constant and equal to a. The velocities of A, B are in directions making angles of α, β respectively with the direction of $\overline{AB}$. Prove that the angular speed of B

15 A lamina is moving in its own plane with constant angular speed ω. If the velocity of a point O of the lamina is $a \cos pt\mathbf{i}+a \sin pt\mathbf{j}$ where a, p are constants and $\mathbf{i}, \mathbf{j}$ are constant orthogonal unit vectors, show that the locus of the instantaneous centre relative to O is a circle of radius a/ω.

16 A rectangle $ABCD$ with $AB = 2a$, $BC = 2b$, has the vertices A, B constrained to move along perpendicular lines OA, OB. If at any instant the angle OBA is equal to θ, show that the velocity of A away from O is $2a \cos \theta\dot{\theta}$ and show also that the velocity of the point of the rectangle with coordinates (X, Y) relative to axes through A parallel to $\overline{OA}, \overline{OB}$, has components of magnitude $(2a\cos\theta - Y)\dot{\theta}$ and $X\dot{\theta}$ parallel to these axes. Deduce that the instantaneous centre is the point of intersection of lines through A, B parallel to $\overline{OB}, \overline{OA}$ respectively.

17 O, P are points of a lamina moving in its own plane with spin $\boldsymbol{\omega}$. If $\mathbf{u}, \mathbf{v}$ are the velocities of O, P respectively and $\mathbf{r}$ is the position vector of P relative to O, prove that (i) $\dot{\mathbf{r}} = \boldsymbol{\omega}\wedge\mathbf{r}$; (ii) $\dot{\mathbf{v}} = \dot{\mathbf{u}}+\dot{\boldsymbol{\omega}}\wedge\mathbf{r}-\omega^2\mathbf{r}$.

VIII

APPLICATIONS OF VECTORIAL METHODS IN TWO-DIMENSIONAL PARTICLE DYNAMICS

Momentum If at an instant, a particle of mass m has a velocity $\mathbf{v}$ then the vector $\mathbf{p}$ equal to the product $m\mathbf{v}$ defines *the linear momentum* of the particle at that instant.

Newton's Second Law of Motion This law which is the foundation of the basic theory of dynamics states that the force acting on a particle is proportional to the rate of change of momentum it produces and has the same direction.

So $$\mathbf{F} \propto \frac{d}{dt}(m\mathbf{v}).$$

When the force $\mathbf{F}$ is expressed in absolute units and the mass m is constant, the law can be written

$$\mathbf{F} = \frac{d}{dt}(m\mathbf{v}) = m\mathbf{a},$$

where $\mathbf{a}$ is the acceleration of the particle.

Ex. 1 *A particle of mass* 1 kg *which is initially at the origin moving with a velocity of* 20 m/s *in the positive direction of the y-axis is acted on by a force whose value at time t* sec *is* $2t\mathbf{i}+2\mathbf{j}$ N. *Find the position vector relative to the origin of the particle at time t.*

Let $\mathbf{v}$, $\mathbf{r}$ be the velocity and position vector of the particle at time t.

Then $$\dot{\mathbf{v}} = 2t\mathbf{i}+2\mathbf{j} \quad \text{as} \quad m = 1.$$

$$\therefore \quad \mathbf{v} = t^2\mathbf{i}+2t\mathbf{j}+\mathbf{u},$$

where $\mathbf{u}$ is the value of $\mathbf{v}$ when $t = 0$; i.e. $\mathbf{u} = 20\mathbf{j}$.

So $$\mathbf{v} = \dot{\mathbf{r}} = t^2\mathbf{i}+(2t+20)\mathbf{j} \text{ m/s},$$

$$\therefore \quad \mathbf{r} = \tfrac{1}{3}t^3\mathbf{i}+(t^2+20t)\mathbf{j}+\mathbf{c},$$

where $\mathbf{c}$ is the value of $\mathbf{r}$ when $t = 0$; i.e. $\mathbf{c} = 0$.

Hence $$\mathbf{r} = \tfrac{1}{3}t^3\mathbf{i}+(t^2+20t)\mathbf{j} \text{ m}.$$

Ex. 2 *A particle moves on a smooth plane curve under gravity; prove that the square of its velocity is proportional to its depth below a certain fixed level.*

If v is the speed of the particle at P, its acceleration is given by

$$\mathbf{a} = v\frac{dv}{ds}\hat{\boldsymbol{\tau}}+\frac{v^2}{\rho}\hat{\mathbf{n}},$$

where $\hat{\boldsymbol{\tau}}$, $\hat{\mathbf{n}}$ are unit vectors along the tangent and inward normal to the curve at P (Fig. 68).

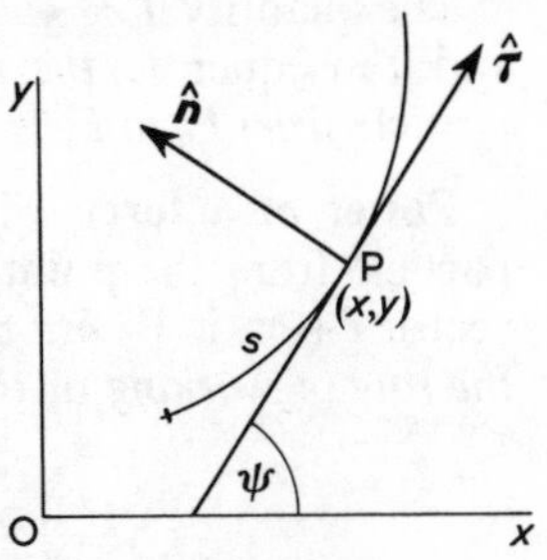

FIG. 68.

As the forces acting on the particle are mg vertically downwards—i.e. in the direction $\overline{YO}$—and the normal reaction R in the direction of $\hat{\mathbf{n}}$, then

$$\mathbf{F} = -mg\sin\psi\hat{\boldsymbol{\tau}}+(R-mg\cos\psi)\hat{\mathbf{n}}.$$

$$\therefore \quad m\left(v\frac{dv}{ds}\hat{\boldsymbol{\tau}}+\frac{v^2}{\rho}\hat{\mathbf{n}}\right) = -mg\sin\psi\hat{\boldsymbol{\tau}}+(R-mg\cos\psi)\hat{\mathbf{n}}.$$

So $$v\frac{dv}{ds} = -g\sin\psi = -g\frac{dy}{ds}.$$

Integrating w.r.t s, $\quad \tfrac{1}{2}v^2 = -gy+c.$

If $v = 0$ when $y = h$, then $c = gh$ and hence

$$v^2 = 2g(h-y).$$

As $(h-y)$ is the depth of the particle below a fixed level, the required result is established.

Work–energy principle Suppose a particle, mass m, which is acted on by a force $\mathbf{F}$ moves from a point P_0, position vector $\mathbf{r}_0$, to a point P_1, position vector $\mathbf{r}_1$. Then as the work done by the force when the particle moves from a point P, position vector $\mathbf{r}$, to a neighbouring point P' with position vector $\mathbf{r}+\delta\mathbf{r}$ is the scalar product $\mathbf{F}\,.\,\delta\mathbf{r}$, the total work done when the particle moves from P_0 to P_1 is given by

$$W = \int_{\mathbf{r}_0}^{\mathbf{r}_1} \mathbf{F}\,.\,d\mathbf{r}.$$

But $\mathbf{F} = m\,d\mathbf{v}/dt$, so

$$W = m\int_{\mathbf{r}_0}^{\mathbf{r}_1}\frac{d\mathbf{v}}{dt}\,.\,d\mathbf{r} = m\int_{t_0}^{t_1}\frac{d\mathbf{v}}{dt}\,.\,\frac{d\mathbf{r}}{dt}dt = m\int_{t_0}^{t_1}\mathbf{v}\,.\,\frac{d\mathbf{v}}{dt}dt$$

$$= m\int_{\mathbf{v}_0}^{\mathbf{v}_1}\mathbf{v}\,.\,d\mathbf{v} = \tfrac{1}{2}m(\mathbf{v}_1^2-\mathbf{v}_0^2) = \tfrac{1}{2}m(v_1^2-v_0^2),$$

where v_0, v_1 are the speeds of the particle at P_0, P_1 respectively.

The quantity $T = \frac{1}{2}mv^2$ is defined as *the kinetic energy* of the particle, and consequently *the total work done by the force* **F** *in moving the particle from* P_0 *to* P_1 *is equal to the gain of kinetic energy of the particle.*

Power of a force The work done by a force **F** when moving a particle from the point P, position vector **r**, to the point P', position vector $\mathbf{r}+\delta\mathbf{r}$, is $\mathbf{F}\,.\,\delta\mathbf{r}$. So if the time taken for this displacement in δt, *the rate of working* or *the power* of **F** is given by

$$\lim_{\delta t\to 0}\frac{\mathbf{F}\,.\,\delta\mathbf{r}}{\delta t} = \mathbf{F}\,.\,\frac{d\mathbf{r}}{dt} \quad \text{or} \quad \mathbf{F}\,.\,\mathbf{v},$$

where **v** is the velocity of the particle at P.

Ex. 3 *Show that the rate of increase of the kinetic energy of a particle moving under a force* **F** *is equal to the power of* **F**.

Let $T = \frac{1}{2}\text{mv}^2$ be the K.E. of the particle of time t. Then the rate of increase of T is given by

$$\frac{dT}{dt} = \frac{1}{2}m\frac{d}{dt}(v^2) = \frac{1}{2}m\frac{d}{dt}(\mathbf{v}^2) = m\mathbf{v}\,.\,\frac{d\mathbf{v}}{dt}$$

$$= m\frac{d\mathbf{v}}{dt}\,.\,\mathbf{v} = \mathbf{F}\,.\,\mathbf{v}, \quad \text{the power of } \mathbf{F}.$$

Conservative forces—potential energy If the work done by a force or system of forces acting on a particle in moving the particle slowly from a point P_0 to a point P_1 is independent of the path taken between P_0 and P_1, the force or system of forces is said to be *conservative.* In such a case, the *potential energy* V is defined as the work done by the force or forces in moving the particle from its existing position to some standard position.

Take for example the earth's gravitational field. If $\hat{\mathbf{d}}$ is a unit vector in the upward vertical direction, the gravity force acting on a particle, mass m, is $-mg\hat{\mathbf{d}}$, where g can be assumed constant. Consequently the work done by gravity in moving the particle from P_0 to P_1

$$= \int_{\mathbf{r}_0}^{\mathbf{r}_1} -mg\hat{\mathbf{d}}\,.\,d\mathbf{r} = -mg\hat{\mathbf{d}}\,.\int_{\mathbf{r}_0}^{\mathbf{r}_1} d\mathbf{r}$$

$$= mg\hat{\mathbf{d}}\,.\,(\mathbf{r}_0-\mathbf{r}_1).$$

As this expression involves only the position vectors of P_0, P_1 and not the path between, it follows that the earth's gravity field is conservative. Moreover, as $\hat{\mathbf{d}}\,.\,(\mathbf{r}_0-\mathbf{r}_1)$ is equal to the depth of P_1 below P_0, it follows that the potential energy of the particle at a point P is mgh, where h is the height of P above some standard position.

Conservation of energy *For a particle moving in a conservative field of force the sum of the kinetic and potential energies is constant.* This important principle follows at once from the results just obtained; for if V, T represent the potential and kinetic energies of the particle then the work done by the forces acting on the particle when it moves from P_0 to P_1 is $V_0 - V_1$. Also the work done in the same interval by the forces has been shown to be equal to $T_1 - T_0$.

Hence $$V_0 - V_1 = T_1 - T_0,$$

or $$V_0 + T_0 = V_1 + T_1.$$

Impulse—momentum principle The *impulse* **I** *of a force* **F** acting on a particle, mass m, during a time interval t_0 to t_1 is defined as the change of linear momentum produced.

So if $\mathbf{v}_0$, $\mathbf{v}_1$ are the velocities of the particle at the beginning and end of the time interval,

$$\mathbf{I} = m(\mathbf{v}_1 - \mathbf{v}_0).$$

But $$\int_{t_0}^{t_1} \mathbf{F}\,dt = m\int_{t_0}^{t_1} \frac{d\mathbf{v}}{dt}\,dt = m\int_{\mathbf{v}_0}^{\mathbf{v}_1} d\mathbf{v} = m(\mathbf{v}_1 - \mathbf{v}_0).$$

$\therefore$ the impulse $$\mathbf{I} = \int_{t_0}^{t_1} \mathbf{F}\,dt.$$

So *the impulse of a force is the time-integral of the force.*

If **F** is very large and the interval $(t_1 - t_0)$ very small but in such a way that the time-integral of **F** is finite, **F** is spoken of as an *impulsive force* and is measured by its impulse—i.e. the change of momentum it produces.

Ex. 4 *A particle of mass* 50 g *is struck a blow which changes its velocity from* $\mathbf{v}_0 = 10\mathbf{i} + 20\mathbf{j}$ *cm/s to* $\mathbf{v}_1 = 16\mathbf{i} + 8\mathbf{j}$ *cm/s. Find the impulse of the blow.*

$$\begin{aligned}\text{Impulse of blow} &= \text{change of momentum produced}\\ &= 50(\mathbf{v}_1 - \mathbf{v}_0)\\ &= 50(6\mathbf{i} - 12\mathbf{j}) \quad\text{or}\quad 100(3\mathbf{i} - 6\mathbf{j}) \text{ units.}\end{aligned}$$

Angular momentum Let **r** be the position vector of a moving particle P, mass m, relative to a fixed origin O. Then if the velocity of P is $\mathbf{v}(=\dot{\mathbf{r}})$, the linear momentum **p** of P is a vector in the direction of **v** of magnitude mv. The vector moment **H** of **p** about O defined as in the case of a force vector is given by

$$\mathbf{H} = \mathbf{r} \wedge m\mathbf{v}.$$

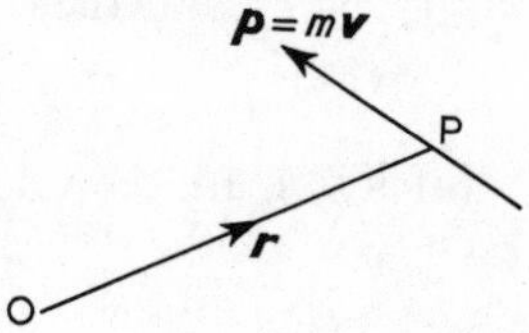

FIG. 69.

This *moment of momentum* of the particle about O is called *the angular momentum* of the particle about O.

The rate of change of the angular momentum is

$$\frac{d\mathbf{H}}{dt} = m\frac{d}{dt}(\mathbf{r} \wedge \mathbf{v}) = m(\dot{\mathbf{r}} \wedge \mathbf{v} + \mathbf{r} \wedge \dot{\mathbf{v}})$$

$$= m\mathbf{r} \wedge \dot{\mathbf{v}} \quad \text{or} \quad \mathbf{r} \wedge \mathbf{F}, \quad \text{as} \quad \dot{\mathbf{r}} \wedge \mathbf{v} = \mathbf{v} \wedge \mathbf{v} = 0,$$

i.e. *the rate of change of the angular momentum of a particle about a fixed point O is equal to the moment about O of the resultant force acting on the particle.* Consequently if the moment of the resultant force about O is zero, the angular momentum of the particle about O is constant.

Ex. 5 *A particle P moves under the action of a central force* $\mathbf{F}$ *acting in the direction $\overline{PO}$ where O is a fixed point. Prove that P moves on a plane curve.*

As the moment of $\mathbf{F}$ about O is zero, the angular momentum of the particle about O is constant.

Hence $\mathbf{r} \wedge \mathbf{v}$ is a constant vector, assuming m is constant.

As $\mathbf{r} \wedge \mathbf{v}$ is a vector normal to the plane of $\mathbf{r}$ and $\mathbf{v}$, it follows that this plane must be fixed and consequently that P moves on a plane curve.

Systems of particles The dynamical principles established in the case of a single particle will now be extended to a system of particles. Before doing so it is necessary to define what is known as the centre of mass of a set of particles.

Centre of mass The centre of mass of a set of particles of masses $m_1, m_2, m_3, \ldots$ situated at points with position vectors $\mathbf{r}_1, \mathbf{r}_2, \mathbf{r}_3, \ldots$ is the point G whose position vector $\bar{\mathbf{r}}$ is given by

$$\bar{\mathbf{r}} = \frac{m_1\mathbf{r}_1 + m_2\mathbf{r}_2 + m_3\mathbf{r}_3 + \ldots}{m_1 + m_2 + m_3 + \ldots} = \frac{\Sigma m\mathbf{r}}{\Sigma m}.$$

The following important results follow

(i) if the position vectors of the masses $m_1, m_2, m_3, \ldots$ relative to G are $\mathbf{r}'_1, \mathbf{r}'_2, \mathbf{r}'_3, \ldots$, then

$$\Sigma m\mathbf{r}' = 0; \quad \Sigma m\dot{\mathbf{r}}' = 0 \quad \Sigma m\ddot{\mathbf{r}}' = 0.$$

(ii) if $\bar{\mathbf{v}}, \bar{\mathbf{a}}$, are the velocity and acceleration of G and $\mathbf{v}_1, \mathbf{a}_1$; $\mathbf{v}_2, \mathbf{a}_2$; $\mathbf{v}_3, \mathbf{a}_3$; ... are the respective velocities and accelerations of the separate masses,

$$\bar{\mathbf{v}}\Sigma m = \Sigma m\mathbf{v}; \quad \bar{\mathbf{a}}\Sigma m = \Sigma m\mathbf{a}.$$

Ex. 6 *Particles P_1, P_2 of masses* 5 *and* 10 *units respectively have position vectors $\mathbf{r}_1$, $\mathbf{r}_2$ given by $\mathbf{r}_1 = t^2\mathbf{i}+t\mathbf{j}$, $\mathbf{r}_2 = 4t\mathbf{i}+t^3\mathbf{j}$, where t is the time. Find (i) the position vector; (ii) the velocity; (iii) the acceleration of the centre of mass of the particles when $t = 2$.*

$$\bar{\mathbf{r}} = \tfrac{1}{15}(5\mathbf{r}_1+10\mathbf{r}_2) = \tfrac{1}{3}[(t^2+8t)\mathbf{i}+(t+2t^3)\mathbf{j}].$$

When $t = 2$, $\quad \bar{\mathbf{r}} = \tfrac{1}{3}[20\mathbf{i}+18\mathbf{j}].$

Also $\quad \bar{\mathbf{v}} = \tfrac{1}{15}(5\dot{\mathbf{r}}_1+10\dot{\mathbf{r}}_2) = \tfrac{1}{3}[(2t+8)\mathbf{i}+(1+6t^2)\mathbf{j}].$

When $t = 2$, $\quad \bar{\mathbf{v}} = \tfrac{1}{3}[12\mathbf{i}+25\mathbf{j}].$

Similarly

$$\bar{\mathbf{a}} = \tfrac{1}{3}[2\mathbf{i}+12t\mathbf{j}] = \tfrac{1}{3}[2\mathbf{i}+24\mathbf{j}] \text{ when } t = 2.$$

Alternatively we could have used the results $\bar{\mathbf{v}} = \dot{\bar{\mathbf{r}}}$; $\bar{\mathbf{a}} = \dot{\bar{\mathbf{v}}}$.

Linear momentum Considering a system of particles defined as above then the total linear momentum $\mathbf{P}$ of the system is given by

$$\mathbf{P} = \Sigma m\dot{\mathbf{r}} \quad \text{or} \quad \Sigma m\mathbf{v}.$$

But Σmv is equal to $\bar{\mathbf{v}}\Sigma m$ or $M\bar{\mathbf{v}}$, where M is the sum of the masses of the particles and $\bar{\mathbf{v}}$ is the velocity of the centre of mass. Consequently *the total linear momentum of the system is equal to the linear momentum of a single particle of mass equal to the total mass of the system moving with the velocity of the centre of mass.*

The rate of change of linear momentum

$$\frac{d}{dt}\Sigma m\dot{\mathbf{r}} = \Sigma m\ddot{\mathbf{r}} \quad \text{or} \quad \Sigma m\mathbf{a}.$$

But $\Sigma m\mathbf{a}$ is equal to $M\bar{\mathbf{a}}$, where $\bar{\mathbf{a}}$ is the acceleration of the centre of mass of the system.

So $\quad \Sigma m\ddot{\mathbf{r}} = M\bar{\mathbf{a}}.$

Now if the particle P, mass m, with position vector $\mathbf{r}$ is subject to an external force $\mathbf{F}$ and an internal force $\mathbf{F}'$, where by Newton's third law, $\Sigma\mathbf{F}'$ for all the particles of the system is zero, then

$$m\ddot{\mathbf{r}} = \mathbf{F}+\mathbf{F}'$$

$$\therefore \quad \Sigma m\ddot{\mathbf{r}} = \Sigma\mathbf{F}+\Sigma\mathbf{F}' = \Sigma\mathbf{F}.$$

Hence $\quad M\bar{\mathbf{a}} = \Sigma\mathbf{F},$

i.e. *the acceleration of the centre of mass of a system of particles is equal to the sum of the external forces acting on the particles divided by the total mass of the system.*

Conservation of linear momentum *If for a system of particles there is no resultant component of external force in any particular direction, then the linear momentum of the system in that direction is constant.*

As
$$\Sigma m\ddot{\mathbf{r}} = \Sigma \mathbf{F},$$
so in any particular direction say $\overline{OX}$ in which the magnitudes of the components of $\mathbf{r}$ and $\mathbf{F}$ are respectively x and F_x,
$$\Sigma m\ddot{x} = \Sigma F_x.$$
Hence if $\Sigma F_x = 0$ then $\Sigma m\ddot{x} = 0$ and consequently $\Sigma m\dot{x}$, the linear momentum of the system in the direction $\overline{OX}$, is constant.

Ex. 7 *Particles of masses* 5, 2, 3 *kg are moving in the x–y plane under the actions of forces* $4\mathbf{i}-\mathbf{j}$, $2\mathbf{i}+4\mathbf{j}$, $-3\mathbf{i}-2\mathbf{j}$ *N respectively. Find the acceleration of the centre of mass of the particles.*

Here
$$M = \Sigma m = 10 \text{ kg}; \ \Sigma \mathbf{F} = 3\mathbf{i}+\mathbf{j} \text{ N}.$$
Hence the acceleration of the centre of mass is
$$\bar{\mathbf{a}} = \tfrac{1}{10}(3\mathbf{i}+\mathbf{j}) \text{ m/s}^2.$$

Kinetic energy The kinetic energy T of a system of particles is equal to $\frac{1}{2}\Sigma m\dot{\mathbf{r}}^2$. Now if P is the position at time t of a general particle, mass m, of the system and G is the centre of mass where
$$\overline{OP} = \mathbf{r}; \qquad \overline{OG} = \bar{\mathbf{r}}; \qquad \overline{GP} = \mathbf{r}' = \mathbf{r}-\bar{\mathbf{r}},$$
then
$$T = \tfrac{1}{2}\Sigma m(\dot{\bar{\mathbf{r}}}+\dot{\mathbf{r}}')^2$$
$$= \tfrac{1}{2}\Sigma m\dot{\bar{\mathbf{r}}}^2 + \Sigma m\dot{\bar{\mathbf{r}}}\,.\,\dot{\mathbf{r}}' + \tfrac{1}{2}\Sigma m\dot{\mathbf{r}}'^2.$$
But
$$\Sigma m\dot{\bar{\mathbf{r}}}\,.\,\dot{\mathbf{r}}' = \dot{\bar{\mathbf{r}}}\,.\,\Sigma m\dot{\mathbf{r}}' = 0 \quad \text{as} \quad \Sigma m\dot{\mathbf{r}}' = 0.$$
$$\therefore \quad T = \tfrac{1}{2}M\dot{\bar{\mathbf{r}}}^2 + \tfrac{1}{2}\Sigma m\dot{\mathbf{r}}'^2.$$

So the K.E. of a system of particles is equal to the K.E. of a single particle of mass equal to the total mass of the system and moving with the centre of mass together with the K.E. of the system in its motion relative to the centre of mass.

Ex. 8 *Prove that the K.E. of masses* m_1, m_2 *is equal to* $\frac{1}{2}(m_1+m_2)\bar{\mathbf{v}}^2 + \frac{1}{2}m_1m_2\mathbf{v}^2/(m_1+m_2)$, *where* $\bar{\mathbf{v}}$ *is the velocity of their centre of mass and* $\mathbf{v}$ *is the relative velocity of* m_1 *to* m_2.

We have
$$T = \tfrac{1}{2}m_1\mathbf{v}_1^2 + \tfrac{1}{2}m_2\mathbf{v}_2^2,$$
where $\mathbf{v}_1, \mathbf{v}_2$ are the velocities of the masses.

$$\therefore \quad (m_1+m_2)T = \tfrac{1}{2}m_1^2\mathbf{v}_1^2+\tfrac{1}{2}m_2^2\mathbf{v}_2^2+\tfrac{1}{2}m_1m_2(\mathbf{v}_1^2+\mathbf{v}_2^2)$$
$$= \tfrac{1}{2}(m_1\mathbf{v}_1+m_2\mathbf{v}_2)^2-m_1m_2\mathbf{v}_1\,.\,\mathbf{v}_2+\tfrac{1}{2}m_1m_2(\mathbf{v}_1^2+\mathbf{v}_2^2)$$
$$= \tfrac{1}{2}(m_1\mathbf{v}_1+m_2\mathbf{v}_2)^2+\tfrac{1}{2}m_1m_2(\mathbf{v}_1-\mathbf{v}_2)^2.$$

But $m_1\mathbf{v}_1+m_2\mathbf{v}_2 = (m_1+m_2)\bar{\mathbf{v}}$ and $\mathbf{v}_1-\mathbf{v}_2 = \mathbf{v}$.

$$\therefore \quad T = \tfrac{1}{2}(m_1+m_2)\bar{\mathbf{v}}^2+\tfrac{1}{2}m_1m_2\mathbf{v}^2/(m_1+m_2).$$

Angular momentum The angular momentum $\mathbf{H}$ of a system of particles about a fixed point O is given by

$$\mathbf{H} = \Sigma\mathbf{r}\wedge m\dot{\mathbf{r}}.$$

So the rate of change of angular momentum about O

$$\dot{\mathbf{H}} = \Sigma\dot{\mathbf{r}}\wedge m\dot{\mathbf{r}}+\Sigma\mathbf{r}\wedge m\ddot{\mathbf{r}}$$
$$= \Sigma\mathbf{r}\wedge m\ddot{\mathbf{r}}, \quad \text{as} \quad \Sigma\dot{\mathbf{r}}\wedge m\dot{\mathbf{r}} = 0.$$

But $m\ddot{\mathbf{r}} = \mathbf{F}+\mathbf{F}'$, where $\mathbf{F}$, $\mathbf{F}'$ are the external and internal forces acting on the general particle, mass m.

$$\therefore \quad \dot{\mathbf{H}} = \Sigma\mathbf{r}\wedge\mathbf{F}+\Sigma\mathbf{r}\wedge\mathbf{F}',$$

and as $\Sigma\mathbf{r}\wedge\mathbf{F}'$, the sum of the moments of these internal forces about O, is zero, then

$$\dot{\mathbf{H}} = \Sigma\mathbf{r}\wedge\mathbf{F}.$$

Or, *the rate of change of angular momentum of a system of particles about a fixed point is equal to the sum of the moments of the external forces acting on the system about that point.*

Conservation of angular momentum *If the sum of the moments of the external forces acting on a system of particles about a fixed point is zero, then the angular momentum of the system about that point is constant.*

For if $\sum\mathbf{r}\wedge\mathbf{F} = 0$, then $\dot{\mathbf{H}} = 0$ and so the angular momentum $\mathbf{H}$ is constant.

Ex. 9 *Prove that the rate of change of angular momentum of a system of particles about its centre of mass G is equal to the sum of the moments of the external forces acting on the system about G.*

As in general, G will not be a fixed point, the result just obtained does not immediately apply.

With the notation used previously, the angular momentum about G is

$$\bar{\mathbf{H}} = \Sigma\mathbf{r}'\wedge m\dot{\mathbf{r}},$$

so

$$\dot{\bar{\mathbf{H}}} = \Sigma\dot{\mathbf{r}}'\wedge m\dot{\mathbf{r}}+\Sigma\mathbf{r}'\wedge m\ddot{\mathbf{r}}.$$

But $$\Sigma\dot{\mathbf{r}}'\wedge m\dot{\mathbf{r}} = \Sigma(\dot{\mathbf{r}}-\dot{\bar{\mathbf{r}}})\wedge m\dot{\mathbf{r}}$$
$$= -\dot{\bar{\mathbf{r}}}\wedge\Sigma m\dot{\mathbf{r}} = -\dot{\bar{\mathbf{r}}}\wedge M\dot{\bar{\mathbf{r}}} = 0.$$
$$\therefore\quad \dot{\bar{\mathbf{H}}} = \Sigma\mathbf{r}'\wedge m\ddot{\mathbf{r}}$$
$$= \Sigma\mathbf{r}'\wedge(\mathbf{F}+\mathbf{F}') = \Sigma\mathbf{r}'\wedge\mathbf{F}$$
$$= \text{moment of external forces about } G.$$

Impulsive forces Suppose a system of particles is acted upon by a set of impulsive forces $\Sigma\mathbf{I}$; any internal impulsive forces $\Sigma\mathbf{I}'$ set up in the system will be equal and opposite in pairs and so neutralise each other.

If $\mathbf{v}$ is the velocity of the general particle, mass m, after the impulses and $\mathbf{v}_0$ its original velocity, then

$$\Sigma\mathbf{I} = \Sigma m\mathbf{v} - \Sigma m\mathbf{v}_0$$
$$= M\bar{\mathbf{v}} - M\bar{\mathbf{v}}_0,$$

where $\bar{\mathbf{v}}, \bar{\mathbf{v}}_0$ are the final and original velocities of the centre of mass of the system.

Hence *the motion of the centre of mass of the system is that of a particle of mass equal to that of the system positioned at the centre of mass and acted upon by the set of impulses.*

The moment of the impulses about an origin O is

$$\Sigma\mathbf{r}\wedge\mathbf{I} = \Sigma\mathbf{r}\wedge m(\mathbf{v}-\mathbf{v}_0)$$
$$= \Sigma\mathbf{r}\wedge m\mathbf{v} - \Sigma\mathbf{r}\wedge m\mathbf{v}_0$$
$$= \mathbf{H}-\mathbf{H}_0.$$
$$= \text{the increase in angular momentum about } O,$$

i.e. *the sum of the moments about a point of the impulses acting on the particles of the system is equal to the increase in the angular momentum of the system about that point.*

Ex. 10 *Particles of equal masses m are attached to the ends of a light rod AB which is free to move on a smooth horizontal table. The system is set in motion by an impulse $\mathbf{I}$ applied to the particle at A in the plane of the table. Show that the impulsive reaction in the rod has a magnitude of $\frac{1}{2}\hat{\mathbf{e}}\,.\,\mathbf{I}$, where $\hat{\mathbf{e}}$ is a unit vector in the direction $\overline{AB}$.*

Let the impulsive thrust in the rod AB have a magnitude J; then the impulsive reactions on the masses at A, B are $-J\hat{\mathbf{e}}, J\hat{\mathbf{e}}$ respectively. If the velocities of the particles at A, B immediately after the impulse are $\mathbf{v}_1, \mathbf{v}_2$ respectively,

$$\mathbf{I} - J\hat{\mathbf{e}} = m\mathbf{v}_1$$

and

$$J\hat{\mathbf{e}} = m\mathbf{v}_2.$$

Taking the scalar products of both sides of these equations with $\hat{\mathbf{e}}$ and subtracting,

$$\hat{\mathbf{e}} \,.\, (\mathbf{I} - J\hat{\mathbf{e}}) - \hat{\mathbf{e}} \,.\, J\hat{\mathbf{e}} = m(\hat{\mathbf{e}} \,.\, \mathbf{v}_1 - \hat{\mathbf{e}} \,.\, \mathbf{v}_2)$$
$$= 0,$$

as the particles must have equal velocity components along the rod.

$$\therefore \quad \hat{\mathbf{e}} \,.\, \mathbf{I} - 2J = 0,$$

or

$$J = \tfrac{1}{2}\hat{\mathbf{e}} \,.\, \mathbf{I}.$$

EXAMPLES 8

1 A force of $15\mathbf{i} + 20\mathbf{j}$ N acts on a particle of mass 5 kg, find the magnitude of the acceleration of the particle.

2 A particle of mass 20 kg, initially at rest, is acted on by a constant force of $50\mathbf{i} + 100\mathbf{j}$ N. Find the velocity and kinetic energy of the particle after it has been moving for 2 s.

3 At time t s a force has a value of $3t^2\mathbf{i} - 2\mathbf{j}$ N. If the force acts on a particle of unit mass initially at rest, find the velocity of the particle when $t = 5$.

4 A particle of mass 2 kg moves from rest at a point A to a point B under the action of a force $\mathbf{F} = 3\mathbf{i} + 4\mathbf{j}$ N and a force $\mathbf{R}$ which has a direction normal to $\overline{AB}$. If the points A, B have coordinates $(1, -1), (4, 2)$ respectively find the total work done by the forces and deduce the speed of the particle when it reaches B. Assume the length unit is 1 m.

5 A force $\mathbf{F}$ is acting on a particle which has a velocity $\mathbf{v}$. If $\mathbf{F} = 50\mathbf{i} - 10\mathbf{j}$ N and $\mathbf{v} = 4\mathbf{i} - \mathbf{j}$ m/s, find the power of $\mathbf{F}$.

6 A particle of mass 5 kg is moving with a velocity of $10\mathbf{i} - 2\mathbf{j}$ m/s when it is acted on by an impulse of $15\mathbf{i} + 20\mathbf{j}$ units. Find the new velocity of the particle.

7 A body of mass 50 kg moving with a velocity of $10\mathbf{i}$ m/s is struck a blow which changes its velocity to $20\mathbf{i} - 5\mathbf{j}$ m/s. Find the magnitude and direction of the impulse of the blow.

8 An impulse $\mathbf{I}$ acting on a particle, mass m, initially at rest gives it a velocity $\mathbf{v}$; show that the kinetic energy produced is $\frac{1}{2}\mathbf{I} \,.\, \mathbf{v}$.

9 Particles of masses $m, 2m$ are moving with velocities $2\mathbf{v}, \mathbf{v}$ respectively. What is the velocity of the centre of mass of the particles?

10 Particles of masses 5, 8, 3 g are at points with position vectors $2\mathbf{i} + \mathbf{j}$, $3\mathbf{i} - \mathbf{j}$, $-4\mathbf{i} + \mathbf{j}$ respectively. Find the position vector of the centre of mass of the particles.

11 Show that the mass centre of three particles, masses 2, 3, 5 g, in motion in a plane with velocities of $5\mathbf{i}+\mathbf{j}$, $\mathbf{j}$, $-2\mathbf{i}-\mathbf{j}$ cm/s respectively is at rest.

12 A particle of unit mass originally at rest at the origin is acted on by a force whose value at time t s is $10(\cos\frac{1}{5}\pi t\mathbf{i}+\sin\frac{1}{5}\pi t\mathbf{j})$ N. Find the position vector of the particle relative to the origin when $t = 5$.

13 A particle of mass 20 g has a velocity of $4\mathbf{i}+3\mathbf{j}$ cm/s. Find the angular momentum of the particle about (i) the origin; (ii) the point (2, 1), at the instant when the particle is at the point (3, 4).

14 An impulse $\mathbf{I}$ acting on a particle changes its velocity from $\mathbf{v}_0$ to $\mathbf{v}_1$. Show that the kinetic energy of the particle increases by an amount $\frac{1}{2}\mathbf{I}\,.\,(\mathbf{v}_0+\mathbf{v}_1)$.

15 A particle P of mass 10 g is projected in a plane from a point distant 20 cm from the origin O with a velocity of 20 cm/s at right angles to $\overline{OP}$. If the particle is subject only to a force in the direction $\overline{PO}$, find the angular speed of OP when $OP = 10$ cm.

16 Equal particles attached to the ends of a light rod are moving freely on a smooth horizontal table. Prove that the mid-point of the rod moves with constant speed in a straight line.

17 Particles of masses m_1, m_2, moving in a plane, collide and coalesce. Show that the loss of kinetic energy is $\frac{1}{2}m_1m_2\mathbf{v}^2/(m_1+m_2)$, where $\mathbf{v}$ is the relative velocity of one particle to the other before the collision.

18 Masses m_1, m_2, m_3 initially at rest at points in a plane move under the actions of mutually attractive forces proportional to the product of masses and inversely proportional to the square of the distance of separation. Show that the centre of mass of the particles remains at rest.

19 Particles A, B of masses $m, 2m$ are moving in a plane with velocities $2\mathbf{v}$, $-\mathbf{v}$ respectively when they collide and coalesce. Find (i) the impulse on A; (ii) the loss of kinetic energy.

20 A particle P moves in a plane under a force $\omega^2\overline{PO}$ per unit mass where O is a fixed origin. If the initial position of the particle is A and its initial velocity is represented by $\omega\overline{OC}$, show that at time t, $\overline{OP} = \overline{OA}\cos\omega t+\overline{OC}\sin\omega t$.

21 Particles P, Q of masses m_1, m_2 attract each other with a force proportional to the product of their masses and inversely proportional to the square of the distance between them. If the position vectors of P, Q at time t are $\mathbf{r}_1, \mathbf{r}_2$ respectively, show that $m_1\ddot{\mathbf{r}}_1+m_2\ddot{\mathbf{r}}_2 = 0$ and deduce that the centre of mass of the particles moves with constant velocity. If $PQ = \mathbf{r}$, show that $\ddot{\mathbf{r}} = -k\hat{\mathbf{r}}/r^2$, where $\hat{\mathbf{r}}$ is the unit vector in the direction $\overline{PQ}$ and k is a constant.

22 Particles of masses m_1, m_2 are attached to the ends A, B of a light rod. Impulses $\mathbf{I}_1, \mathbf{I}_2$ are simultaneously applied to m_1, m_2 respectively, show that the impulsive reaction of the rod on m_1 is

$$\hat{\mathbf{n}}\frac{m_1m_2}{m_1+m_2}\,.\left(\frac{\mathbf{I}_2}{m_2}-\frac{\mathbf{I}_1}{m_1}\right),$$

where $\hat{\mathbf{n}}$ is the unit vector in the direction $\overline{AB}$.

23 A particle P moves under the action of a central force μ/r^2 per unit mass directed towards the origin O where r is the distance of the particle from O at time t. If θ is the angle $\overline{OP}$ makes with a fixed direction at time t, $\hat{\mathbf{r}}$ is a unit vector in the direction $\overline{OP}$ and $\hat{\mathbf{s}}$ is a unit vector normal to $\overline{OP}$ in the direction θ increasing, establish the following results: (i) $\ddot{\mathbf{r}} = -\mu\hat{\mathbf{r}}/r^2$; (ii) $2\dot{\mathbf{r}}\,.\,\ddot{\mathbf{r}} = -2(\mu/r^2)(\dot{r}\hat{\mathbf{r}}+r\dot{\theta}\hat{\mathbf{s}})\,.\,\hat{\mathbf{r}} = -2(\mu/r^2)\dot{r}$; (iii) $v^2 = 2\mu/r+c$, where v is the speed of the particle and c a constant.

24 If G is the centre of mass of a system of particles, prove that the angular momentum of the system about a fixed point O is equal to the angular momentum about O of a particle of mass equal to that of the system moving with G together with the angular momentum of the system about G.

25 O is a fixed point and S is a moving point whose position vector relative to O is $\mathbf{s}$. If $\mathbf{P}$ is the linear momentum and $\mathbf{H}, \mathbf{H}'$ the angular momenta about O, S respectively of a system of particles, prove that $\mathbf{H} = \mathbf{s}\wedge\mathbf{P}+\mathbf{H}'$.

26 The centre of mass G of a set of particles in motion has a velocity $\bar{\mathbf{v}}$ and the angular momentum of the system about G is $\mathbf{H}$. Show that the angular momentum of the system about a point A whose position vector relative to G is $\mathbf{a}$ is $\mathbf{H}-\mathbf{a}\wedge M\bar{\mathbf{v}}$, where M is the total mass of the system.

27 With the notation of ex. 25, show that $\dot{\mathbf{H}}' = \mathbf{L}-\dot{\mathbf{s}}\wedge\mathbf{P}-\mathbf{s}\wedge\mathbf{R}$ where $\mathbf{R}$ is the sum of the external forces acting on the system and $\mathbf{L}$ is the moment of these forces about O. Deduce that the rate of change of angular momentum about the moving point $\mathbf{S}$ is $\mathbf{L}'-\dot{\mathbf{s}}\wedge\mathbf{P}$, where $\mathbf{L}'$ is the moment of the external forces acting on the system about S.

ANSWERS

EXAMPLES 1a (page 6)

2. 0. **3.** (i) $\mathbf{a}+\mathbf{b}$; (ii) $-(\mathbf{a}+\mathbf{b})$; (iii) $\mathbf{b}-\mathbf{a}$. **4.** 5. **5.** (i) $\mathbf{b}-\mathbf{a}$; (ii) $\mathbf{a}-\mathbf{b}$; (iii) $\frac{1}{2}(\mathbf{a}+\mathbf{b})$. **6.** $\sqrt{5}$; $\sqrt{130}$; 13; $\sqrt{101}$. **7.** (i) $\mathbf{a} = -\mathbf{c}$; (ii) $\mathbf{b} = \mathbf{d}$; (iii) $\mathbf{a}+\mathbf{b}$; (iv) $\mathbf{a}-\mathbf{d}$; $\mathbf{b}$ or $\mathbf{d}$. **10.** (i) $\frac{1}{3}(2\mathbf{a}+\mathbf{b})$; (ii) $\frac{1}{5}(3\mathbf{a}+2\mathbf{b})$. **13.** 5; $\tan^{-1}\frac{4}{3}$ to $\overline{OX}$. **16.** Yes. **18.** $\mathbf{b}-\mathbf{a}$.

EXAMPLES 1b (page 11)

1. $\frac{5}{2}(\sqrt{3}\mathbf{i}+\mathbf{j})$. **2.** (i) 5; (ii) 2; (iii) $\sqrt{29}$; (iv) 1; (v) 1; **3.** $10\mathbf{i}-5\mathbf{j}+6\mathbf{k}$. **4.** $\sqrt{14}$. **5.** 3; $\frac{1}{3}, -\frac{2}{3}, \frac{2}{3}$. **6.** 6. **7.** $-\frac{4}{3}$. **8.** (i) $\sqrt{13}$; (ii) $\sqrt{58}$; (iii) $4\sqrt{2}$. **9.** (i) $a = 3, b = -4$; (ii) $a = 2, b = -1, c = 3$; (iii) $a = 2, b = -1$. **10.** (i) $\sqrt{94}$; $8/\sqrt{94}, -2/\sqrt{94}, 3/\sqrt{94}$; (ii) $\sqrt{114}$; $-5/\sqrt{114}, -8/\sqrt{114}, 5/\sqrt{114}$. **11.** (i) $8\mathbf{i}-8\mathbf{j}+4\mathbf{k}$; (ii) $2\mathbf{i}+6\mathbf{j}+4\mathbf{k}$; (iii) $l\mathbf{i}+m\mathbf{j}+n\mathbf{k}$. **12.** $\frac{1}{3}(2\mathbf{i}-2\mathbf{j}+\mathbf{k})$. **13.** $\frac{5}{3}(\mathbf{i}+2\mathbf{j}-2\mathbf{k})$.

14. $\frac{1}{\sqrt{41}}(2\mathbf{i}+\mathbf{j}+6\mathbf{k})$. **15.** $\sqrt{105}$; $-5/\sqrt{105}, -8/\sqrt{105}, 4/\sqrt{105}$.

16. $\frac{1}{2}(2+3\sqrt{3}), \frac{1}{3}(2\sqrt{3}-3)$. **17.** 1:3. **18.** (i) $\sqrt{33}$; $2/\sqrt{33}, -5/\sqrt{33}, 2/\sqrt{33}$; (ii) $\frac{1}{5}(4\mathbf{i}-3\mathbf{j})$. **19.** $a = 4, b = -4$. **21.** $\frac{1}{\sqrt{69}}(-7\mathbf{i}+2\mathbf{j}-4\mathbf{k})$.

23. $\sqrt{\{(x_1+x_2)^2+(y_1+y_2)^2+(z_1+z_2)^2\}}$; $(x_1+x_2)/r, (y_1+y_2)/r, (z_1+z_2)/r$ where $r = \sqrt{\{(x_1+x_2)^2+(y_1+y_2)^2+(z_1+z_2)^2\}}$. **24.** (i) $\frac{1}{2}(7\mathbf{i}-\mathbf{j}-\mathbf{k})$; (ii) $\frac{1}{3}(11\mathbf{i}-3\mathbf{k})$. **25.** $\overline{PQ} = \mathbf{a}+2\mathbf{b}$; $\overline{QR} = 3\mathbf{a}+6\mathbf{b}$. **26.** $\mathbf{r} = 2\mathbf{i}-\mathbf{j}+2\mathbf{k}$. **28.** (2, 3); 1.

EXAMPLES 2a (page 18)

1. (i) 6, $6\sqrt{3}$; (ii) $\sqrt{2}, \sqrt{2}$; (iii) 0, 40; (iv) $-\frac{1}{2}\sqrt{3}, \frac{3}{2}$; (v) -1, 1. **2.** (i) 60; (ii) 60; (iii) 60; (iv) -60; (v) -60. **3.** (i) $60\sqrt{3}\hat{\mathbf{n}}$; (ii) $-60\sqrt{3}\hat{\mathbf{n}}$; (iii) $60\sqrt{3}\hat{\mathbf{n}}$; (iv) $-60\sqrt{3}\hat{\mathbf{n}}$; (v) $60\sqrt{3}\hat{\mathbf{n}}$. **5.** $16\mathbf{k}$. **6.** (i) perependicular; (ii) perpendicular; both zero. **8.** At right angles. **9.** $\mathbf{a} \wedge \mathbf{b}$. **21.** 0.

EXAMPLES 2b (page 24)

1. (i) 1, $-3\mathbf{i}+3\mathbf{j}+6\mathbf{k}$; (ii) -2, $\mathbf{i}+2\mathbf{j}-3\mathbf{k}$; (iii) 2, $-4\mathbf{k}$; (iv) 1, $-\mathbf{i}-6\mathbf{j}-16\mathbf{k}$; (v) -1, $\mathbf{i}-2\mathbf{j}+2\mathbf{k}$. **2.** (i) 6; (ii) -3; (iii) 8; (iv) 7; (v) 3. **3.** (i) $9\mathbf{i}-9\mathbf{j}-18\mathbf{k}$; (ii) $-3\mathbf{i}-6\mathbf{j}+9\mathbf{k}$; (iii) $12\mathbf{k}$; (iv) $3\mathbf{i}+18\mathbf{j}+48\mathbf{k}$; (v) $-3\mathbf{i}+6\mathbf{j}-6\mathbf{k}$. **5.** (i) $1/\sqrt{15}$; (ii) 5/21; (iii) $-4/\sqrt{154}$; (iv) $-11/15$; (v) 2/39. **6.** (i) $6/\sqrt{85}$; (ii) $2\sqrt{2/3}$;

(iii) $\sqrt{\frac{2}{3}}$. **8.** (i) $-\mathbf{k}$; (ii) $-\mathbf{j}$; (iii) $-\dfrac{1}{\sqrt{2}}(\mathbf{j}+\mathbf{k})$; (iv) $\dfrac{1}{\sqrt{90}}(4\mathbf{i}+5\mathbf{j}+7\mathbf{k})$.

10. (i) $\sqrt{2}$; (ii) $1/\sqrt{3}$; (iii) $1/\sqrt{14}$ in direction of $-\mathbf{a}$. **11.** (i) $14\mathbf{i}-10\mathbf{j}+9\mathbf{k}$; (ii) $13/\sqrt{3}$. **14.** $45\mathbf{k}$. **17.** (i) $\pm\dfrac{1}{\sqrt{14}}(\mathbf{i}-3\mathbf{j}+2\mathbf{k})$;

(ii) $\pm\dfrac{1}{\sqrt{377}}(9\mathbf{i}-10\mathbf{j}-14\mathbf{k})$; (iii) $\pm\dfrac{1}{\sqrt{110}}(5\mathbf{i}+6\mathbf{j}-7\mathbf{k})$.

19. $[yw-z(v+x\omega)]\mathbf{i}+[z(u-y\omega)-xw]\mathbf{j}+[x(v+x\omega)-y(u-y\omega)]\mathbf{k}$.

21. $\pm\dfrac{1}{2\sqrt{3}}[(1-\sqrt{3})\mathbf{i}+(1+\sqrt{3})\mathbf{j}-2\mathbf{k}]$, $\pm\dfrac{1}{2\sqrt{3}}[(1+\sqrt{3})\mathbf{i}+(1-\sqrt{3})\mathbf{j}-2\mathbf{k}]$.

24. (i) 2; (ii) 8; (iii) 0. **25.** (i) $-3\mathbf{i}-\mathbf{j}+2\mathbf{k}$; (ii) $16\mathbf{i}-11\mathbf{j}+7\mathbf{k}$; (iii) $20\mathbf{i}-\mathbf{j}+2\mathbf{k}$. **28.** **a** parallel to plane of **b** and **c**.

31. **b** is normal to the plane of **a** and **c**. **33.** **a** parallel to **b**; **c** parallel to **d**; **a**, **b**, **c**, **d** all parallel to same plane. **34.** $y = [\mathbf{d}, \mathbf{c}, \mathbf{a}]/[\mathbf{b}, \mathbf{c}, \mathbf{a}]$, $z = [\mathbf{d}, \mathbf{a}, \mathbf{b}]/[\mathbf{c}, \mathbf{a}, \mathbf{b}]$.

EXAMPLES 3a (page 30)

1. (i) $\frac{1}{2}\mathbf{a}$; (ii) $\frac{2}{5}\mathbf{a}$; (iii) $3\mathbf{a}$; (iv) $-\mathbf{a}$. **2.** $\overline{OP} = \frac{1}{8}(3\mathbf{a}+5\mathbf{b})$, $\overline{OQ} = \frac{1}{2}(5\mathbf{b}-3\mathbf{a})$, $\overline{PQ} = \frac{15}{8}(\mathbf{b}-\mathbf{a})$. **3.** $2\mathbf{b}-\mathbf{a}$, $4\mathbf{b}-3\mathbf{a}$, $3\mathbf{b}-2\mathbf{a}$. **4.** (i) $\frac{1}{2}(\mathbf{a}+\mathbf{b})$; (ii) $\mathbf{c}-\mathbf{a}$; (iii) $\frac{1}{2}(\mathbf{b}-\mathbf{a})$; (iv) $\frac{1}{2}(\mathbf{a}-\mathbf{c})$; (v) $\frac{1}{10}(3\mathbf{b}+5\mathbf{c}+2\mathbf{d})$. **5.** $\mathbf{d} = \mathbf{a}+\mathbf{c}-\mathbf{b}$; $\frac{1}{2}(\mathbf{a}+\mathbf{c})$, $\frac{1}{3}(2\mathbf{a}-\mathbf{b}+2\mathbf{c})$. **6.** 1:3. **7.** $\mathbf{d} = 2\mathbf{b}+\mathbf{c}-2\mathbf{a}$; $\frac{1}{3}(2\mathbf{b}+\mathbf{c})$.

8. $\frac{1}{3}(\mathbf{a}+\mathbf{b}+\mathbf{c})$. **9.** $\frac{1}{2}(\mathbf{r}-\mathbf{q})$. **10.** $\overline{BC}^2 = (\mathbf{c}-\mathbf{b})^2$. **15.** $\frac{1}{2}\mathbf{d}$, $\frac{1}{2}(\mathbf{b}+2\mathbf{d})$.

17. $\overline{CB} = -\mathbf{a}-\mathbf{c}$, $\overline{CA} = \mathbf{a}-\mathbf{c}$. **23.** $\overline{AC} = \mathbf{b}+\mathbf{d}$, $\overline{BD} = \mathbf{d}-\mathbf{b}$.

26. $\overline{AC} = \mathbf{b}+\mathbf{d}$, $\overline{BP} = \frac{1}{4}(4\mathbf{d}-\mathbf{b})$. **31.** $\mathbf{d} = \mathbf{a}+2(\mathbf{c}-\mathbf{b})$, $\mathbf{e} = 2\mathbf{a}-3\mathbf{b}+2\mathbf{c}$, $\mathbf{f} = 2\mathbf{a}-2\mathbf{b}+\mathbf{c}$.

EXAMPLES 3b (page 36)

1. (i) 4; (ii) 8; (iii) 4; (iv) 1; (v) 0. **2.** (i) $4\mathbf{i}-\mathbf{j}-3\mathbf{k}$; (ii) $12\mathbf{i}+2\mathbf{j}+3\mathbf{k}$; (iii) $18\mathbf{i}+10\mathbf{j}-\mathbf{k}$; (iv) $-5\mathbf{i}+\mathbf{j}-12\mathbf{k}$; (v) $-3a^2\mathbf{i}-3a^2\mathbf{j}$.

3. (i) $\sqrt{3}$; $-\dfrac{1}{\sqrt{3}}, \dfrac{1}{\sqrt{3}}, -\dfrac{1}{\sqrt{3}}$; (ii) 3; $-\frac{1}{3}, -\frac{2}{3}, \frac{2}{3}$; (iii) 7; $-\frac{6}{7}, \frac{2}{7}, -\frac{3}{7}$;

(iv) 2; 0, 0, -1; (v) $a\sqrt{3}$; $\dfrac{1}{\sqrt{3}}, -\dfrac{1}{\sqrt{3}}, -\dfrac{1}{\sqrt{3}}$. **4.** (i) $\sqrt{14}$; $-\dfrac{1}{\sqrt{14}}, \dfrac{2}{\sqrt{14}}, -\dfrac{3}{\sqrt{14}}$; (ii) $3\sqrt{6}$; $-\dfrac{1}{\sqrt{6}}, -\dfrac{1}{\sqrt{6}}, \dfrac{2}{\sqrt{6}}$; (iii) 1; 1, 0, 0. **5.** (i) $\dfrac{1}{\sqrt{3}}$;

(ii) $-\dfrac{1}{2\sqrt{3}}$; (iii) $\dfrac{3}{5\sqrt{2}}$; (iv) $\dfrac{1}{\sqrt{30}}$. **7.** (i) $\frac{1}{7}(3\mathbf{i}-2\mathbf{j}+6\mathbf{k})$; (ii) $\mathbf{i}$;

(iii) $-\frac{1}{3}(2\mathbf{i}+\mathbf{j}+2\mathbf{k})$. **9.** $AB:CD = 1:2$. **10.** (i) $-\dfrac{1}{\sqrt{3}}$; (ii) 0;

(iii) $\dfrac{7}{2\sqrt{21}}$; (iv) $\dfrac{1}{\sqrt{5}}$. **11.** $\frac{1}{3}(2\mathbf{i}+6\mathbf{j}+\mathbf{k})$. **12.** $\frac{5}{3}\mathbf{i}$. **13.** $(\frac{7}{5}, \frac{6}{5}, -\frac{1}{5})$.

14. $\frac{1}{\sqrt{3}}(\mathbf{i}+\mathbf{j}+\mathbf{k})$. **15.** (i) 4; (ii) $-2\mathbf{i}+\mathbf{j}-2\mathbf{k}$; $\frac{4}{5}$; Area $= \frac{3}{2}$.

16. (i) $AB = \sqrt{6}$, $AC = \sqrt{5}$, $BC = \sqrt{17}$; $\cos A = -\frac{3}{\sqrt{30}}$, $\cos B = \frac{9}{\sqrt{102}}$,

$\cos C = \frac{8}{\sqrt{85}}$. **17.** $\frac{1}{\sqrt{77}}(4\mathbf{i}-5\mathbf{j}-6\mathbf{k})$. **18.** $\Delta = \frac{1}{2}\overline{AB}\wedge\overline{AC}$;

$\frac{1}{2}(-6\mathbf{i}+3\mathbf{j}-7\mathbf{k})$. **19.** (i) $\frac{1}{2}\pi$; (ii) $\cos^{-1}\frac{1}{\sqrt{3}}$. **21.** $-\frac{1}{\sqrt{26}}(\mathbf{i}+3\mathbf{j}+4\mathbf{k})$.

22. (i) 1; (ii) 87; (iii) $\frac{400}{9}$. **24.** $2/\sqrt{14}$. **26.** $40/3\sqrt{2}$. **28.** 30.

29. $\frac{1}{1+\lambda}[(\lambda+2)\mathbf{i}+(\lambda-1)\mathbf{j}+(\lambda+3)\mathbf{k}]$; $\frac{1}{9}(8\mathbf{i}+11\mathbf{j}+7\mathbf{k})$. **30.** $\frac{1}{9}(14\mathbf{i}-\mathbf{j}+8\mathbf{k})$.

31. $(2, \frac{1}{2}, \frac{3}{2})$.

EXAMPLES 4a (page 44)

1. (i) $\mathbf{r} = \mathbf{a}+\lambda(\mathbf{b}-\mathbf{a})$; (ii) $\mathbf{r} = \mathbf{b}+\lambda(\mathbf{a}-\mathbf{b})$; (iii) $\mathbf{r} = \mathbf{a}+\lambda[\frac{1}{2}(\mathbf{b}+\mathbf{c})-\mathbf{a}]$; (iv) $\mathbf{r} = \mathbf{a}+\lambda(\mathbf{c}-\mathbf{b})$. **2.** (i) $\mathbf{r} = \mathbf{i}+\mathbf{j}-\mathbf{k}+\lambda(\mathbf{i}-2\mathbf{j})$; (ii) $\mathbf{r} = -\mathbf{i}+2\mathbf{j}+\lambda(3\mathbf{i}+\mathbf{j}-\mathbf{k})$; (iii) $\mathbf{r} = 2\mathbf{i}+2\mathbf{j}+\mathbf{k}+\lambda(3\mathbf{i}-\mathbf{j}-\mathbf{k})$; (iv) $\mathbf{r} = 2\mathbf{i}+\mathbf{j}-\mathbf{k}+\lambda(2\mathbf{i}+\mathbf{j}+3\mathbf{k})$. **3.** (i) $\mathbf{r} = \lambda 2\mathbf{a}$; (ii) $\mathbf{r} = \mathbf{a}+\lambda(2\mathbf{b}-\mathbf{a})$; (iii) $\mathbf{r} = \mathbf{a}+\mathbf{b}+\lambda(-2\mathbf{b})$; (v) $\mathbf{r} = \mathbf{a}+2\mathbf{b}+\lambda(\mathbf{a}-\mathbf{b})$. **4.** $-\mathbf{i}+6\mathbf{j}$.

5. $\frac{1}{3}(-\mathbf{b}+2\mathbf{c})$. **6.** (i) $\mathbf{r} = \lambda(\mathbf{c}-\mathbf{b})$; (ii) $\mathbf{r} = \mathbf{c}-\lambda\mathbf{b}$; (iii) $\mathbf{r} = \frac{1}{2}(\mathbf{b}+\mathbf{c})-\lambda\mathbf{b}$; (iv) $\mathbf{r} = \mathbf{c}-\mathbf{b}+\lambda(\mathbf{b}-\frac{1}{2}\mathbf{c})$; (v) $\mathbf{r} = \mathbf{c}+\lambda(2\mathbf{b}-\mathbf{c})$. **7.** (i) $\mathbf{a}+\mathbf{b}$; (ii) $\mathbf{b}-\mathbf{a}$; (iii) $\mathbf{i}+\mathbf{j}$; (iv) $\frac{2}{3}(\mathbf{a}+\mathbf{b})$; (v) $2\mathbf{i}-\mathbf{j}+\mathbf{k}$. **8.** $\mathbf{r} = \mathbf{i}+\mathbf{j}+\mathbf{k}+\lambda(2\mathbf{i}-2\mathbf{j}+\mathbf{k})$; $\mathbf{r} = a\mathbf{i}+b\mathbf{j}+c\mathbf{k}+\lambda(l\mathbf{i}+m\mathbf{j}+n\mathbf{k})$. **11.** (i) $\mathbf{r} = \lambda(\mathbf{b}+\mathbf{c})$; (ii) $\mathbf{r} = \frac{1}{2}\mathbf{b}+\mu(\mathbf{c}-\mathbf{b})$.

12. $\mathbf{r} = \mathbf{b}+m(\frac{1}{2}\mathbf{c}-\mathbf{b})$, $\mathbf{r} = \mathbf{c}+n(\frac{1}{2}\mathbf{b}-\mathbf{c})$. **13.** (i) $\mathbf{r} = \lambda(\mathbf{c}+\mathbf{d})$; (ii) $\mathbf{r} = \mathbf{b}+\lambda(\frac{1}{2}\mathbf{d}-\mathbf{b})$; (iii) $\mathbf{r} = \frac{1}{2}\mathbf{c}+\lambda(\mathbf{b}+\mathbf{d}-\mathbf{c})$.

14. $\mathbf{r} = 3\mathbf{i}-2\mathbf{j}+\lambda(-\mathbf{i}+6\mathbf{j})$; $\mathbf{r} = \mathbf{i}+\mathbf{j}+\mu(\frac{3}{2}\mathbf{i})$; $\frac{1}{4}(7\mathbf{i}+4\mathbf{j})$. **15.** $\frac{4}{7}$.

16. $\mathbf{r} = \mathbf{b}+\lambda(\frac{1}{3}\mathbf{c}-\mathbf{b})$; $\mathbf{r} = \mathbf{c}+\mu(\frac{1}{3}\mathbf{b}-\mathbf{c})$; 3:1.

17. (i) $\mathbf{r} = 2\mathbf{i}-\mathbf{j}+\mathbf{k}+\lambda(-\mathbf{i}+2\mathbf{j}-3\mathbf{k})$; (ii) $\mathbf{r} = -\mathbf{i}+3\mathbf{j}+\mathbf{k}+\lambda(\mathbf{i}-\mathbf{j}+\mathbf{k})$; (iii) $\mathbf{r} = \mathbf{j}+\mathbf{k}+\lambda(4\mathbf{i}+2\mathbf{j}+\mathbf{k})$. **21.** $\frac{4}{9}$. **24.** $\mathbf{r} = \lambda(2\mathbf{i}+\mathbf{j}+\mathbf{k})$, $\mathbf{r} = \lambda(-2\mathbf{i}-\mathbf{j}-\mathbf{k})$. **25.** (i) $\frac{1}{3}(\mathbf{b}+\mathbf{c}+\mathbf{d})$; (ii) $\frac{1}{3}(\mathbf{c}+\mathbf{d})$; (iii) $\mathbf{r} = \lambda(\mathbf{b}+\mathbf{c}+\mathbf{d})$; $\mathbf{r} = \mathbf{b}+\mu(\mathbf{c}+\mathbf{d}-3\mathbf{b})$; $\frac{1}{4}(\mathbf{b}+\mathbf{c}+\mathbf{d})$. **26.** (i) $\mathbf{r} = t(23\mathbf{i}-4\mathbf{j}-\mathbf{k})$; (ii) $\mathbf{r} = \mathbf{i}+\mathbf{j}+\mathbf{k}+t(-\mathbf{k})$; (iii) $\mathbf{r} = 4\mathbf{i}+4\mathbf{j}+t(\mathbf{i}+\mathbf{j})$. **28.** $\sqrt{2}$. **30.** $\frac{1}{3}a\sqrt{6}$.

32. $\frac{1}{11}(15\mathbf{i}+16\mathbf{j}-10\mathbf{k})$. **36.** $\frac{1}{\sqrt{3}}$. **39.** $\sqrt{\frac{1}{2}(b^2+c^2-d^2)}$.

EXAMPLES 4b (page 53)

1. (i) $\mathbf{r} = s(\mathbf{i}+2\mathbf{j}+\mathbf{k})+t(-2\mathbf{i}+\mathbf{j}+2\mathbf{k})$; (ii) $\mathbf{r} = 2\mathbf{i}+\mathbf{j}+2\mathbf{k}+s(-2\mathbf{i}+2\mathbf{j}-3\mathbf{k})+t(\mathbf{i}-\mathbf{j}+2\mathbf{k})$; (iii) $\mathbf{r} = -\mathbf{i}+\mathbf{j}+s(4\mathbf{i}+2\mathbf{j}+3\mathbf{k})+t(3\mathbf{i}-2\mathbf{j}-2\mathbf{k})$; (iv) $\mathbf{r} = 3\mathbf{i}+\mathbf{j}-4\mathbf{k}+s(-\mathbf{i}-2\mathbf{j}+6\mathbf{k})+t(-6\mathbf{i}+\mathbf{j}+5\mathbf{k})$; (v) $\mathbf{r} = a\mathbf{i}+s(-a\mathbf{i}+a\mathbf{j})+t(-a\mathbf{i}+a\mathbf{k})$. **2.** $\mathbf{r} = \mathbf{i}+\mathbf{j}+\mathbf{k}+s(2\mathbf{i}+\mathbf{j})+t(\mathbf{i}-\mathbf{j}+2\mathbf{k})$.

3. (i) $\mathbf{r} = s(\mathbf{i}+\mathbf{j}+\mathbf{k})+t(\mathbf{i}-\mathbf{j}-\mathbf{k})$;
(ii) $\mathbf{r} = \mathbf{i}-2\mathbf{j}+s(\mathbf{j}-\mathbf{k})+t(2\mathbf{i}+3\mathbf{k})$; (iii) $\mathbf{r} = 2\mathbf{i}+\mathbf{j}-3\mathbf{k}+s\mathbf{i}+t(3\mathbf{i}-\mathbf{j}-2\mathbf{k})$;
(iv) $\mathbf{r} = a\mathbf{i}+s(b\mathbf{j}+c\mathbf{k}-a\mathbf{i})+t(b\mathbf{j}-c\mathbf{k})$. **4.** (i) $\mathbf{r}.(2\mathbf{i}-\mathbf{j}+2\mathbf{k}) = 18$;
(ii) $\mathbf{r}.(\mathbf{i}+\mathbf{j}+\mathbf{k}) = 6$; (iii) $\mathbf{r}.(2\mathbf{i}+\mathbf{j}-2\mathbf{k}) = 9$; (iv) $\mathbf{r}.(p\mathbf{i}+q\mathbf{j}+r\mathbf{k}) = p^2+q^2+r^2$.
5. (i) $\mathbf{r}.(2\mathbf{i}-\mathbf{j}+2\mathbf{k}) = 3$; (ii) $\mathbf{r}.(6\mathbf{i}-3\mathbf{j}-2\mathbf{k}) = 13$; (iii) $\mathbf{r}.(2\mathbf{i}+2\mathbf{j}+\mathbf{k}) = 4$.
7. $\mathbf{r} = s\mathbf{i}+t\mathbf{j}$ or $\mathbf{r}.\mathbf{k} = 0$; $\mathbf{r} = \frac{1}{2}(7\mathbf{i}-\mathbf{j})$. **8.** $\mathbf{r}.(3\mathbf{i}-2\mathbf{j}+2\mathbf{k}) = 0$.
9. (i) $\frac{1}{\sqrt{3}}, \frac{1}{\sqrt{3}}, \frac{1}{\sqrt{3}}; \frac{1}{\sqrt{3}}$; (ii) $-\frac{1}{3}, \frac{2}{3}, \frac{2}{3}; \frac{2}{3}$; (iii) $-\frac{6}{7}, \frac{2}{7}, -\frac{3}{7}; \frac{1}{7}$.
10. $\mathbf{r} = \mathbf{i}-2\mathbf{j}+\mathbf{k}+\lambda(-\mathbf{i}+5\mathbf{j}-3\mathbf{k})$; $\mathbf{r} = s(4\mathbf{j})+t(2\mathbf{i}+\mathbf{k})$; $(\frac{4}{5}, -1, \frac{2}{5})$.
13. (i) $\pm\frac{1}{\sqrt{3}}(-\mathbf{i}+\mathbf{j}+\mathbf{k})$; (ii) $\pm\frac{1}{\sqrt{38}}(2\mathbf{i}+3\mathbf{j}+5\mathbf{k})$; (iii) $\pm\frac{1}{\sqrt{6}}(2\mathbf{i}+\mathbf{j}-\mathbf{k})$;
(iv) $\pm\frac{1}{\sqrt{150}}(2\mathbf{i}-11\mathbf{j}-5\mathbf{k})$; (v) $\pm\frac{1}{\sqrt{398}}(9\mathbf{i}+11\mathbf{j}-14\mathbf{k})$;
(vi) $\pm\frac{1}{\sqrt{83}}(-3\mathbf{i}+7\mathbf{j}+5\mathbf{k})$. **14.** $\mathbf{i}+\mathbf{j}+\mathbf{k}$. **16.** $2\frac{1}{6}$ units. **17.** $\frac{1}{\sqrt{7}}$.
19. $\cos^{-1}\frac{4}{\sqrt{414}}$. **20.** $\frac{2}{\sqrt{3}}$; same side. **21.** same side.
23. $\mathbf{r}.(2\mathbf{i}+2\mathbf{j}+\mathbf{k}) = 4$; $\frac{7}{3}$. **25.** $\mathbf{r} = \mathbf{i}+\mathbf{j}+\mathbf{k}+s(2\mathbf{i}+\mathbf{j}+\mathbf{k})+t(\mathbf{j}-\mathbf{k})$.
26. (i) $\mathbf{r} = s(2\mathbf{i})+t(2\mathbf{j}+2\mathbf{k})$; (ii) $\mathbf{r} = 2\mathbf{k}+s(2\mathbf{i}+\mathbf{j}-2\mathbf{k})+t(2\mathbf{j}-\mathbf{k})$;
(iii) $\frac{8}{\sqrt{29}}$; (iv) $\cos^{-1}\frac{1}{\sqrt{58}}$. **27.** $\mathbf{r} = \frac{1}{2}\mathbf{i}-\frac{1}{2}\mathbf{j}+2\mathbf{k}+s(\mathbf{i}+3\mathbf{j}+2\mathbf{k})+$
$t(-3\mathbf{i}-3\mathbf{j}+4\mathbf{k})$. **32.** (i) $\frac{4}{\sqrt{34}}$; (ii) $\frac{6\sqrt{34}}{17}a$.

EXAMPLES 5a (page 60)

1. (i) $10\mathbf{j}$ cm/s; (ii) $-4\mathbf{i}$ N; (iii) $\pm\frac{8}{5}(-3\mathbf{i}+4\mathbf{j})$ m/s;
(iv) $3(-5\mathbf{i}+12\mathbf{j})$ N; (v) $10(\mathbf{i}-\sqrt{3}\mathbf{j})$ N.
2. (i) $5\sqrt{2}$ km/h in direction $\overline{OP}$ where P is the point $(-1, -7)$; (ii) as (i) with $P(1, 7)$. **3.** 21 cm/s: $\frac{6}{7}, \frac{3}{7}, -\frac{2}{7}$. **4.** $\sqrt{1961}$ N in the direction $\overline{OP}$ where P is the point $(-44, -5)$. **5.** $P = \frac{80}{3}\sqrt{3}$, $Q = \frac{160}{3}\sqrt{3}$ N.
6. $2\sqrt{18}$ km/h; $-\frac{1}{\sqrt{18}}, -\frac{1}{\sqrt{18}}, -\frac{4}{\sqrt{18}}$. **9.** $\overline{AD}$; the direction of $\overline{AD}$ or $\overline{DA}$.
10. $N\theta^\circ E$ where $\theta = \sin^{-1}(w\sin\varphi)/v$; s/R where $R = \sqrt{(v^2-w^2\sin^2\varphi)}-w\cos\varphi$.
11. $-(\mathbf{r}_1+\mathbf{r}_2)$. **12.** (i) $\mathbf{P}+\mathbf{Q}+\mathbf{R}+\mathbf{S} = 0$; (ii) $\overline{AB}$ or $\overline{BA}$; (iii) $\overline{BA}$ or $\overline{AB}$.
13. $3000\sqrt{74}$ m/s; $\frac{1}{\sqrt{74}}, \frac{3}{\sqrt{74}}, -\frac{8}{\sqrt{74}}$. **15.** $10\left(\mathbf{i}-\frac{1}{\sqrt{3}}\mathbf{j}\right)$ km/h, where $\mathbf{i}, \mathbf{j}$ are unit vectors in the directions E and N. **17.** $3(3\mathbf{i}+\sqrt{3}\mathbf{j})$ km/h, where $\mathbf{i}, \mathbf{j}$ are unit vectors in the directions W and S. **20.** $2\sqrt{59}$ N; $\frac{7}{\sqrt{59}}, \frac{1}{\sqrt{59}}$,

$\dfrac{3}{\sqrt{59}}$. **21.** $S\theta°E$ where $\theta = \tan^{-1} 2$. **22.** $AP/PC = 7/3$, $BQ/QC = 3/1$;

$\mathbf{r} = -40$. **24.** $4\sqrt{55}$ N. **26.** (i) zero; (ii) $q = r = 1$.

27. $\frac{2}{7}, -\frac{3}{7}, \frac{6}{7}$. **28.** $2\sqrt{\frac{29}{3}}$ N; $-\dfrac{2}{\sqrt{29}}$. **29.** $3(\mathbf{i}-2\mathbf{k})$ cm/s; $2\sqrt{22}$ cm.

EXAMPLES 5b (page 68)

1. (i) 7 J; (ii) 1 J; (iii) -13 J; (iv) 0; (v) $(Xx+Yy+Zz)$ J.
2. $5(2\sqrt{3}-1)$ J. **3.** -3 J. **5.** (i) $\mathbf{k}$; (ii) $3(-\mathbf{i}+5\mathbf{j}+9\mathbf{k})$; (iii) $10(\mathbf{i}+4\mathbf{j}+3\mathbf{k})$; (iv) $24(-4\mathbf{i}-3\mathbf{j}+3\mathbf{k})$; (v) $(yZ-zY)\mathbf{i}+(zX-xZ)\mathbf{j}+(xY-yX)\mathbf{k}$. **6.** $2(5\mathbf{i}-17\mathbf{j}-13\mathbf{k})$; -26 N m. **7.** 460 J.
8. (i) $20(2\mathbf{i}+2\mathbf{j}-\mathbf{k})$; (ii) $20(-9\mathbf{i}-2\mathbf{j}+8\mathbf{k})$ N m. **9.** 18 units.
10. (i) 0; point lies on line of action of force; (ii) $\dfrac{98}{\sqrt{3}}$ units. **11.** 25 units.
12. $11\sqrt{5}$ N. **13.** (i) 3, 5, 7, 13 units; (ii) 96 units. **14.** $\frac{160}{3}$ N m.
16. (i) $20(-7\mathbf{i}-2\mathbf{j}+9\mathbf{k})$; 180 N m. **17.** 29 J. **18.** mid-point.
21. 7 N; $\sqrt{173}$ N cm. **22.** zero. **23.** $aF/\sqrt{2}$. **24.** equivalent to a couple.
26. $\mathbf{G}-\mathbf{a}\wedge\mathbf{R}$.

EXAMPLES 6a (page 76)

1. 0; $2\mathbf{i}+3\mathbf{j}+4\mathbf{k}$. **2.** (i) $2\mathbf{i}-\mathbf{j}$; (ii) $\dfrac{1}{\sqrt{2}}$. **3.** $\frac{1}{2}a\sqrt{(8+\pi^2)}$. **4.** $8(-\mathbf{i}+\mathbf{j})$.
5. (i) $3\mathbf{i}+4t\mathbf{j}$; (ii) $4\cos t\mathbf{i}-3\sin t\mathbf{j}$; (iii) $e^t\mathbf{i}-e^{-t}\mathbf{j}+\mathbf{k}$; (iv) $-b\omega\sin\omega t\mathbf{i}+b\omega\cos\omega t\mathbf{j}$. **6.** (i) $(2+2t)\mathbf{i}+2t\mathbf{j}+\mathbf{k}$; (ii) $6t^2-4t+2$; (iii) $3t^2\mathbf{i}-(4+4t^3)\mathbf{k}$; (iv) $4(2t+t^3)$. **7.** (i) $\sqrt{6}$; (ii) $7/\sqrt{6}$; (iii) 3. **8.** $F[-\{2\sin 2t(1+\alpha t)+\alpha\cos 2t\}\mathbf{i}+\{2\cos 2t(1+\alpha t)-\alpha\sin 2t\}\mathbf{j}]/m_0(1+\alpha t)^2$. **9.** (i) $2\mathbf{r}\,.\dfrac{d\mathbf{r}}{ds}$; (ii) $2\dfrac{d\mathbf{r}}{ds}\,.\dfrac{d^2\mathbf{r}}{ds^2}$;

(iii) $\left(2\mathbf{r}\,.\dfrac{d\mathbf{r}}{ds}\right)\dfrac{d\mathbf{r}}{ds}+\mathbf{r}^2\dfrac{d^2\mathbf{r}}{ds^2}$; (iv) $\left(\dfrac{d\mathbf{r}}{ds}\right)^2+\mathbf{r}\,.\dfrac{d^2\mathbf{r}}{ds^2}$; (v) $\mathbf{r}\,.\dfrac{d^2\mathbf{r}}{ds^2}$ **10.** (i) $\dfrac{d\mathbf{a}}{dt}\,.\,\mathbf{u}$;

(ii) $\dfrac{da}{dt}\mathbf{a}+a\dfrac{d\mathbf{a}}{dt}$; (iii) $2a\dfrac{da}{dt}\mathbf{a}+a^2\dfrac{d\mathbf{a}}{dt}+\mathbf{u}\wedge\dfrac{d^2\mathbf{a}}{dt^2}$. **11.** $6\mathbf{i}+e\mathbf{j}+\mathbf{k}/\sqrt{2}$.

12. (i) $2\mathbf{i}+6t\mathbf{j}+12t^2\mathbf{k}$; (ii) $-\cos t\mathbf{i}-\sin t\mathbf{j}-4\sin 2t\mathbf{k}$; (iii) $-4\sin 2t\mathbf{i}-9\cos 3t\mathbf{j}+e^t\mathbf{k}$. **17.** $\{-\sin\theta\mathbf{i}+\cos\theta\mathbf{j}\}\dot{\theta}=\{\cos(\frac{1}{2}\pi+\theta)\mathbf{i}+\sin(\frac{1}{2}\pi+\theta)\mathbf{j}\}\dot{\theta}$. **19.** (i) $t^3\mathbf{i}-2t^2\mathbf{j}+t\mathbf{k}+\mathbf{c}$; (ii) $-\cos t\mathbf{i}+\sin t\mathbf{j}+t^2\mathbf{k}+\mathbf{c}$; (iii) $e^t\mathbf{i}-e^{-t}\mathbf{j}+\mathbf{c}$.
20. $\frac{1}{2}t^2-\frac{1}{4}t^4+\frac{1}{2}(\log t)^2+c$. **21.** $\frac{1}{2}\mathbf{q}\wedge\mathbf{p}$. **22.** 3. **24.** $1-1/\sqrt{2}$.
25. (i) $\mathbf{r}=\mathbf{A}e^{2t}+\mathbf{B}e^{-t}$; (ii) $\mathbf{r}=\mathbf{A}+\mathbf{B}e^t$; (iii) $\mathbf{r}=e^{2t}(\mathbf{A}+\mathbf{B}t)$; (iv) $\mathbf{r}=e^t(\mathbf{A}\cos t+\mathbf{B}\sin t)$.

EXAMPLES 6b (page 81)

1. $6\mathbf{i}+2\mathbf{j}+2\mathbf{k}$; $\sqrt{17}$. **2.** (i) $2u\mathbf{i}$, $2v\mathbf{j}$, $2w\mathbf{k}$; (ii) $vw(\mathbf{i}+\mathbf{j}+\mathbf{k})$, $uw(\mathbf{i}+\mathbf{j}+\mathbf{k})$, $uv(\mathbf{i}+\mathbf{j}+\mathbf{k})$; (iii) $w\cos u\mathbf{j}+\sin v\mathbf{k}$, $\sin w\mathbf{i}+u\cos v\mathbf{k}$, $v\cos w\mathbf{i}+\sin u\mathbf{j}$; (iv) $we^{wu}\mathbf{j}+ve^{uv}\mathbf{k}$, $we^{vw}\mathbf{i}+ue^{uv}\mathbf{k}$, $ve^{vw}\mathbf{i}+ue^{wu}\mathbf{j}$.

3. (i) $-\dfrac{c}{\sqrt{2}}(\mathbf{i}+\mathbf{j})$; (ii) $\dfrac{c}{\sqrt{2}}\mathbf{k}$. **7.** $y(x^2+y^2)^{-\frac{3}{2}}(y\mathbf{i}-x\mathbf{j})$; $x(x^2+y^2)^{-\frac{3}{2}}(-y\mathbf{i}+x\mathbf{j})$

8. (i) $\cos v\mathbf{i}+\sin v\mathbf{j}$; (ii) $-u\sin v\mathbf{i}+u\cos v\mathbf{j}+c\mathbf{k}$; (iii) 0; (iv) $-\sin v\mathbf{i}+\cos v\mathbf{j}$; (v) $-u\cos v\mathbf{i}-u\sin v\mathbf{j}$; (vi) 0; (vii) $c\sin v\mathbf{i}-c\cos v\mathbf{j}+u\mathbf{k}$.

9. (i) $\mathbf{i}+\mathbf{j}+\mathbf{k}$; (ii) $2x\mathbf{i}+2y\mathbf{j}+2z\mathbf{k}$; (iii) $(2xy^2+2xz^2)\mathbf{i}+(2yz^2+2yx^2)\mathbf{j}+(2zy^2+2zx^2)\mathbf{k}$. **13.** (i) $-x\sin y$; (ii) $\mathbf{k}$. **16.** $\varphi=\frac{1}{2}(x^2+y^2+z^2)+c$.

19. 0.

EXAMPLES 7a (page 91)

1. $2t\mathbf{i}+3t^2\mathbf{j}$; (ii) $2\mathbf{i}+6t\mathbf{j}+4t^3\mathbf{k}$; (iii) $e^t\mathbf{i}-e^{-t}\mathbf{j}+\mathbf{k}$; (iv) $\cos t\mathbf{i}-\sin t\mathbf{j}+2\cos 2t\mathbf{k}$. **2.** (i) $b\omega\mathbf{j}$; (ii) $-a\omega\mathbf{i}$. **3.** $\sqrt{82}$.

4. $-3\mathbf{i}+2\mathbf{j}$. **5.** $3\sin 2t(-3\sin t\mathbf{i}+2\cos t\mathbf{j})$. **6.** (i) $2t\mathbf{i}+3t^2\mathbf{j}+4t^3\mathbf{k}$, $2\mathbf{i}+6t\mathbf{j}+12t^2\mathbf{k}$; (ii) $\cos t\mathbf{i}-\sin t\mathbf{j}+\mathbf{k}$, $-\sin t\mathbf{i}-\cos t\mathbf{j}$; (iii) $-\mathbf{a}e^{-t}$, $\mathbf{a}e^{-t}$; (iv) $2\cos 2t\mathbf{a}-2\sin 2t\mathbf{b}$, $-4\sin 2t\mathbf{a}-4\cos 2t\mathbf{b}$. **9.** $4\sqrt{13}$; parallel to $\overline{OP}$ where P is the point (2, 3). **10.** (i) 1, $2t$; (ii) e^t, $-e^{-t}$; (iii) $\omega\cos\omega t$, $\omega\sin\omega t$. **14.** (i) $a\omega$, 0; (ii) 0, $2a\omega^2$.

15. $\dfrac{a}{4\theta}\left(\dfrac{2}{\theta^2}-1\right)$, $-\dfrac{a}{2\theta^2}$. **20.** $2\lambda^2r^3-\dfrac{\mu^2\theta^4}{r}$, $\lambda\mu r\theta^2+\dfrac{2\mu^2\theta^3}{r}$. **23.** Parallel to the line $y=x\tan\theta$. **28.** $(\ddot{x}-2\omega\dot{y}-x\omega^2)\mathbf{i}+(\ddot{y}+2\omega\dot{x}-y\omega^2)\mathbf{j}$.

EXAMPLES 7b (page 98)

1. (i) 14 rad/s; $6(-\mathbf{i}+2\mathbf{k})$ cm/s. **2.** $\pm 5(\mathbf{i}+2\mathbf{j}-2\mathbf{k})$ rad/s.
3. $12\sqrt{5}$ cm/s. **4.** $4(-4\mathbf{i}+27\mathbf{j}+11\mathbf{k})$ cm/s. **5.** $\sqrt{142}$ cm/s.
6. $-6\mathbf{i}+14\mathbf{j}+8\mathbf{k}$ cm/s. **7.** 77/169 rad/s. **9.** -20, -31 cm/s; $(-\frac{5}{12}, \frac{1}{3})$. **10.** $3(-14\mathbf{i}+12\mathbf{j}-9\mathbf{k})$ cm/s.

EXAMPLES 8 (page 109)

1. 5 m/s^2. **2.** $5\mathbf{i}+10\mathbf{j}$ m/s; 1250 J. **3.** $125\mathbf{i}-10\mathbf{j}$ m/s.
4. 21 J; $\sqrt{21}$ m/s. **5.** 210 W. **6.** $13\mathbf{i}+2\mathbf{j}$ m/s.

7. $250\sqrt{5}$ units; parallel to $2y+x=0$. **9.** $\frac{4}{3}\mathbf{v}$. **10.** $\frac{11}{8}\mathbf{i}$. **12.** $\dfrac{250}{\pi^2}(2\mathbf{i}+\pi\mathbf{j})$.

13. (i) $-140\mathbf{k}$ units; (ii) $-180\mathbf{k}$ units. **15.** 4 rad/s. **19.** (i) $-2m\mathbf{v}$; (ii) $3mv^2$.

INDEX